CAMBRIDGE LIBRARY COLLECTION

Books of enduring scholarly value

Medieval History

This series includes pioneering editions of medieval historical accounts by eye-witnesses and contemporaries, collections of source materials such as charters and letters, and works that applied new historiographical methods to the interpretation of the European middle ages. The nineteenth century saw an upsurge of interest in medieval manuscripts, texts and artefacts, and the enthusiastic efforts of scholars and antiquaries made a large body of material available in print for the first time. Although many of the analyses have been superseded, they provide fascinating evidence of the academic practices of their time, while a considerable number of texts have still not been re-edited and are still widely consulted.

Yorkshire Deeds

Published between 1909 and 1955, this ten-volume collection contains deeds relating to all of Yorkshire, from the twelfth to the seventeenth century. The deeds are of local historical interest, and provide topographical, philological and genealogical information, as well as insights into daily life. The majority of the records here are presented as abstracts, while documents in the vernacular that are of greater interest or importance are printed in full. Where possible, the documents are dated. Thorough background information and discussion of the deeds is included, as are notable physical descriptions, in particular of the seals. Each volume concludes with an index of people and places. Published in 1940, Volume 8 was edited by Charles Travis Clay (1885–1978). The majority of the deeds found here are from the collection of Lord Allendale. This volume also contains documents relating to the North and East Ridings from the collection of the Duke of Norfolk.

T0382294

Cambridge University Press has long been a pioneer in the reissuing of out-of-print titles from its own backlist, producing digital reprints of books that are still sought after by scholars and students but could not be reprinted economically using traditional technology. The Cambridge Library Collection extends this activity to a wider range of books which are still of importance to researchers and professionals, either for the source material they contain, or as landmarks in the history of their academic discipline.

Drawing from the world-renowned collections in the Cambridge University Library and other partner libraries, and guided by the advice of experts in each subject area, Cambridge University Press is using state-of-the-art scanning machines in its own Printing House to capture the content of each book selected for inclusion. The files are processed to give a consistently clear, crisp image, and the books finished to the high quality standard for which the Press is recognised around the world. The latest print-on-demand technology ensures that the books will remain available indefinitely, and that orders for single or multiple copies can quickly be supplied.

The Cambridge Library Collection brings back to life books of enduring scholarly value (including out-of-copyright works originally issued by other publishers) across a wide range of disciplines in the humanities and social sciences and in science and technology.

Yorkshire Deeds

VOLUME 8

EDITED BY CHARLES TRAVIS CLAY

CAMBRIDGE UNIVERSITY PRESS

Cambridge, New York, Melbourne, Madrid, Cape Town,
Singapore, São Paolo, Delhi, Mexico City

Published in the United States of America by Cambridge University Press, New York

www.cambridge.org
Information on this title: www.cambridge.org/9781108058476

© in this compilation Cambridge University Press 2013

This edition first published 1940
This digitally printed version 2013

ISBN 978-1-108-05847-6 Paperback

This book reproduces the text of the original edition. The content and language reflect
the beliefs, practices and terminology of their time, and have not been updated.

Cambridge University Press wishes to make clear that the book, unless originally published
by Cambridge, is not being republished by, in association or collaboration with, or
with the endorsement or approval of, the original publisher or its successors in title.

THE YORKSHIRE
ARCHÆOLOGICAL SOCIETY

Founded 1863   Incorporated 1893

RECORD SERIES

Vol. CII

FOR THE YEAR 1940

YORKSHIRE DEEDS

VOL. VIII

EDITED BY

CHARLES TRAVIS CLAY, F.S.A.

PRINTED FOR THE SOCIETY

1940

Printed by
THE WEST YORKSHIRE PRINTING CO. LIMITED,
WAKEFIELD.

YORKSHIRE DEEDS

Vol. VIII

CONTENTS

ILLUSTRATION

INTRODUCTION

The ownership of the documents printed in this volume is as follows :

Viscount Allendale, Bretton Park, Wakefield, Nos. 41, 43, 48-58, 61, 136-141, 151-159, 162-201, 204A, 215-216, 234, 236, 250-251, 321-329, 423, 435-498, 520-521.

Bradford Public Libraries (Misc. MSS.), Nos. 3, 62, 65-66, 233, 256-257, 316, 434.

Lord Derwent, Hackness Hall, Scarborough, Nos. 208-210.

The Duke of Leeds (Hornby Castle Muniments in custody of Y.A.S.), Nos. 16-25, 143-148, 202, 219-232, 247, 261-270, 317-320, 330, 378, 384-419, 506-519.

The Duke of Norfolk, Arundel Castle, Nos. 2, 4-15, 42, 47, 59-60, 63, 142, 161, 203-204, 206-207, 213-214, 217-218, 237, 241-246, 248-249, 252-255, 258-260, 309-310, 331-343, 383, 420-422, 424-428, 430-432, 499-505.

Sir Thomas Pilkington, Chevet Park, near Wakefield, Nos. 1, 67-101, 235, 433.

Mr. J. H. Priestley, Carver Clough, Rishworth, near Halifax, No. 40.

The Richmond Corporation, No. 271.

Mr. J. M. Spencer-Stanhope, Cannon Hall, Barnsley, Nos. 311-315.

Mr. W. M. Staveley (collection in custody of Y.A.S.), Nos. 44-45, 64, 238-240, 274-308, 344-377, 379.

The Hon. Mrs. A. M. P. Stopford, Hillgrove Farm, Cookham Dean, Berkshire, Nos. 211-212.

The Rev. P. M. Williams, The Vicarage, Thorner, Nos. 380-382.

Sir William Worsley, Hovingham Hall, Nos. 102-135.

The Yorkshire Archæological Society, Nos. 26-39, 46, 160, 205, 272-273; in custody, Nos. 149-150, 429.

The abstracts of the deeds were made for the most part when the material was being collected for volume vii, which was published in 1932, or shortly afterwards. They have been laid aside while other volumes of the Record Series were in course of publication. In some cases they complete the collections which were begun in earlier volumes. Thus, instalments of Lord Allendale's large collection have been printed in volumes v to vii; and in the present volume the collection for the period earlier than 1550 is completed, except for a large number of miscellaneous documents of comparatively minor importance such as bonds.

The second and final instalments of Sir Thomas Pilkington's deeds relating to Chevet, and Sir William Worsley's relating to North Cliff, and a further instalment of the early documents from the Hornby Castle collection, started in volume vii, are included in the present volume. Of other collections the most important is that belonging to the Duke of Norfolk. It deals with several places in the North and East Ridings, and throws much light on the family of Fauconberg of Rise, which acquired a portion of the lands of the Brus fee when the distribution among the coheirs was made in 1272 after the death of Peter de Brus III. These deeds form part of the large collection of muniments which is now at Arundel Castle, and was formerly stored in the house where King George III was born behind Norfolk House in St. James's Square. It was through the kindness of Mr. R. C. Wilton, the custodian of the muniments, that the collection was made known to me, and facilities for dealing with them were provided.

It is primarily due to Mr. T. S. Gowland that the interesting collection belonging to Mr. W. M. Staveley, and relating mainly to Ripon and North Stainley, is made available—a collection which has now been deposited with the Society in safe custody. It contains two early original charters dealing with land granted to Fountains abbey (nos. 344, 345), and two documents issued by Wolsey (nos. 301, 302). The miscellaneous documents belonging to the Bradford Public Libraries became available through Mr. W. Robertshaw; those belonging to the vicar of Thorner through Mr. G. E. Kirk; the scroll of charters belonging to Mr. Spencer-Stanhope, and some additional documents which he found at Chevet, through Mr. W. E. Preston; the document belonging to the Richmond Corporation through Mr. G. W. Waine; and that lent by Mr. J. H. Priestley through Mr. J. W. Houseman. In a letter of April 1933 Mrs. Stopford, the owner of nos. 211, 212, which she then kindly lent me for transcription, informed me that they came to her through the Pashley family of Stainton, near Doncaster,[1] from whom she is descended. Lastly, among the documents belonging to our Society, special mention must be made of the charter of William de Mala Palude, canon of York (no. 205), which was formerly in the Phillipps collection. Some notes are given in the Appendix on certain points to which it gives rise, and it is suggested that the extreme limits of date are 1197-1201. It is reproduced as a frontispiece to the volume, in a collotype made by the Oxford University Press.

§ 2.

It is pleasant to find in any collection documents which go beyond the normal type of the grant of real property, or which contain details of interest in other fields. Details relating to

[1] For a pedigree of this family see Hunter, *South Yorkshire*, i, 259.

domestic architecture, as at Blacker Hall (no. 137), or to the cost of keeping boys at school at Thorpe Salvin in the early fifteenth century (no. 406), are certainly unusual. Corrodies were not always monastic; and a lay agreement for one (no. 391) gives specific details for food, clothes and bedding. At Skelton a quit-claim of a toft and croft was made by an oath on the gospels in the presence of the parishioners of the church (no. 331). When a parent at Woolley made over property in 1387 to his son on the latter's marriage, it required a deed for the son to allow his father to dwell there for the next six months (no. 493); and another document shows the unsuccessful nature of a marriage in its first year when the bridegroom had not been well ordering and "dandellyng" his wife (no. 325). Nos. 133 and 134 give examples of the symbolic livery of seisin in the sixteenth century by the handle or latch of the door. And a salmon in Lent was a suitable rent for a plot and some fishing at Linthorpe (no. 237).

A good example of the rare use of the words *post conquestum* in the style of Richard II is given in the dating clause of a Chevet document (no. 91); and this is the subject of a brief footnote. No. 119 gives the name of an unknown prior of North Ferriby; no. 217 an early list of tenants at Hunmanby; and no. 271 some details relating to the post-dissolution history of the Franciscans at Richmond. A detailed calendar of charters, the subject of an indenture in 1311 (no. 383), is welcome to those who are interested in the partition of the Brus inheritance.

Because their seals were unknown, those who issued a certain notification (no. 407) procured the seals of the local archdeacon and rural dean to be fixed to it; but unfortunately these are missing.

As usual most of the originals are in Latin; but a few are in French, including two dealing with forestry arrangements, and containing clauses of which satisfactory translations are not easy to make (nos. 2, 389). Fifteenth-century deeds in English are usually given *in extenso* (*e.g.*, nos. 125, 126, 361, 413), or else certain clauses of interest are given in the original spelling (*e.g.*, nos. 99, 415).

Field-names and local names abound; and such sections as those relating to Barforth, Bishopton, Chevet, Drax, Flockton, Markington, Ravenfield, Richmond, Skelton, Thorner, Whorlton and Woolley provide a large number. Following the usual custom in these volumes field-names are indexed in their respective alphabetical order in the general index, and in the index to this volume they are printed in italics, so that those who are engaged in compiling lists of Yorkshire field-names can detect them readily, while those who are primarily interested in the field-names of a particular township can refer to the pages on which that township occurs. On the other hand street-names and place-names in towns such as Richmond, Ripon, Wakefield and York, are included in entries in the index relating to the particular town.

In the identification of places, especially for the purposes of the index, it is a pleasure to record the great help derived from the two volumes of the English Place-name Society dealing with the North and East Ridings and the city of York. Richard and Geoffrey de Birsay, Bursay, or Byrsay, and other members of the family, occur in the section relating to North Cliff, and then later on the name occurs as a surname without the 'de.' It is clear from these references and from the forms given in the Place-name volume for the East Riding (p. 234), that the surname is derived from the place Bursea in the wapentake of Harthill—probably meaning 'pool near the shed.' In the West Riding a manor with a place-name interest is that of Rykenild Thorpe. In a footnote in the previous volume (vol. vii, p. 165) it was noted that Hunter supposed it to be an earlier form of the name Thorpe Salvin, but that the evidence of these deeds shows that there were two distinct manors. The place Thorpe Salvayne occurs as early as 1255 (vol. vii, no. 481), and in the present volume (no. 413) we find mention of the lordship of Thoroph Rekynyll in 1480, with the two places separately mentioned in the same document in 1349 and 1383 (nos. 390, 404). The deeds also show that the Salvain family were lords of Thorpe Rykenyld (nos. 387-9 etc.); and it is evident that the early history of the two places requires further investigation, which was perhaps made by the late William Farrer in his manuscripts dealing with the honour of Tickhill. The Salvain family were interested in another place named Thorpe—Thorpe by Langeton; and this is shown to be Thorpe Langton, co. Leicester (no. 419). But it is not always possible to provide a conclusive proof of an identification. The Grimston of no. 205 is doubtful; and the only practical suggestion for the Wyten in no. 503 seems to be Whitton, co. Lincoln. In dealing with collections of documents relating mainly to Yorkshire it is often not only pleasant, but imperative, to penetrate into other counties.

It only remains to record the thanks of the Society to the owners of the various collections for their permission to print abstracts, and to those whose good offices I have mentioned in an earlier part of this introduction. My thanks are also due to Mr. C. T. Flower, the Deputy Keeper of the Public Records, for advice on some particular points; to Mr. E. W. Crossley for many facilities in connection with documents belonging to the Society; and to our Librarian, Mr. W. Hebditch, for his ready help in examining the proofsheets, and for several useful suggestions.

CHARLES CLAY.

11, TITE STREET,
CHELSEA.
June, 1940.

YORKSHIRE DEEDS.

Acaster Selby.

1. Martinmas [Nov. 11], 1314. Agreement between Thomas Ketel and Alice his wife of Acastre on one part, and William in the Gaylle and Aubreye his wife on the other, by which the former demised to the latter, their heirs and assigns, five acres of land with appurtenances in Acastre,[1] which Hugh son of Robert had held of Thomas (*de me*) for a term of years; for a term of twenty-one years, rendering yearly 5s. of silver, half at Martinmas and half at Whitsuntide, the first payment to begin at Whitsuntide 1315, for all secular service. Mutual seals to either part of the indenture. Witnesses, Hugh son of William, John the smith, William Bernard, Henry Saumpson, Walter de Henlay, Nicholas de Fiskergate. (*Sir Thomas Pilkington*).

Aislaby (Whitby).

2. Christmas, 14 Richard II [1390]. Sale[2] by Sir Philip Darcy, lord de Menyll, to Peter del Launde, John Nikson of Asilby, Thomas *othe Hall* of the same, and John Yunge of the same, of all his wood lying between the holding of Peter del Launde and *le Ragarth* of Asilby, namely, Blapot, *le Oldepark* and Symfeld, except all the margins (*bordurez*) of Halhyll, the margin *del Oldepark*, and the margin of Blapot; rendering at the following feast of the Invention of the Cross 10*li*. of silver, and when the auditor should be at Asilby for the accounts about the following Michaelmas 10*li*. of silver. The purchasers should leave ....[3] small and handsome at the view of the parker, and leave as many holly-trees; and should inclose all the said woods at their own cost for five years after the following feast of the Invention of the Cross, and have the enjoyment of the issue of the wood for a year after the said feast . . . ., and do their cutting [?] before then under forfeiture of all the wood left in *le spryng*;[4] and they

---

[1] There seems no doubt this is Acaster Selby. A William Ketel of Acaster Selby issued a charter to Selby abbey, in which land belonging to Thomas in le Gaile is mentioned (*Selby Coucher*, i, 323); and the present grantor, as Thomas Ketil of Nether Acaster [*i.e.* Acaster Selby; *cf. Yorks. Deeds*, i, 5], issued a charter to the abbey in 1315 (*Selby Coucher*, i, 329). He died before May 18, 1316 when Alice his widow made an agreement (*ibid.*).

[2] In French.

[3] Two words '[?] claguez wayuerez.'

[4] Probably meaning a plantation of young trees.

should lose all the wood left therein for their said forfeiture. Mutual seals to either part of the indenture. Asilby.

Dorso : Also the said Peter del Launde was bound to inclose all *le spryng* between the park and Whitby, which he had purchased of the lord, for four years after Michaelmas, 14 Richard II, at his own cost. (*Duke of Norfolk*, Misc., II, iii, No. 16).

Alwoodley.

3. Sept. 1, 20 Henry VIII [1528]. Grant by William Fraunke of Alwodley, esq., to Perceval Fraunke, clerk, of a yearly rent of 40s. from his manor of Alwodley; for the term of the grantee's life; with power to distrain in the grantor's manor if the rent should be forty days in arrear. Alwodley. (*Bradford Public Libraries*, Misc. MSS.).

Ampleforth.

4. Saturday after St. Gregory [March 12], 1326[-7]. Quit-claim by Alice formerly wife of Hugh de Nonewyk, in her widow-hood, to Geoffrey de Fyngale and his assigns of all right in all the assart of Clarice in the field of Ampleford, which she formerly had of the demise of Geoffrey del Bek; to hold for her life; also quit-claim of all right in another assart of Clarice, which had formerly belonged to Adam de London of Ampleford; which assart the said Geoffrey had of the demise of Hugh her husband, containing twenty-three acres of arable land; to hold for her life, rendering to her and her heirs a rose in the time of roses for all services. Witnesses, Thomas de Etton, Richard de Pykering, William Starre, John de Neuton, Robert de Cuton. Oswaldekirk in Rydale.[1] (*Duke of Norfolk*, Misc., II, ii, No. 16).

5. Wednesday the Annunciation of the B.V.M. [March 25], 1327, 1 Edward III. Whereas Alice formerly wife of Hugh de Nonewyk had quitclaimed to Geoffrey de Fyngale and his assigns all right in all the assarts of Clarice in the field of Ampleford in the territory (*sola*) of Oswaldekirk, John son of Michael de St. Andrew confirmed this quitclaim, willing that Geoffrey should hold the said assarts with their appurtenances and profits without contradiction by him or his heirs. Witnesses, Richard Huntyngton, William de Horneby of York, John de Harum. York. (*Ibid.*, II, ii, No. 17).

[1] Seal : red wax, round, ¾ in.; a bird; * IE SVY PRIVE.

North Anston.

6. St. Nicholas [Dec. 6], 1321, 15 Edward [II]. Grant by Robert Attehesches of Dynigton to Thomas Woderof of the same, his heirs and assigns, of an acre of land in parcels (*particulariter*), lying in the east field of Anstan in the place called Birkys, with appurtenances. Witnesses, Thomas Cailly, Stephen de Eyuill of Northanstan, William Hasquil of the same, John ad fontem of Dynigton, Alan Woderof of the same. Dinigton.[1] (*Duke of Norfolk*, Misc., II, ii, No. 12).

7. Saturday before St. John of Beverley [April 30], 1323. Grant by Robert Attehesches of Dynington to William son of Gregory de Tatewick, his heirs or assigns, of an acre of land in parcels (*particulariter*), lying in the east field of Northanstan in the place called Birkys, with appurtenances. Witnesses, Thomas Caily, Stephen de Eyuile, William Hascul, John ad fontem, Alan Woderof. Dynington.[2] (*Ibid.*, II, ii, No. 14).

Appleton=le=Moors.

8. Sunday in mid-Lent [April 2], 1318. Grant by Mabel daughter of Richard son of Benedict de Wodappelton to Stephen son of Margery her sister, his heirs or assigns, of all her land which fell to her by hereditary right after the death of Simon her brother, namely four acres of land with appurtenances in the vill and territory of Wodappelton;[3] also the reversion of a toft lying between the toft of Walter son of Benedict on one side and that of William son of Jueta on the other, together with eight acres of arable land lying throughout the whole field of Wodappelton, which toft and eight acres John son of David had given to Richard her father, with the yearly rents of 6*d.* from the tenement lying between the land of the abbot of St. Mary, York and the toft formerly belonging to Savaric in the said vill, and 5*d.* yearly rent from a plot of land which John son of Hervey had formerly held in the territory of Wodappelton; the toft [*etc.*] being held by Margery her sister for life of her gift. Witnesses, William son of Benedict, John son of Simon, William son of John, William Laundely,

---

[1] Fragment of seal of white wax.

[2] Seal: yellow-brown wax, pointed oval, 1 × ⅝ in.; a bird; legend chipped and rubbed.

[3] This is not given as a form of Appleton-le-Moors, par. Lastingham, in *Place-Names of N.R.* (English Place-Name Soc.), p. 59; but is so given in *V.C.H.*, *N.R.*, i, 525. Certainly St. Mary's abbey possessed land there; and a deed issued by a William son of Savari de Apelton in 1236, which relates to Appleton-le-Moors (*Y.A.J.*, xii, 97), suggests that the present identification is correct, in view of the occurrence of the name Savaric. The witness Stephen de Edeston [Edstone] to the following deed points in the same direction.

John son of Walter de Wodappelton. Wodappelton.[1] (*Duke of Norfolk*, Misc., II, ii, No. 8).

9. Friday after Corpus Christi, 19 Edward III [May 27, 1345]. Grant by John de Fauconberge of Skelton, knt., to Simon son of William de Rydale and his heirs, of the messuage and eight acres of land with appurtenances in Wodappelton, which he had of the gift and feoffment of Stephen son of Margaret; to hold for life of the grantor and his heirs, rendering yearly 12*s.* of silver at Whitsuntide and Martinmas in equal portions for all services, with reversion to the grantor. The grantee to maintain the messuage and land at his own cost in as good state or better. Mutual seals to either part of the indenture. Witnesses, Stephen son of William son of Benedict, Stephen de Edeston, William Laundel, John son of Isabel, John de Thorne. Wodappelton.[2] (*Ibid.*, II, iii, No. 3).

Arnold (E.R.)

10. Quitclaim[3] by Peter de Faukenberge and the freemen of Norh'kirlae and Rut',[4] namely, Philip de Norhkirlae, Laurence de Rut', Simon Folebert, to the nuns of Swina of any right in the lands called Milnehol' and Cornuwra, and in a meadow adjacent in the territory of Harnaal'. The nuns could inclose the said lands with a dike, sow and improve them yearly at will, and possess the meadow with its crop for their own uses. Grant also that they should have a free way as they were wont to do through the grantors' lands for their ploughs and other business, for their animals taken to and fro for cultivating the land, and their carts carrying the fruits both of the cultivated land and the meadow, so that, however, if the said men should incur loss by reason of the nuns or their animals in corn or meadow it should be made good by the view of lawful men chosen by either side. Grant by Peter, then rector of the house of Swina, and Sybil,[5] the prioress, and the convent to the said men of Norkirlae[6] and of Rut' that after

[1] Seal : red wax, round, ⅞ in.; blurred; possibly a hare riding a dog.
[2] Seal : red wax, round, ¾ in.; a gnome-like figure standing to the dexter, between the letters V S; legend . . . . . PART . .
[3] The word *Cirograephum* cut through, idented.
[4] North Skirlaugh and Rowton, which with Arnold now form a township.
[5] There were two prioresses of that name in the middle part of the 13th century. The first, who occurs in a fine of 1236, was the successor of Helewise, who occurs in a fine of 1226 (*Yorks. Fines*, 1218-31, p. 97; *ibid.*, 1232-46, p. 43). The second, who occurs in fines of 1246, 1251, 1252, was the successor of Maud, who occurs in fines of 1240-41 (*ibid.*, 1232-46, pp. 86, 94, 151; *ibid.*, 1246-72, pp. 48, 88). The occurrence of P., rector of Rise, as a witness, suggests that the present document is earlier than *c.* 1251, when Sir Peter de Fauconberge presented W. de Beverle to the church, by a deed witnessed by Sir Andrew de Fauconberge (*Reg. Gray*, p. 265).
[6] Written *Rorkirlae*.

they (the nuns) had carried the crops both of the cultivated land and meadow of Milnehol' and Cornewra the said men should have entry to the lands and exit in one place with their animals for feeding down the pasture of the said lands until sowing time or until the lands and meadows ought to be inclosed, and then the nuns could close again such entry. The said Peter and Sybil, appointed as proctors of the nuns, undertook to observe the agreement and affixed the priory seal (*sigillum ecclesie*); and Peter de Facunberge on behalf of himself and the men made the same undertaking and affixed their seals. Witnesses, Sir Sayer de Sutt[on], William de Henna, Andrew de Faukenberg, Peter de Wist[?ou], knts., William, steward of Rise, P., parson of Rise, John de Fribois, Richard de Wllingham, Thomas de Sut', Henry Coleman[1]. (*Duke of Norfolk*, Misc., II, i, No. 23).

11. St. Nicholas, 3 Edward II [Dec. 6, 1309]. Quitclaim by William de Grymmesby and Agnes his wife to Sir Walter de Faucumberg of Skelton, his heirs or assigns, of all right in a toft and croft and one bovate of land with appurtenances in the vill and territory of Arnale in Holdrenesse, which John de Henna,[2] father of the said Agnes, had held of the gift of Hugh de Arnale in frank-marriage with Margery, Agnes's mother. Witnesses, Sir Herbert de Sancto Quintino, Sir Henry de Faucumberg, knts., William Hautayn, Stephen Hautayn, Ralph de Merton, William son of John de Wythornwyk, Walter Northinby of Ryse. Ryse.[3] (*Ibid.*, II, ii, No. 5).

Aughton (Aston).

12. Sunday after St. Dunstan [May 25], 1315. Grant by Robert son of Ralph de Pecto of Acton to Robert son of John le Coupar of the same, his heirs or assigns, for a sum of money given beforehand, of an acre of land with appurtenances in the territory of Acton, lying in *le Westestedis* between the land of John son of Nicholas on either side and abutting on Goselinridding at one end, and on *le Helintre b . . . h'*[4] at the other. Witnesses, Joylenus de Neutona, John de Ullay, John son of Nicholas de Astona, Ralph Ellot, Robert Freman of Acton, John son of Goselin of the same. Acton.[5] (*Duke of Norfolk*, Misc., II, ii, No. 7).

13. Sunday after the Purification of the B.V.M. [Feb. 8], 1320[-1]. Grant by Agnes daughter of Alexander son of Gocelin

---

[1] Tag for one seal, missing. Endorsed in a medieval hand : Holdernesse . Arnale.

[2] The initial letter not very clearly written.

[3] Two tags; one seal remains : white wax, round, ¾ in.; a hawk preying over a bird; legend rubbed.

[4] Torn; perhaps *busch*.

[5] Seal : brown wax, round, ⅞ in.; a cross; S' ROBERTI.

de Pecto of Actona, in her virginity and lawful power, to John son
of Gocelin de Pecto of Acton, his heirs or assigns, of a rood of
land in the field of Acton, lying between the land of Alan the
smith on one side and that of Richard son of John de Aula on
the other, and abutting on Crokesick at one end and on Maheuridding at the other. Witnesses, John son of Nicholas de Astun,
Ralph his son, Matthew de Acton, Alexander son of Gocelin of
the same, Robert Freman of the same. Acton. (*Ibid.*, II, ii, No. 18).

14. Sunday before St. Peter ad vincula, 9 Edward III
[July 30, 1335]. Grant by Alexander son of William de Anstan
to William le Coupar of Actona and Avice his wife and their heirs
or assigns, of all his tenements in Actona which he had of the
feoffment of the said William, as in houses, messuages, tofts,
crofts, meadows, lands, pastures and the services of his tenant,
and other appurtenances in Actona. Witnesses, Hugh de Totehill,
Ralph de Actona, Gilbert de Pokenale, Geoffrey le Sumter of
Actona, John Freman, Hugh son of Joan de Aston. Actona.[1]
(*Ibid.*, II, ii, No. 22).

15. Sunday after the Conversion of St. Paul, 39 Edward
III [Jan. 26, 1364-5]. Grant by John de Popelton, rector of the
church of Aston, to Elizabeth daughter of Geoffrey de Achton of
a toft in the vill of Achton, lying between the toft of Robert de
Poknale on the south and that of Roger Freman on the north,
and five acres of land and a half of arable in the fields of Achton
lying in different places, called *le milner land*; to hold for her life,
and after her death to John de Pimland for life, and after his
death to the heirs of John de Popelton and their assigns. Witnesses, William Westren of Aston, Robert Westren of the same,
Geoffrey Prestsun of the same, Ralph Fischer of Herdwike, Robert
Rosmay of the same. Aston.[2] (*Ibid.*, II, iii, No. 12).

East Ayton.

16. Grant[3] by Alice widow of Richard Francois of Irton to
John Francois, her son, and the heirs of his body, and their heirs
or assigns,[4] of the bovate of land with appurtenances which
Richard son of Alan, her father (*pater meus*), had formerly granted

[1] Seal : yellow wax, round, ¾ in.; a hawk preying over a bird; ✠ ALAS
IE SVRPRIS.
[2] Seal : yellow-brown wax, oval, 1 × ¾ in.; a kneeling figure before the
Virgin and Child; legend is probably S. IOHIS DE POPELTON.
[3] Thirteenth century in date. Tenants named William and Thomas
de Irton, William de Fyshburn and William de Aton occur in 1284-85
(*Feudal Aids*, vi, 78).
[4] 'heredibus suis corpore proprio legitime generatis'; and in the
tenendum clause 'heredibus suis legitimo thoro gneratis et eorum heredibus
uel assignatis.'

with her in frank-marriage to Richard Francois formerly her husband; which bovate lay in the territory of Aton between the two bovates which Almotus son of Ivo de Clocton had in the same vill throughout all the field; to hold of the grantor and her heirs, with all easements in meadows, feedings, ways, paths and other places belonging thereto, rendering yearly to Richard Francois, her son, and his heirs a pair of white gloves at Christmas for all secular services; with reversion to the grantor and her heirs in default of issue. Witnesses, William de Irton, Thomas his son, William de Fisseburn, Richard de Wassand, Robert his brother, John son of William de Irton, William son of Walter de Aton.[1] (*Duke of Leeds*, Hornby Castle Muniments, Ayton, No. 1).

17. Sunday after the Purification of the B.V.M., 14 Richard II [Feb. 5, 1390-1]. Grant by Thomas de Nuby of Scardeburgh, son and heir of Thomas de Nuby, formerly of Scardeburgh, to Roger Alaynson of Semer, his heirs and assigns, of a bovate of land with appurtenances in Aton in Pykeringlyth on the east side of the water of Derwent, which had descended to him by hereditary right after the death of the said Thomas his father, and which lay throughout the field of the said vill between the land of William son of John Nelson on one side and that of John de Bulmer son of John de Bulmer formerly son of Michael de Bulmer on the other; with all meadows, pastures, turbaries and easements within the vill and without. Witnesses, William del Chaumbre of Aton, Thomas de Anlakby of the same, John de Bulmer of the same, John Rikman of Irton, William Baty, John Westend of Irton, John de Rotse of Semer, William de Ryton of the same. Aton on the east side of the water of Derwent. (*Ibid.*, No. 2).

18. Nov. 5, 18 Richard II [1394]. Grant by Roger Alanson of Semer and Agnes his wife to Sir John de Kyme, vicar of the church of Semer, and John de Wylton, chaplain, of a bovate of land with appurtenances lying in the fields of Aton in Pykerynglyth on the east side of the water of Derwente, between the land of John Bulmer of Aton on one side and that of William Jakson of Scardeburgh on the other. Witnesses, William Harome, John Lassy, Robert Brytte, William del Chambere, John Bulmer. [A]ton in Pykerynglyth.[2] (*Ibid.*, No. 3).

19. Nov. 12, 18 Richard II [1394]. Grant by John de Kyme, vicar of the church of Semer, and John de Wylton, chaplain, to

[1] Seal : greenish-brown wax; pointed oval, 1¼ × ¾ in.; a star-shaped device; ✠ S'. ALISCIE . . . . ANS . AS. The document is endorsed in a seventeenth-century hand : A deed of the oxg. of Land purchased of Wm. Dowsland in East Aiton.

[2] Two tags for seals : a fragment of one alone remains apparently the same as the first to the next deed.

Roger Alanson of Semer and Agnes his wife, of the same premises [*as in the preceding deed*], which they had of their grant and feoffment; to hold for their lives and that of the survivor, with remainder to John Bellard, son and heir of John Megson of Staxton, and Alice his wife and the heirs of their bodies, and reversion in default of issue to the right heirs of Roger Alanson. [*Same witnesses*[1] *and place*].[2] (*Ibid.*, No. 4).

20. Nov. 30, 5 Henry VIII [1513]. Grant[3] by William Douslande of Aton in Pikerrynglith on the east side of the water called Darwent, *husbondman*, to Peter Percy of Scardeburgh, gent., and John Barnard of Weyrthropp, esquire (*valecto*), their heirs and assigns, of a bovate of arable land lying in the fields and territory of Aton, with all appurtenances far and near. Also appointment of William Peynder and Thomas Stubbeys of the same, *husbondmen*, as joint attorneys to deliver seisin. Witnesses, Thomas Webster, Thomas Baxster, Thomas Lofthouse, William Cuke, William Webster. Semar. (*Ibid.*, No. 5).

21. Oct. 16, 20 Henry VIII [1528]. Grant[4] by Thomas Kylbourne of Ayton in Pikeringlithe to William Clarke of Ayton aforesaid, his heirs and assigns, of a cottage with toft and croft adjacent, and all easements, as it lay in the said vill in breadth between the land formerly belonging to Robert Sudberye on the [west] and the toft of the chapel of the B.M. of Ayton on the east, and in length from (*ad*) the water of Derwente on the north as far as the ditch called *le Colwathe* on the south. Witnesses, Ralph Bukton of Aiton aforesaid, gent., Ralph Stubbez and John Stubbez of the same, *husbandmen*. Ayton.[5] (*Ibid.*, No. 7).

22. Nov. 4, 32 Henry VIII [1540]. Grant by John Seirge of Ayton in Pikerynglith to Thomas Constable and Robert Foster of Tadcastre, gent., their heirs and assigns, of his three messuages with crofts and four bovates of land, with appurtenances in the vill and territories of Estayton in Pikerynglith. Also appointment of John Brompton and William Bovell as joint attorneys to enter and deliver seisin. Ayton. (*Ibid.*, No. 9).

[1] Bulmer is described as of Aton.

[2] Two tags for seals : (1) brown wax, round, *c.* ⅞ in.; the sacred monogram; chipped; (2) a fragment.

[3] Also, same day, release by the same to the same of all right in the same; the bovate described as lying between the land of [*blank*] on one side and that of [*blank*] on the other; Barnard described as of Werthropp, yeoman; same witnesses and place (*Ibid.*, No. 6).

[4] Also, same day, appointment by the same (Kilbourne) of John Stubbez *alias* Jenkyn Stubbez as attorney to enter and deliver seisin; same seal. (*Ibid.*, No. 8).

[5] Seal : red wax; round, 1 in.; a shield of arms, a bend between three fleurs-de-lis; SIGILLV[M] WILL'I REVILL. At the foot of the deed is the name Cawod and a notarial mark.

23. Feb. 1, 35 Henry VIII [1543-4]. Grant by Christopher Russell of Lincoln, cook (*coquus*), for a sum of money given beforehand, to Robert Forstar of Tadcastre, gent., his heirs and assigns, of his messuage or tenement and close of pasture adjacent in Aton in Pikerynglith, as it extended in length from the highway towards the north as far as the land called *lez Shorthawers hylles* towards the south, and in breadth between the land formerly belonging to William Stratour towards the west and the land of the king, lately parcel of the priory of Wikam, towards the east; and also his plot of meadow lying in the field of Yrton called *lez Hawers*, which plot was named *le Grisepole* as it extended in length and breadth; with all their appurtenances lately in the tenure of Ralph Stubbys. Also appointment of Thomas Constable and Robert Brompton as joint attorneys to enter and deliver seisin. Witnesses to sealing, [?]Henry Coke, John Maynman, Richard [*blank*].

At the foot : William Snawdun of the city of Lincoln, notary public (notarial mark), and Thomas Watson, *literatus* (mark).

Dorso : Seisin delivered, June 26, 36 Henry VIII [1544], by Thomas Constable, *gentylman* ; witnesses, Robert Lacy, William Bouell, bailiff (*balay*) of Ayton, John Brompton, Robert Collynson, Robert Hopper, John Neylson, Richard Haystyngs. (*Ibid.*, No. 10).

24. In the name of God Amen the xixth day of Aprill anno domini 1592.[1] I George Goston of Aton within the parisshe of Seamer in the countie of Yorke husbandman callinge to mynd the incertentie of this transitorie life do ordain & make this my laste will & testament in maner & forme followinge. First I committe my soule into the handes of Almightie God my maker trustinge surelie that through & for Jesus Christes sake my redemer and saviour he will receive it into his glorie & place it in the companie of holye Angells & blessed. And my bodie to be buried within the churchyard of Seamer aforesaid, belevinge accordinge to the article of our faithe that at the daie of the generall resurreccion I shall receive it again by the mightie power of God, not weake corruptible & mortall as it is nowe, but incorruptible immortall & perfect. And my temperall goodes I dispose as followethe. Firste I give & bequeathe to my sonne Roberte Goston my house garthe & crofte & ii oxganges of arable land medowe & pasture & all & singuler the appurtenances sett lyinge & beinge within the towne & territories of Aton aforesaid to have & to hold the said house [*etc.*] unto my said sonne Robert Goston & to the heires male of his bodie lawfullie begotten, and for lacke of siche issue to my sonne Henrie Goston & to his heires for ever. And albeit I do give my lands unto my said sonne Roberte I will that he shall have his porcion of my goodes & chattells notwithstandinge.

[1] Probate copy. Probate annexed, 5 Sept. 1592; and administration granted to Pottes.

Item I give to the residewe of my children 6*li*. 13*s*. 4*d*. equallie to be devided emongste them viz. to euerye one of them xxxiiis. 4*d*. Item I give to Roberte Goston my brother 20*s*. and to my father in law William Pottes[1] 20*s*. And to Philippe Douslandes children a yowe.[2] The residewe of all my goodes I give to my sonne Henrie Goston and to my doughters Agnes Esabell & Ellis whom I do ordain & make my full ioynte & hole executors of this my will. And I do desyer the said William Pottes my father in law & my said brother Roberte Goston to be supervisors hereof. Witnesses hereof Roberte Hall, Philippe Dousland, William Maland and Thomas Headley with sundrie others.

This codicill made & annexed to this laste will and testamente of me the said George Goston the viiith daie of Auguste in the yeare of our Lord above written viz. I do committe the tuicion & governmente of my sonne Roberte Goston & of the residewe of all my children to the above named William Pottes my father in lawe onlie. Witnesses hereof as also of the will the said William Maland & Thomas Headley with others. (*Ibid*., No. 11).

25.   Feb. 20, 1627[-8], 3 Charles I.   Demise[3] by Edward Warham of Osmington, co. Dorset, esq., to Robert Gate of the city of Lincoln, gent., in consideration of the sum of 450*li*., of the impropriate chapel or chapelry of East Ayton, parcel of the rectory or impropriate parsonage of Seymour in Pickering Lyth, with the tithe lathe or barn, stables, garth and glebe lands belonging, and all manner of tithe corn, hay, wool, and lamb and all other tithes within the titheable grounds of the said chapel, except those of a farm in Ayton called Paustons farm already demised for lives to Henry Mompesson of Seymour, gent.; to hold from the following Lady Day for a term of eighty years, if the said Robert, Eleanor his wife or Robert his son should live so long, paying yearly at

[1] Copy of the will and testament of William Pottes of Ayton in Pickringelythe, husbandman, dated Nov. 18, 1592, is in the same collection; it is a long document, with many references to his children and grandchildren; George Goston had married his dau. Anne. (*Ibid*., No. 12).

[2] Ewe.

[3] In English. Also the counterpart of the indenture; (*sd*.) Edw: Warham; witnesses, Henry Mompesson, John Naper, William Fitzharbert, Henry Mompesson, jun., William Keble and another, not deciphered; endorsed with a memorandum that on Feb. 13, 1631 Henry Mompesson, gent., by Henry Mompesson, jun., received 450 *li*. from Mr. Edward Warham by the hands of Sir Robert Naper, jun., the receipt being by the appointment of Mr. Robert Gates, in the presence of Henry Mompesson and Henry Mompesson, jun. (*Ibid*., No. 13A). Also, March 2, 7 Charles I [1631-2], resignation by Gate to Sir Robert Naper, jun., of Luton Hoe, co. Bedford, knt., of the same chapel and premises so demised, in consideration of 450*li*.; Seamer so spelt; in one place the term is stated to have been for ninety-nine years; (*sd*.) Rob. Gate; witnesses, Henry Mompesson, Samuel [?] Ward, John Blacoe (mark), George Smithe; seal of red wax, a shield of arms, probably per pale three lions rampant. (*Ibid*., No. 14). These are the arms of Gate given in *V.C.H.*, *N.R.*, ii, 485. For the interest of the Gate family in the rectory of Seamer see that section in the present volume.

Michaelmas a peppercorn if demanded, and to the king the yearly rent or fee-farm of 8*li*. 6*s*. 8*d*. Upon condition that if within five years Warham desired to redeem the lease, giving one year's notice and paying back the purchase money, the demise should be void. (*sd*.) Robert Gate.

Dorso : sealed in the presence of Henry Mompesson, Francis [?] Romer, John Sidnam (mark). (*Ibid*., No. 13).

Barforth.

26. Grant[1] and quitclaim by Peter de Barnhou to Sir John de Bereford, his lord, his heirs or assigns, of all the land which he had held of him, with his chief messuage and all other appurtenances, in the vill and territory of Bereford;[2] together with all escheats which could fall to him from his mother or others, and all liberties and easements belonging to the land within the vill of Bereford and without. Witnesses, Sir Roald son of Roald, Sir Henry his brother, Robert de Wicliue, Robert de Aldelin, Richard Ruter, Robert son of Walter de Thorp, Geoffrey Noreis, Warin de Bereford, William the smith, Geoffrey son of Chiuenor, Roald son of Warin.[3] (*Y.A.S.*, M^D 161A, Barforth, No. 1).

27. Confirmation by master Gilbert de Forsete, vicar of Gilling, to Sir John de Bereford, his heirs or assigns, of the gift of Warin son of William the smith of Bereford of all the land with a messuage and appurtenances which Warin had given to Sir John in the vill and territory of Bereford, in accordance with an agreement drawn up between them; Sir John, his heirs or assigns, to pay yearly to God and the church of St. Cuthbert of Forsete and to the confirmor during life and his successors 12*d*. sterling on St. Cuthbert's day in Lent for all secular service. Witnesses, Geoffrey Norrensis of Bereford, Eborard de Tindale in Bereford,[4] Geoffrey his brother, Ralph de Boleton, Geoffrey de Carleton, Roald de Bereford, Ralph de Deping', William de Tesdale.[5] (*Ibid*., No. 2).

28. Grant by Maud widow of Robert de Stapilton to Benedict her son, his heirs or assigns, in her widowhood, of eight acres of land with appurtenances in the territory of Berford and a moiety

[1] Also, attached, another charter in the same terms with the addition of Emma wife of Sir John de Bereford as joint grantee; same witnesses, Norais so spelt; same seal; written in quite a different hand. (No. 1A).
[2] Several Barforth deeds are pd. in *Pudsay Deeds*, pp. 290 *et seq*, with which this series can be compared.
[3] Seal : green wax, pointed oval, 1⅜ × 1 in.; a floral device; ✠ SIGIL' PETRI D' BARNH'V.
[4] Dead in 1266 according to *Pudsay Deeds*, p. 292.
[5] Seal : white wax, pointed oval, *c*. 1¾ × 1¼ in.; a floral device; SIGIL . . . .; badly broken.

of her toft and croft in the same vill on the south side next the toft formerly belonging to Robert Gerewel, namely, half an acre at Hwyteflat, a rood at Layrougate, half an acre at Thrimhowes, a rood at Demmingis, a rood in Watelandis, a rood and a half at Cotegarht, a rood at Dorthanhow, a rood at Syke, a rood and a half in two places at Forteborem, a rood and a half at Graystan, half a rood at Heggeraue, a rood in Hardengys, half a rood in Crukengis, half an acre at Butte, a rood and a half beyond the road, half a rood on Tytelesacre, a rood and a half on Estflatestan, a rood on Crumbacre, a rood at Netaldewaht and at Lynlandendis, half a rood in Lynlandis, three roods and a half in Wynstunhalw of the same land, half a rood at Toftendis, a rood in Furacris, a rood at Thornougate, half a rood at Dolfinhow and at Wythebusce, and half a rood at Byrthinsty; with all easements within the vill of Berford and without; for a sum of money given in her need; rendering yearly to the church of St. Cuthbert of Forset 1*d.* on St. Cuthbert's day in Lent for all secular service, suit of court and demand; warranty against all men and women. Witnesses, master Gilbert, vicar of Forset, John de Forset, lord of Berford, Geoffrey Norrays, Roger de Walmesford, Warin de Berford, Roald his son, Geoffrey son of Chyuenor, Robert his son, Rayner son of Seman, Everard de Tyndale.[1] (*Ibid.*, No. 3).

29. Grant and quitclaim by Geoffrey Norrais of Berford to Benedict de Berford and his heirs of his rent of 8*d.* which Benedict had given him for the land of Peter Berrid in the fields of Berford, and of the land itself; Benedict to pay 5*d.* yearly to the altar of St. Cuthbert of Forset on St. Cuthbert's day in Lent for all services. Witnesses, Sir Adam, vicar of Gilling, Harsculf (*Arquiuo*) de Cleseby, Everard de Tindal, Robert Chiuenor, Roald son of Warin de Berford, the writer of the writing. (*Ibid.*, No. 4).

30. Grant by Geoffrey Norrays of Bereford to Andrew de Bereford, clerk, his heirs or assign, of part of his land in the fields of Bereford, namely, a rood and a half in the east marshes towards the field of Appilby by the land formerly belonging to Robert son of Geoffrey son of Cheuenor, two and a half roods on Haluthbank, half a rood at Noutestilis, a rood by his meadow in Wynistonhaluth, all his land at Berewardhaker, half the share of his land on Lange-banke towards the east, half a rood in *le Bothe* at Holegathe, which Geoffrey the miller had held of the said Geoffrey, and an acre at Akeinahou lying in different places which Alexander Morel had held of the said Geoffrey; to hold of the grantor and his heirs, with all easements within the vill of Bereford and without; for a sum of money given beforehand, rendering yearly 1*d.* within the octave of Christmas for all services. Witnesses, Harscul de Cleseby,

---

[1] Seal : brown wax, oval, *c.* 1½ × 1¼ in.; a floral device; much broken.

Robert de Bereford, Roald son of Warin of the same, Everard de Tyndale, Robert son of Geoffrey Cheuenor, Ralph de Depping', Hugh the clerk.[1] (*Ibid.*, No. 5).

31. Grant by Geoffrey Norays of Bereford to Andrew the clerk of Bereford, his heirs or assign, of part of his land in the fields of Bereford, namely, two and a half roods on Haulebanc', half a rood on Notestilis, a rood by his meadow in Wynistunhaul', and all his land at Berewardhakyr'; to hold of the grantor and his heirs, with all easements within the vill of Bereford and without; for a sum of money given beforehand in his great need; rendering yearly 1*d.* within the octave of Christmas for all other services. Witnesses, Harsculf de Clesiby, Alan the clerk of the same, Warin de Bereford, Roald his son, Everard de Tyndale, Geoffrey his brother, Robert son of Geoffrey Cheuenor, Ralph de Depping', William de Tesedale, Hugh the clerk.[2] (*Ibid.*, No. 6).

32. Confirmation by Geoffrey son of Geoffrey Norrensis of Bereford to Andrew de Bereford, his heirs or assigns, of all the lands with appurtenances which Andrew had acquired of the gift or sale of Geoffrey the confirmor's father in the vill and territory of Bereford. Witnesses, Harsculf de Cleseby, Warin de Bereford, Roald his son, Eborard de Tindale, Geoffrey his brother, Ralph de Deping', William de Tesdale, Adam Hoppescort, Hugh de Bereford, clerk.[3] (*Ibid.*, No. 7).

33. Grant by Geoffrey son of Geoffrey Norays to Benedict son of Maud de Bereforht, his heirs or assigns, of his plot (*particulam*) under Langebanke near Langebanke in Linelandes towards the west, and his plot in Scortebothem belonging to a bovate of land in the territory of Bereforht; to hold of the grantor and his heirs, with all easements belonging to so much land within the vill and without, free from all service. Witnesses, Roald son of Warin, Everard de Tindall', Alan son of Geoffrey Norays, Robert Chiuenor, Simon de Tindall'. (*Ibid.*, No. 8).

34. Quitclaim and confirmation by Geoffrey Norais son of Geoffrey Norais of Bereford of all the lands and pastures which his father had sold to Sir John his lord in the fields of Bereford; warranty to Sir John against all men and women. Witnesses, Michael de Latun, Robert his son, Alan de Latun, John his son, Gerard de Bous, Laurence de Girlingtun, Nicholas his son, Robert de Torp, John his son, Warin de Bereford, Roald his son, Everard

[1] Seal : dark green wax; pointed oval, 1½ × 1 in.; a fleur-de-lis; ✠ SIGILL [GAL]FRIDI N'RRAIS.
[2] Same seal as to the preceding deed.
[3] Seal : green wax; pointed oval, 1½ × 1 in.; a bird displayed; SIGIL' GALF'ID FIL' GALF'ID.

de Tind[al], Hugh his son, Geoffrey de Tind[al], Waldef his son,
Geoffrey son of Cheuenor, Robert his son, William the smith,
Warin his son.[1] (*Ibid.*, No. 9).

35. Grant by Alan son of Geoffrey le Norrays of Bereford
to Harsculf de Cleseby, his heirs and assigns, of a toft and croft
with meadow belonging which he had of the gift of Geoffrey le
Norrays his father in the vill of Bereford, namely, between the
toft of Roald son of Warin and a certain toft of Geoffrey, the
grantor's brother; also the service of Eborard de Tindale for half
an acre of land in the territory of Bereford under Langebanc, for
which Eborard was wont to render to him ½*d.* yearly at Christmas;
and the service of Hugh son of the said Eborard for half an acre
there, for which Hugh was wont to render to him an arrow at the
same term; and the service of Joan the grantor's sister for two
acres and a rood of land under Sceld in the same territory, for
which she was wont to render to him 1*d.* at the same term; to hold
of the grantor and his heirs, with all easements; rendering yearly
1*d.* at Christmas for all demands. Witnesses, Sir John le Breton,
Sir Warin de Scaregile, William de Salkoc, Richard de Muleton,
bailiff of Richmond, master John de Manefeld, Eborard de Tindale,
Hugh his son, Andrew de Bereford, Benedict de Stapelton, Robert
son of Geoffrey Cheuenor of Bereford, Simon de Tindale, Waldeve
his brother.[2] (*Ibid.*, No. 10).

36. Grant by Robert son of Geoffrey son of Cheuenor of
Bereford to Harsculf de Cleseby, his heirs and assigns, of an acre
and a rood of land with appurtenances in the territory of Bereford,
namely on Nettelhoulandes between the land of the prioress of
Ellerton and that of Andrew de Bereford; to hold of the grantor
and his heirs, with all easements; for a sum of money given beforehand; rendering yearly to the grantor and his heirs within the
vill of Bereford if they were present, and if not present to the
chapel of St. Mary of Bereford three roses at the Nativity of St.
John the Baptist for all other secular services. Witnesses, Robert
de Wycliue, Michael de Thorp', Laurence de Girlington, Walter
de Uluington, Robert Gretheued, Gerard de Boghes, Geoffrey
son of Geoffrey le Norrays of Bereford, Eborard de Tindale, Hugh
his son, Simon de Tindale, Andrew de Bereford, Benedict son of
Maud de Stapelton, William Bateman.[3] (*Ibid.*, No. 11).

37. Grant by Robert son of Geoffrey son of Cheuenor to
Robert son of Sir John de Bereford, his heirs or an assign at will,

[1] Seal : green wax; shield-shaped with rounded top, 1⅛ × ⅞ in.; a bird;
✠ SIGILL' G'F'I FIL' : G. NORI.
[2] Seal : green wax, pointed oval, 1⅜ × ⅞ in.; a fleur-de-lis; ✠ SIG'L .
ALANI . NORRASIS.
[3] Seal : red wax, pointed oval, 1½ × 1 in.; some objects not deciphered;
✠ SIGIL' ROBERTI FIL' GALFRID' B.

of an acre of his land in the fields of Bereford, lying on Likehou; to hold of the grantor and his heirs, with all appurtenances and easements within the vill of Bereford and without; rendering yearly an iron arrow at Easter for all services. Witnesses, Harscul' de Cleseby, Roald son of Warin de Bereford, Everard de Tyndale, Andrew de Bereford, clerk, Geoffrey son of Geoffrey Norrays of the same, Benedict son of Maud, Hugh the clerk. (*Ibid.*, No. 12).

38. Martinmas [Nov. 11], 1301. Agreement between William de Gerford and Henry de Chirch, by which William demised to Henry, his heirs or assigns, an acre of land in the territory of Berford, lying on Roberdhow between the lands of Sir Richard de Hodelston on either side; for a sum of money given beforehand; to hold for a term of twenty years of the chief lord of the fee; with all easements within the vill of Berford; rendering yearly to William, his heirs or assigns, a rose in summer for all other services, suits of court and demands. A payment of 20s. to be made in default of warranty. Mutual seals to either part of the indenture. Witnesses, William de Persebrig', Henry son of Roald, Robert son of Hugh, William Bikeman, Geoffrey son of Benedict, Simon de Tindale.[1] (*Ibid.*, No. 13).

39. Grant by William de Gerford to Geoffrey son of Bene- dict de Berford and Isabel his wife, and his heirs or assigns, of eight acres of land and half a rood, and a piece of meadow in the field of Berford, of which one and a half acres lay on Alneakerbanck, one and a half roods on Hegeraw, three roods in *le Halow* between the land of Sir Robert de Clesby and that of Sir Richard de Hodels- ton, one and a half roods in Linelandes between the land of the said Sir Robert and that of the grantee, a rood at Netewath between the land of the said Sir Robert and the land of Gerwell, half an acre in Bakestanecraftes between the land of the said Sir Robert and that of Robert son of Hugh, an acre under Lang- banck between the land of the said Sir Robert and that which Geoffrey son of Walden had of Robert son of Hugh, one and a half roods at Burtrebusk by the land of Geoffrey son of Benedict, three and a half roods at Flaustane between the land of William Bikeman and that of Robert son of Hugh, half an acre on Peshow by the land of the prioress of Ellerton, half an acre at Dorthankeld by the meadow of the said prioress, one and a half roods at Sitel- saker between the land of Gerwell and that of John de Deping, one and a half roods by Holgate, one and a half roods in *le Sou* . . *akers* between the land of Sir Richard de Hodelston and that of the said prioress, and all the meadow lying in a place called Croukeing; to hold of the chief lords of the fee, with all easements within the vill of Berford and without; rendering yearly to the chief

---

[1] Seal : yellow wax, round, ⅜ in; not deciphered. Endorsed: *Le Escrit Hanne.*

lords of the fee a rose in the time of roses for homage, reliefs, escheats, wardships, suits of court and other services. Witnesses, John del Hey of Forseth, Hugh Greteheued of Caldewell, Adam son of Thomas of the same, William son of William of the same, John son of Henry de Appelby, Robert son of Geoffrey of the same, Robert son of Hugh de Berford, Philip de Eryum of the same, John son of Joye of the same, Geoffrey son of Walden of the same, William son of Walter de Melsamby, Geoffrey son of Eudo de Carleton.[1] (*Ibid.*, No. 14).

Barkisland.

40. March 11, 13 Edward IV [1472-3]. Grant[2] by William Hagh of Skyrehous to John Gleydehill son of Robert Gleydehill, his heirs and assigns, of a messuage lately built within the township of Barkysland called Lytill Hevyn, with all lands and tenements, meadows and pastures with appurtenances belonging thereto, in the tenure of the said Robert for a term of years; rendering yearly 2s. of lawful money of England at Whitsuntide and Martinmas in equal portions for all secular services; with power to distrain if the rent should be in arrear for forty days; and as security for tenure the grantee to have power to distrain to the value of 13s. 4d. in the grantor's messuages, lands and tenements called Boterworth in the tenure of John Henryson the elder. Mutual seals to either part of the indenture.[3] Witnesses, John Romsden of Sykehous, John Tounhend, Robert Wylkynson. Barkysland. (*J. H. Priestley, esq.*).

Barnsley.

41. March 28, 10 Henry VII [1495]. Grant by Henry Eueryngham of Staynburgh, esq., to Alexander Hudson of Bernesley, his heirs and assigns, of all his purparty of his garden in Bernesley on the west side, abutting on the messuage of Richard Bosewell on the west side of the said garden, containing in breadth therefrom ten ells, and in length twenty-seven and a half ells between the messuage of the grantee on the south and north; rendering yearly 4d. at Whitsuntide and Martinmas in equal portions. Witnesses, Richard Keresford of Bernesley, John Webster the younger of the same, William Bayly of the same. Bernesley.[4] (*Lord Allendale*, Barnsley, No. 2).[5]

[1] Seal : green wax, round, ¾ in.; a lion passant; * SVM LEO FORTIS.
[2] Also a contemporary draft or copy, not executed. Variations in spelling, Haygh, Gleydhyll, Buterworth, Sikehouse. Also, on the following day, appointment of Thomas Elistonys as attorney to deliver seisin; seal, red wax, small, letter W.
[3] Tag for seal, missing.
[4] Seal : red wax; blurred.
[5] No 1 of this series was printed in vol. vi.

Bilton (E.R.)

42. Thursday, St. Peter in cathedra, 15 Edward III [Feb. 22, 1340-1]. Indenture between Sir John de Faucumberge, lord of Skelton, and Sir Walter de Faucumberge of Biltoun, by which the former demised to the latter a plot of meadow in Biltoun called Riseland in Holdernes, for a term of fourteen years beginning at the above date; rendering yearly a clove-gillyflower (*clauum gariophili*) at Christmas if demanded. Mutual seals.[1] Rise. (*Duke of Norfolk*, Misc., II, iii, No. 2).

Bingley.

43. Oct. 12, 1386, 10 Richard II. Demise by Richard de Ilkelay, chaplain, and Thomas Machon of Horton, the elder, to John Chartres of Bynglay and Alice his wife, of all their lands and tenements which they had of the grant and feoffment of the said John in the vill of Bynglay; to hold with appurtenances for their lives, with remainder to Richard, John's son, and Isabel his wife, daughter of John de Bollyng, and the heirs of their bodies; with remainder, in default of issue, to John de Bollyng and John Chartres and their heirs in equal portions. Mutual seals to either part of the indenture.[2] Witnesses, Nicholas de Stansfeld, Simon Mauht, William de Baildon. Bynglay. (*Lord Allendale*, Bingley, No. 7).[3]

Bishopton (Ripon).

44. Grant by Christian formerly wife of Richard de Kelinghale, in her widowhood and lawful power, to Robert de Biscopton, clerk, his heirs or assigns, for a sum of money given beforehand in her need, of the rood of land lying together at Martinflat in the field of Biscopton and abutting on Grauelay, with appurtenances; rendering yearly to her and her heirs a rose at the Nativity of St. John the Baptist for all secular service. Witnesses, John de Biscopton, John son of Robert, John Frere, John called Prest, John son of Robert de Clother[um]. (*W. M. Staveley, esq.*, Bishopton, No. 1).

45. Thursday the eve of the Apostles Simon and Jude [Oct. 27], 1300. Grant by Robert son of Walter de Hyltona to John Frere of Rypon and Robert his son, and the heirs of Robert's

[1] Seal : red wax, round, ¾ in.; beneath a helm a shield of arms, a lion rampant; legend rubbed. After acquiring Skelton the main line of the Fauconberg family adopted the Brus arms, *argent, a lion rampant azure*.
[2] Two tags; one seal remains : white wax, round, ¹⅜ in.; a shield of arms, blurred; legend contains the letters DE . VOR; broken at the top.
[3] Nos. 1-6 of this series were printed in vol. vi.

body, of a messuage in Biscoptona with a toft and croft, eight acres of land and an acre of meadow in the fields and territories of Byscoptona, Rypon and Stodleyroger, which he had of the grant of John son of Robert de Biscoptona; also three tofts, a plot with a barn built thereon, twelve acres and three roods of land with appurtenances in Biscoptona and a moiety of a [?][1] at Elum in the same vill, of which two acres lay at Eskbyri between the land of William de Clouthrum and that of John de Biscoptona, one acre at Bylardley by the land of Adam Maresch[al], three acres at Henryran, two acres at Ryflatte, two acres and one rood at Uppeandoune, one acre at Thykthorndale, one acre and one rood at Doweranes, and one rood at Northmancroftys; also 4s. yearly rent from a burgage in Skelgate in the vill of Rypon which John de Caue was holding of the grantor's grant in fee; with all easements and profits within the said vills and without; to hold of the chief lords of the fee; with remainder, in default of issue, to the right heirs and assigns of John Frere and Margery his wife. Witnesses, Patrick de Braffertona, bailiff of Rypon, William de Clouthrum, John de Ebor', Richard Huberd, William the dyer, John de Ilketona, Adam Maresch[al]. Rypon. (*Ibid.*, No. 2).

Bolton Percy.

46.   Invention of the Cross, 16 Richard II [May 3, 1393]. Release[2] by John de Somerby, chaplain, to William Gascryk, his heirs and assigns, of all right in all the lands, tenements, rents and services, with appurtenances in the vills and territories of Barton on Humbre, Barowe and South Feriby which had formerly belonged to Henry de Barton, rector of the church of Bolton Percy, except twenty-one acres of land with appurtenances in the vill of Barton which had descended to the said Henry by hereditary right; which lands [*etc.*] William Gascryk lately had of the livery and surrender of the said Henry; also [all right] in all the messuages and reversions which the said William had of the feoffment of Sir William Mountaigne, rector of the church of Barghton, co. Lincoln, and Thomas Aunger, in the said vill of Barton. Witnesses, William Barker, Robert Ryuill', John de Cawod, William Sampson, William de Driffeld, Robert de Feriby. Bolton Percy.[3] (*Y.A.S.*, M[D] 150).

Braworth (Skutterskelfe).

47.   Friday after the octave of Easter [April 9], 1350. Grant by Nicholas Gower of Sexhow, John his brother, William Gower

---

[1] *dunerii* or perhaps *dimerii*.

[2] This deed was found in a parcel mainly of later deeds relating to the family of Barraclough of Brookfoot in Southowram. Although it relates to lands in Lincolnshire it shows the place from which a rector of Bolton Percy derived his name.   [3] Fragments of seal of red wax.

of Ingelby, and John de Mydilton on Leuen, jointly and severally, to John son of Stephen de Barton and his heirs of a yearly rent of 100s. from all their lands and tenements in Braithwath in Cliueland, which had formerly belonged to Sir John de Barton, knt., and Joan his wife; with power to the grantee to enter the premises notwithstanding the feoffment made to them, should the rent be in arrear at the two terms of Whitsuntide and Martinmas. Witnesses, Thomas Sturmy, Robert del How, John son of Cecily de Stokesley, Robert de Chambre. Stokeslay.[1] (*Duke of Norfolk*, Misc., II, iii, No. 5).

West Bretton.

48. Exaltation of the Cross [Sept. 14], 1317. Indenture by which the abbot and convent of Byland (*Bella Landa*) demised to master John de Dronefeld ten acres of land in the territory of Bretton, namely, those which they had of the grant of Peter son of Orm de Bretton;[2] to hold for a term of twenty years, rendering yearly to the abbot and convent and their successors 3s. sterling in equal portions at Whitsuntide and Martinmas; should John die within the term the premises to revert to the abbot and convent. John promised his faithful aid in all the business of the house.[3] Byland. The abbot and convent and John affixed their seals.[4] Witnesses[5] [*blank*]. (*Lord Allendale*, Bretton, No. 57).[6]

49. Saturday after the Assumption of the B.M., 19 Edward III [Aug. 20, 1345]. Grant by John Agson of Emlay to Laurence son of John de Dronsfeld, his heirs or assigns, of a tenement with toft and croft and gardens lying in the vill of Westbretton, and

[1] Two seals remaining on tongues of the parchment : (1) black wax, round, *c.* 1 in.; a shield of arms, on a bend three dogs passant; legend chipped or rubbed; (2) rubbed. These arms are a variant of those on a seal used by John son of John Gower of Sexhow in 1379 (see Mr. Brown's note in *Y.D.*, i, 135).

[2] See vol. vi, No. 33.

[3] Predictus vero magister Johannes promisit quod fideliter et fiducialiter stabit pro domo de Bellalanda et personis eiusdem domus in consilio et auxilio et negocia dicte domus sicut sua propria negocia erga quoscumque pro posse suo fideliter et sine malo ingenio procurabit et faciet expediri.

[4] Presumably to either part of the indenture. One tag for a seal, missing.

[5] Hiis testibus; and nothing follows.

[6] Nos. 1-54 of this series were printed in vols. v and vi, with the exception of No. 9 which is printed in this volume. No. 55 is a repetition of the quitclaim made by Christopher Dronsfeld to Richard Wentworth on 30 April 1433, which is printed in vol. vi, No. 55; it is dated on the feast of St. Dunstan the Archbishop, 26 Henry VI [May 19, 1448], and witnessed by Robert Waterton, knt., William FitzWilliam, Nicholas FitzWilliam, John Haryngton, Edmund FitzWilliam, esqs.; seal, red wax, signet, a ram passant. The reason for this repetition may perhaps be due to an acquisition of the premises by Dronsfeld under the terms of a deed of June 1434 (vol. vi, No. 57) and his subsequent alienation of them to Wentworth. The premises lay in West Bretton and elsewhere.

half an acre of land called Kerlandes lying in the field of the same; rendering yearly to John de Bretton and his heirs or assigns 8*d*. at Easter, 3*d*. at Whitsuntide, and 3*d*. at Martinmas for all services. Witnesses, John de Dronsfeld, Edmund de Dronsfeld, John Erkyn, William Erkyn, Nicholas Erkyn, Nicholas Burdon, Adam Blakeburn. Westbretton. (*Ibid.*, No. 58).

50. Oct. 3, 1430, 9 Henry VI. Feoffment by Maud, countess of Cambridge,[1] to Richard Wentworth and the heirs of his body of all her manor of Westbretton with appurtenances, and all the lands and tenements, rents, reversions and services, advowsons of churches and chantries, with appurtenances which she had in the vills and hamlets of Westbretton, Lytulbretton, Sandall, Hegheholand, Kimberworth,[2] Ingbrechworth, Fryth, Carre hows, and Steynton, all of which she lately had of the grant and feoffment of Agnes late wife of John Wentworth of Northelmesall, esq., jointly with Richard Flynthill, who had released to her all his right therein; with remainder, in default of issue, to Thomas Wentworth, William Wentworth, and Ralph Wentworth for their lives and the life of the survivor, without impeachment of waste; and remainder to the right heirs of the said Agnes. Also appointment of John Dowebyggyng and John Capetour as her joint attorneys to deliver seisin. Witnesses, John Melton, Thomas Savill, Robert Watterton, knts., Thomas Clarell, Ralph Makerell, John Bosevyll, Robert Rokeley, John Haryngton, Thomas Wombewell, esqs. At our castle of Cunnesburghe.[3] (*Ibid.*, No. 59).

51. Dec. 14, 2 Henry VIII [1510]. Whereas[4] Thomas Wentworth of Westbretton, esq., son and heir of Matthew Wentworth, on the one part, and James Langley, esq., and Elizabeth his wife, late wife and executrix of the said Matthew Wentworth, on the other part, stood bound to each other in 100*li*. by their writing dated the preceding Oct. 31 to keep the award[5] of master Herry Machill, doctor, and master John Underwod, bachelor of law, in the disputes concerning the testament and administration of goods of the said Matthew, the said arbitrators gave their award as follows : James and Elizabeth to enjoy all the goods and chattels belonging to Matthew at the time of his death in accordance with his testament, and Thomas to deliver to them all such goods as he had, except such things as he could prove to be "heirelomes"; James and Elizabeth to deliver to Thomas all the plate bequeathed

---

[1] See vol. vi, p. 15*n*. In that vol. are printed the grant to her by Agnes widow of John Wentworth, and sister and one of the heirs of Sir William Dronsfield, in Oct. 1425 (vol. vi, No. 51), and Flynthill's release to her, including land in Wickersley, on May 19, 1430 (vol. vi, No. 54).
[2] Cumberworth (see vol. vi, p. 16*n*).
[3] Tag for seal, missing.
[4] In English.
[5] "Laude, arbitriment, awarde and jugement."

to him, and pay all bequests and debts; Elizabeth to have the keeping of Anne Wentworth and Bettres Wentworth, daughters of Matthew and Elizabeth, until their marriage or lawful age, and have yearly for their finding meat and "arament" at the sight of Thomas, William Wentworth of Sprotbrught and Thomas Friston of Altoft; Thomas to have the bargain of Calthorn and Haukwode according to indentures between Robert Waterton, esq., and Matthew Wentworth, esq., dated Sept. 12, 17 Henry VII [1501], and find sufficient surety to James and Elizabeth to discharge them of the bargain, and for the bargain to pay to the said William Wentworth and Thomas Friston to the use of the said Anne and Bettres "in partie of their childs parte" 16*li*. 17*s*. 5*d*.; and James and Elizabeth likewise to deliver for the same purpose 29*li*. 16*s*. 7*d*.; provided that "if eny dett be a newly clamyd provid and recouered of the said James and Elisabeth that it be alowed unto theym of the hoole goods." Witness, Henrie Machell. (*Ibid.*, No. 61).

52. Feb. 14, 16 Henry VIII [1524-5]. Feoffment by Richard Burdet of Denbye, esq., and Perceval Adde of Silston, clerk, to Thomas Woderoff, esq., Roger Wentworth, Richard Whetlay, Christopher Bradford, Thomas Wentworth of Gaunton, and Arthur Kay of Wodsom, esq., of all the messuages, lands, tenements, rents and services, meadows, feedings and pastures, with appurtenances in Westbretton, Netherbretton, Elmesall, Claton, and Rotheram, then in the tenure of John Greyn, Richard Walkere, Nicholas Kyrkbye, Robert Hall, Robert Oxle, Edward Mason, John Moere, Richard Hall, William Qwhetlay, Robert Syks, Thomas Trykett, John Norton, Thomas Siks, William Allott, John Campynot, John Oxle, Robert Couden, Richard Masse, and Joan wife of Thomas Jakson, widow, and also a close called Edmondrode in the tenure of Robert Hall and Richard Hall, and a close in Claton in the tenure of Edmund Oxle called Fostall Crofft; to the use of Thomas Wentworth of Westbretton, knt., and Isabel his wife, for their lives, and the heirs male of the body of Sir Thomas; with remainder to the heirs male of the body of Matthew Wentworth, father of Sir Thomas, and remainder to Matthew's right heirs male. Also appointment of Ralph Blaker and John Ward as joint attorneys to enter and deliver seisin. Witnesses, Roger Ameas, esq., Henry Everingham[1] esq., Edmund Oxle, William Dent, Robert Whytfeld, William Wod, Thomas Sigswyk. Westbreton.

Dorso : Seisin delivered to Thomas Woderoff and Roger Wentworth, Feb. 15, in the presence of Roger Ameas, Thomas Wyntworth the younger, Thomas Burdet, Edmund Oxle, William Dent, Robert Grice, William Wod. Adde is described as chaplain. (*Ibid.*, No. 60).

[1] The name seems to be written Eu'igma'; but Everingham was evidently intended. The document, which contains several grammatical mistakes, was not very carefully drawn up.

53. Feb. 14, 21 Henry VIII [1529-30]. Grant by Thomas Wentworthe of Westbretton, knt., to Richard Burdet, esq., and Perceval Adde, clerk, of all the messuages, lands, tenements, rents and services, meadows, feedings and pastures, with appurtenances in Westbretton, Netherbretton, Elmesall, Claton and Rotheram, in the tenure of John Greyn, Richard Walkerr, Nicholas Kyrkbye, Robert Hall, Robert Oxle, Edward Mason, John Moere, Richard Hall, William Qwhetlay, Robert Syks, Thomas Trykett, John Norton, Thomas Sekarr, William Allott, John Campynot, John Oxle, Robert Cowden, Richard Masse, and Joan wife of Thomas Jakson, widow; a close called Edmundroyde in the tenure of Robert Hall and Richard Hall, and a close in Clayton in the tenure of Edmund Oxle called Fostall Crofft. Also appointment of John Walkerr and William Sykes as joint attorneys to enter and deliver seisin. Witnesses, Roger Ameas, esq., Henry Eueryngam, esq., Edmund Oxle, William Dent, Robert Qwytfeld, William Wodd, Thomas Sigswyke. Westbretton. (*sd.*) per me Thomam Wentworth, K.[1] (*Ibid.*, No. 62).

54. July 5, 34 Henry VIII [1542]. Demise by Thomas Wentworth of Parlyngton, co. York, esq., to John Oxlee of Bretton and Thomas Gledhyll, son of Robert Gledhyll, of a messuage in Bretton with all the lands, meadows, woods, closes, pastures and commons, with appurtenances, then in the tenure of the said John Oxlee, from the following Martinmas for a term of twenty-one years, paying yearly 33s. 4d. at Whitsuntide and Martinmas in equal portions, with power to distrain if the rent were in arrear for forty days; the lessees to maintain the tenement, the lessor finding timber for repairs; the lessees to lead yearly 20 dozen of ironstone to Bretton smithy, the lessor paying them therefor as he did to others that led stone for him. Mutual seals. (*Ibid.*, No. 66).

55. March 31, 1 Edward VI [1547]. Release by Walter Pullan of Skotton, esq., to Thomas Wentworth of Westbretton, esq., of all right in the manor of Westbretton, and all other messuages, lands, tenements, and other hereditaments belonging thereto. (*sd.*) per me Walltherum Pulleyn.[2] (*Ibid.*, No. 63).

56. Nov. 5, 5 Edward VI [1551]. Articles of agreement[3] between the lady Isabel Wenttworthe of Hauthwaitt, co. York, widow, and Thomas Wenttworthe of West Brettan, esq., concerning her dower out of the manor and lordship of West Brettan by the death of Sir Thomas Wenttworthe, her late husband. Thomas to have henceforth the receipt of the rents which lady

---

[1] Seal : red wax, a signet, blurred.
[2] Seal : red wax, signet, letters and a bird.
[3] Draft on paper, in English.

Isabel was then having from her tenants, named in a schedule,[1] and pay yearly the said rents to her at Thurnskeughe, at Martinmas and Whitsuntide or within eight days; Thomas to use all the said tenants as his own, "puttynge owtt of ther fermoldes and takinge of grassomes[2] only exceptt," during lady Isabel's life; should she be disposed to come and dwell at the manor of Bretton, Thomas to provide "two honest chambres for her to lye in," in like manner as she had previously; and should Thomas not keep these articles she should enter and receive her rents as she had previously done. (*Ibid.*, No. 65).

57. April 10, 7 Edward VI [1553]. Receipt[3] by Stephen Lasse of Howxton,[4] co. Suffolk, gent., and Frances his wife, one of the daughters of Thomas Wentworth of Bretton Hall, co. York, esq., from Thomas Wentworth of 6*li.* 13*s.* 4*d.* in full payment of 100 marks "for and in the name of the canonicall parte or chylds portion" of the said Frances; and release of all actions, real and personal. (*sd.*) by me Stephann Lacy. (*Ibid.*, No. 56).

58. Nov. 10, 4 & 5 Philip and Mary [1557]. Bond by Elizabeth Allott of Bentlay, widow, and Robert Allott of the same, yeoman, to Matthew Wentworth of Westbretton, esq., in 200 marks to be paid at the following Easter.

Condition : if Elizabeth and Robert kept the terms of an indenture between Matthew Wentworth and them, same date, for the sale of two closes, called Abbott flatt and Burnebanke, with appurtenances in the lordship of Westbretton, and the demise of a tenement or farmhold called Sterlyngbowere and all the lands [*etc.*] belonging, the bond to be void.

Witnesses, Thomas . . . . . , Thomas West, Robart March,[5] William Wheatley, jun., William Syke, Robert Gledyll, Humphrey Newton, John Oxlee, John Hermyttage. (*Ibid.*, No. 64).

Great Broughton (Cleveland).

59. Release by Richard Bolgan and Ellen his wife, for them and Ellen's heirs, to Sir Nicholas de Menill of all right in two tofts and two bovates of land with appurtenances in Magna Brouthton, and in all their other lands and tenements in the same vill; to hold to Sir Nicholas for life and after his death to Nicholas[6]

---

[1] Not annexed to the draft.
[2] Gersums, being fines paid on entry.
[3] In English.
[4] Probably Hoxne; see Copinger's *Suffolk Records*, iii, 220, for an association of a Stephen Lacy with that place.
[5] The first three are signatures. The first is possibly Saivell.
[6] Illegitimate son of Sir Nicholas, who settled a great part of his property on him in 1314 (*Complete Peerage*, new ed., viii, 628).

son of Lucy daughter of Robert de Tweng, and the heirs of his body, with remainder in default of issue to the right heirs of Sir Nicholas. Witnesses, Sir John de Eure, William de Moubrai, William de Hestinges, Geoffrey de Rosels, William de Malteby, Richard de Marton, Robert his brother, Walter Laue, John de Salton.[1] (*Duke of Norfolk*, Misc., II, i, No. 16).

60. Grant by Hugh son and heir of Thomas de Fennewik of Magna Brothton to Sir Nicholas de Menill, knt., of a toft and croft and a bovate of land with appurtenances in Magna Brothton, of which the toft and croft lay between the toft of the abbot of Ryuaus and that which Sir Nicholas had of Richard Bolgan in the same vill, and of the bovate seventeen acres and one rood lay between the land of the abbot of Ryuaus on one side and that which John the reeve of that vill was holding of Sir Nicholas, two roods lay *apud Ouemam*, and one rood at Lynberghflat between the land of John de Saulton and that which the said John the reeve was holding;[2] to hold, in meadows, feedings and pastures, to Sir Nicholas for life, and after his death to Nicholas son of Lucy de Tweng and the heirs of his body, with remainder in default of issue to the right heirs of Sir Nicholas; to hold of the chief lords of the fee. Witnesses, William de Hestinges, William Moubrai, Matthew de Semer, John Gower of Sexhou, Stephen de Gouton. (*Ibid.*, II, i, No. 10).

Bulcliffe (West Bretton).

61. April 12, 35 Henry VI [1457]. Indenture between William FitzWilliam, Nicholas FitzWilliam, and Richard Wyntworth, esqs., on one part, and John of the Syke and Jenet his wife, on the other, witnessing that the former had let to farm to the latter and the heirs male of their bodies a "mese" called Bulclyff, with all lands, "ynges," woods, pastures, commons with the appurtenances belonging thereto, and also the lands belonging to the abbey of Bylond lying within the "presynght" of the said "mese"; to hold, as Elizabeth of Wyntworth lately occupied them, from the following Whitsunday for a term of forty years, paying yearly 100s. in equal portions at Martinmas and Whitsunday, and also to the abbot of Bylond or his assign 4s. in equal portions at the same feasts; power to Richard Wyntworth to distrain for the rent if it should be forty days in arrear; John and Jenet to have "housbote, heybote, ploughbote and waynbote" necessary to serve them during the term. "And also at what tyme the woddes of the seid mese shall be coled[3] or sold the seid Richard or his

[1] Seal : white wax, chipped; a star.
[2] This gives the bovate as eighteen acres.
[3] Cut (*Eng. Dial. Dict.*, s.v. coll.).

heires shall make & reparell all the hegges aboute all the seid woddes for sawyng of the spryng for thre yeres next fouloyng the seid colyng or sale at theire owen propre costs. Also it shall be lefull to the seid John & Jenet & to theire heires male to gete & haue fuell uppon the seid ground for the fyre as of stone or cole competenly to serue theym & theire meney dureyng all the seid terme. Also if the seid John Jenet or their heires male nedeth or will byld uppon the seid ground eny houses for theire ese they shall haue tymbyr & stone uppon the seid ground delyuerd theym such as is there & will serue theym for the seid beldyng duryng the seid terme." The demisees to leave the premises at the end of the term without impeachment of . . . .[1] or hurt[2] of the said Richard. Mutual seals.[3] Witnesses, Richard Dalton, John Tyde, John Yong. (*Lord Allendale*, Bulcliffe, No. 11).[4]

Calverley.

62. Grant by William de Cauuerlay[5] called Scoticus to Simon de Ottel', clerk, in frank-marriage with Alice his daughter, of 15s. worth of yearly rent in Caluerlay, namely, from the land which Simon de Roudon' then held 5s. 6d., from the land which John the fuller then held 5s., from the land which Richard Hunte then held 2s. 6d., from the land which William Harpur then held 12d., and from the land which Thomas son of Menot then held 12d., saving to the grantor wardships, reliefs and other escheats; also free entry within his fee to Simon to make necessary distraints. Bond by the grantor to observe this condition by giving power to the sheriff of Yorkshire to exact half a mark for the fabric of the castle of York. Power to redeem the rent by payment of 9 marks to Simon or his heirs. Witnesses, Sir Henry, vicar of Cauuerl[ay], Sir Alexander, his chaplain, Philip de Ferchelay,[6] Jordan de Wdhall, Geoffrey Luuecoc, John Scoticus, William le Harpur, John the fuller. (*Bradford Public Libraries*, Misc. MSS.).

Canontborpe (Aston).

63. Wednesday the eve of St. John the Baptist, 9 Edward II [June 23, 1316]. Grant by Robert Redser and Margery his wife

[1] Torn; the word begins with 'rep.'

[2] Above the line is inserted 'excepte thay shall not pull no howses downe wyllfully.'

[3] Three slits; two tags; signets, one broken.

[4] Nos. 1-10 of this series were printed in vol. vi.

[5] Calverley. This is the grant mentioned in No. 30 of *Calverley Charters*, Thoresby Soc., which amplifies the arrangements between grantor and grantee for the redemption of the rent; five witnesses are common to the two charters; the present one must have been issued on the same occasion or shortly before No. 30, to which the editors assigned the date *c.* 1260.

[6] Or Ferthelay [Farsley].

to Gilbert Pokenal of Orgraue, his heirs or assigns, of all the tenements with appurtenances which descended to Margery by hereditary right after the death of John de Cranny her father and Margaret her sister at Caunpthorp;[1] with all easements. Witnesses, John de Ullay, William de Orgraue, John son of Nicholas de Aston, Ralph Ellot, William de Byrlayston. Cranem[2] in the parish of Aston. (*Duke of Norfolk*, Box x, No. 76).

Carlton Miniott.

64. Jan. 10, 22 Henry VII [1506-7]. Bond by Robert Wyvell, esq., to Miles Staveley and John Staveley, his son and heir apparent, in 40*li.* to be paid at Whitsuntide if they did not hold all those messuages, tofts, cottages, lands and tenements with appurtenances in Carleton Mynyot, which they lately had of his feoffment, without claim by him, Eleanor his wife and his heirs.[3] (*W. M. Staveley, esq.*, Carlton Miniott, No. 1).

Chevet.

65. Sunday after the Epiphany [Jan. 9], 1316[-7]. Grant by Margery le Normand[4] of Chyuet to Joan her daughter, her heirs and assigns, of her chief messuage in Chyuet with all buildings, and all the lands and tenements, rents and services with appurtenances which she then had in the same, with all right and claim which belonged to her or her heirs, except 3*d.* yearly rent from a tenement called Oliue Yerd and twelve acres of land which she was retaining in her own hand, as they lay in different parts in the territory of Chyuet, of which four acres lay in the south field under *le Heyebalke* towards Notton, four acres lay in the east field towards Walton called Littelferthing, and four acres lay in the west field by *le Grene* on which Cutteloue[5] croft abutted. Witnesses, Thomas de Staynton, Robert his brother, Thomas de Chyuet, Robert Monk of the same, William Gryndenot. Chyuet.[6] (*Bradford Public Libraries*, Misc. MSS.).

66. Saturday, the Annunciation of the B.V.M., 11 Edward II [March 25, 1318]. Appointment by Margery (*Marioria*) le Normaunt of Sir Edmund the chaplain as attorney to deliver seisin to William the tailor of Folby and Joan his wife of eight acres of land and 3*d.* worth of rent, with appurtenances in Cheuet, in accordance with her charter. Cheuet. (*Ibid.*).

[1] Some notes on Canonthorpe are given in *E.Y.C.*, vi, 212.
[2] Apud Cranem.
[3] Fragment of seal on a tongue of the parchment.
[4] She occurs in the series of Chevet deeds printed in vol. vii.
[5] or Cuttelone.
[6] Fragment of seal of white wax.

67.   Sunday before St. Barnabas the Apostle [June 9], 1342. Grant by Thomas son of Stephen Bithebruk of Cheuet to Sir Henry de Crikelston, rector of a moiety of the church of Cottegraue, his heirs or assigns, of all the tenement and bovate of land which Robert Bithebruk his grandfather had formerly purchased of Roger Colloc and Avice his wife in the vill and territory of Cheuet. Witnesses, Robert Munk, William Grindelnot, Roger Bithebruk, Thomas de Wodeson, Adam de Hegrod.   Cheuet.[1]   (*Sir Thomas Pilkington*, Chevet, Series B, No. 20).[2]

68.   Same day.   Grant by Henry de Crigelston, rector of a moiety of the church of Cotgraue, to Thomas son of Stephen Bythebruk and Joan the grantor's sister, in frank-marriage, of all the tenement and land which he had formerly purchased of Robert Ouyot of Walkringham in the vill and territory of Cheuet; to hold to them and the heirs of their bodies, with reversion to the grantor or his right heirs.   Witnesses [*same as to the preceding deed; Heghrod so spelt*].   Cheuet.   (*Ibid.*, No. 21).

69.   St. Barnabas, [June 11], 1342.   Quitclaim by John Isoud and Maud his wife to Thomas son of Stephen Bithebruk of all right in the bovate of land which Robert Bithebruk had formerly purchased of Roger Colloc and Avice his wife, and in the acre of land on *le Merflat* which Robert had purchased of John Grindelnot, [which they held] in the name of dower after the death of Stephen Bithebruk, formerly Maud's husband.[3]   Cheuet.[4]   (*Ibid.*, No. 22).

70.   Thursday, St. Edmund the Archbishop [Nov. 16], 1346. Grant by Robert de Flaxton, rector of the church of Crofton, to Robert Monk of Cheuet and Isabel his wife, of twelve acres of land in the fields of Cheuet, which he had purchased of Roger Bythebrok and Margery his wife, with all easements; to hold to them and the survivor, and after their death to William their son and the heirs of his body, with successive remainders to Roger, William's brother, and Richard his brother and the heirs of their bodies, with reversion to the right heirs of Robert and Isabel.   Witnesses, Robert de Stanton, William de Notton, Thomas le Boysvile, Thomas Monk of Cheuet, Thomas son of Stephen of the same, Adam de Heghrod, Robert de Sandale, chaplain.   Cheuet.[5]   (*Ibid.*, No. 23).

[1] Portion of seal of yellow wax : possibly a hawk preying over a bird.
[2] The first portion of Sir Thomas Pilkington's deeds relating to Chevet, up to the year 1337, was pd. in vol. vii.
[3] *quondam mariti sui.* This clearly indicates Maud, who had apparently married John Isoud after the death of her first husband.
[4] Seal : yellow wax, small, not deciphered.
[5] Seal : white wax, oval, 1 × ⅞ in.; a standing ecclesiastical figure ; poor impression and chipped; legend not deciphered.

71. Friday before St. Andrew the Apostle [Nov. 28], 1348.
Grant by Beatrice, formerly wife of Adam Witbelt of Walton, to
Roger Scot and Alice her daughter in frank-marriage, of all her
messuage with the croft adjacent in the vill of Chift, and all her
lands and meadows in the same, namely, an acre on Cristianrod,
an acre on Drahstaewel, a rood on Wolpit, a rood on Latheclif,
two selions abutting on the ditches of the chapel, an acre on
Aylsirod, half an acre in three selions abutting on *le Lanegat* in
different places, half an acre on Bradlay, half an acre on Adamrod,
half an acre at *le Milnwel*, a rood on Malinrod, a rood by *le thre
grenes* abutting on *le Langat*, a rood by Wetlaygat, half a rood on
End' furlangs, two selions on End' furlangs, a plot of meadow in
le Hardheng, and two plots of meadow in Adamker; also all her
meadow in the great meadow of Walton, namely, one swath[1]
(*swatha*) at *le nuhengthorne*, two swaths in Lefall, and a share of a
swath in *le Drihalges*; for a sum of money given beforehand.
Witnesses, Robert Monk, Thomas Monk his son, Thomas son of
Stephen, Roger Bithebrok, Thomas de Wodussom, John Kyng of
Walton, Adam de Heghrod. Chift. (*Ibid.*, No. 24).

72. Michaelmas [Sept. 29], 1349. Grant by James le
Troumper of Sandale to Beatrice widow of Adam Witbelt of
Walton and Alice her daughter, formerly[2] wife of Roger Scot,
of all the lands, meadows and tenements which he had of the
grant and feoffment of the said Alice[3] in the vills of Cheuet and
Walton; to hold for their lives and the life of the survivor, with
remainder to Joan daughter of Roger Scot and Alice, and the
heirs of her body, with remainder to her right heirs. Witnesses,
Roger Bithebrok of Cheuet, Thomas son of Stephen of the same,
Thomas Grindelnot, Robert Malkynson, Adam de Heghrod.
Cheuet.[4] (*Ibid.*, No. 25).

73. Wednesday, St. Gregory the Pope [March 12], 1353[-4].
Grant by Richard del Yle of Crigeleston to Thomas son of William
Grindenot of Cheuet, and Cecily his wife, and the heirs of their
bodies, of all the tenement, meadows and lands, with appurtenances
which he had of the grant and feoffment of the said Thomas[5]
in the vill and territory of Cheuet; with reversion in default of issue
to Thomas's heirs. Witnesses, John de Mallyng, Roger be la
Brouk, John Grynhod, Thomas son of Stephen, Edmund de
Wethlay. Cheuet. (*Ibid.*, No. 26).

[1] Examples of the word, as a measure of grass land, are given in *O.E.D.*
[2] This shows that Roger Scot had died since Nov. 1348.
[3] This is in the collection, dated Saturday before St. Laurence the
Martyr [Aug. 8], 1349. (*Ibid.*, No. 25A).
[4] Seal : white wax, round ¾ in.; traces of a human face; chipped.
[5] Also in the collection, on the preceding Sunday, same witnesses.
(*Ibid.*, No. 27).

74. Thursday, the Decollation of St. John the Baptist, 27 Edward III [Aug. 29, 1353]. Grant by John de Trafford of Newekroft to Richard son of Gilbert de Haydok, his heirs and assigns, of his capital messuage, with all his lands and tenements, as in lordships, demesnes, wardships, reliefs and escheats, woods and plains, meadows, feedings and pastures, waters, mosses (*mussis*) and marshes, mills and fisheries, with appurtenances in the vill of Cheuete, together with the homage and services of Thomas Munk, Thomas son of William Gryndenote, Roger Bythebrok, and Thomas son of Richard de Cheuete, in respect of the free tenements which they were holding of him in the same vill; also all his lands and tenements with houses and buildings and their appurtenances in the vill of Ryhull, co. York. Urmeston, co. Lancaster. (*Ibid.*, No. 28).

75. Sunday after the Translation of St. Thomas the Martyr [July 11], 1367. Grant by Cecily daughter of Thomas Monk of Chyffte, in her virginity, to Sir Thomas del Stokke, rector of the church of Derton, and Sir Nicholas de Rylay, chaplain, of all the lands and tenements with appurtenances which had fallen to her by hereditary right after the death of Thomas her brother within the bounds of the vills of Cheyfft and Crigelston, with the reversion of all the lands and tenements which Denise who was the wife of Thomas Monk of Chyffte and Katherine who was the wife of Thomas the grantor's brother were holding for life by way of dower within the bounds of the same vills. Witnesses, John de Dronsfeld, John Tours, John de Staynton, Thomas de Doddeworth, Thomas Stevenson of Cheyfft. Cheyfft.[1] (*Ibid.*, No. 29).

76. Tuesday after the Assumption of the B.M. [Aug. 17], 1367. Grant[2] by Thomas del Stokke, rector of the church of Derton and Sir Nicholas de Rylay, chaplain, to Henry de Dernilegh and Cecily his wife, daughter of Thomas Monk of Chyffte, and the heirs of their bodies, of all the lands and tenements and reversions with appurtenances, which they had of the grant of the said Cecily within the bounds of the vills of Chyffte and Crigelston; with remainder in default of issue to Cecily, her heirs or assigns, after Henry's death, or to Henry, his heirs or assigns, after Cecily's death. Witnesses [*same as to the preceding deed*]. At Cheyfft and Crygelston.[3] (*Ibid.*, No. 30).

77. The Purification of the B.V.M. [Feb. 2], 1369[-70]. Grant by Richard de Horsfall to John his brother and Thomas son

---

[1] Same seal as the second to the next deed.
[2] Also the counterpart of the indenture; same seals. (*Ibid.*, No. 31).
[3] Two seals, red wax : (1) round, ⅝ in.; beneath a triple canopy St. Katherine standing and holding a wheel, a female figure on either side of her; (2) oval, 1⅚ × 1⅚ in.; a votary kneeling before the Virgin and Child; * MAT' DEI MEMENTO MEI.

of Stephen Bithebrok of Cheuet, their heirs or assigns, of all his goods, movable and immovable, meadows, lands, pastures and tenements, which he had in the vill and territory of Cheuet, with all appurtenances. Witnesses, Sir John Bosuill, knt., John Kyng of Walton, Sir Thomas de Wodesom, chaplain, John Pelle, William de Walton, chaplain. Cheuet. (*Ibid.*, No. 32).

78. Monday after the Annunciation of the B.V.M., 49 Edward III [March 26, 1375]. Grant by Robert, vicar of Bolton on Dyrne, and William de Walton, chaplain, to Sirs Thomas de Anglehill and Robert Gylmyn, chaplains, of a messuage with buildings and thirteen acres of arable land, with appurtenances in the vill and fields of Cheuet and Walton, which they had of the grant of Magota formerly wife of Roger Bythebroke (*iuxta le Broke*). Witnesses, Thomas de Staynton, Richard de Horsfall, Thomas son of Stephen. Cheuet.[1] (*Ibid.*, No. 33).

79. Michaelmas, 51 Edward III.[2] Grant by Sir Robert del Bruke and Sir William de Walton to Sir John Bosuyll of Chyued, his heirs and assigns, of all the lands and tenements which they had of the grant of Margery wife of Roger Bythebruke (*per le Bruke*) of Chyued in the vill and fields of the same. Witnesses, Thomas son of Stephen de Chyued, John Got of Notton, John Wodword of the same. Chyued. (*Ibid.*, No. 34).

80. April 20, 51 Edward III [1377]. Appointment by William Neuill of Pycale, knt., of John Grenehode of Ketilthorpe, and Thomas Stephenessone of Chete, as attorneys to deliver seisin to Sirs William de Walton and Nicholas de Ryley, chaplains, of a messuage and sixteen acres of land with appurtenances in Chete in accordance with his charter. Rolleston. (*Ibid.*, No. 35).

81. Friday, St. Mark the Evangelist [April 25], 1382. Grant by John Pelle of Crykelston to Sir Richard de Dronsfeld, chaplain, and Henry de Dernylegh,[3] of all the messuages, with buildings, lands and tenements, rents and services, with appurtenances which he had in the vills of Cheyfft, Crykelston, Walton and Sandall by curtesy after the death of Alice daughter of Thomas Monck his wife; to hold for the grantor's life. Witnesses, John de Staynton, Thomas de Whetelay, Thomas de Cheyfft, William

---

[1] Seal: red wax, round, ⅔ in.; a merchant's mark; legend not deciphered; broken at the bottom. Tag for another seal, missing.

[2] This looks like a mistake as the 51st year ended with the king's death in June 1377, and Mich. 1376 was in the 50th year.

[3] On Thursday, St. Philip and St. James [May 1], same year, Henry de Dernelee quitclaimed all right in these premises to Sir Richard Dronsfeld, chaplain; at Berneslay. Seal, red wax, round, ⅛ in.; a flower; legend not deciphered. (*Ibid.*, No. 37).

de Doddeworth, Thomas de Staynton.   Crykelston.[1]   (*Ibid.*,
No. 36).

82.   Wednesday after St. Mark the Evangelist [April 30],
1382.   Quitclaim by Cecily daughter and heir of John Pelle of
Crykelston and of Alice his wife, daughter of Thomas Monk of
Cheyfft, in her virginity, to Sir Richard de Dronsfeld, chaplain,
of all right in the reversion of all the messuages with buildings,
lands and tenements, rents and services, with appurtenances which
could fall to her within the townships (*villat'*) of Cheyfft, Crykelston, Walton, and Sandall, and which the said Richard had of the
grant of her father; also in the reversion of all the messuages [*etc.*]
which Sir John Bosseuile, knt., was holding in the name of dower
in the same vills of the grant of Katherine wife of Thomas Monk
the younger and Denise wife of Thomas Monk of Cheyfft the
elder. Witnesses, John de Staynton, Thomas de Staynton, Richard
de Keuerisforth, William de Doddeworth, Thomas de Whetelay
of Woluelay. Crykelston.[2]   (*Ibid.*, No. 38).

83.   Sunday after the Invention of the Cross [May 4], 1382.
Grant by Richard de Dronsfeld, chaplain, to Sirs John Howell,
perpetual vicar of Sandale, William de Walton, chaplain, and
John de Wodroff, of all the lands and tenements, rents and services,
with reversions, which he had within the townships of Chyeft,
Crykelston, Walton and Sandale of the grant of John Pell of
Crykelston and of Cecily, daughter and heir of the said John
Pell and Alice his wife, daughter of Thomas Monk of Cheyft.
Witnesses, Thomas Bosuyll of Ardeslay, John de Dronsfeld, John
de S[t]aynton, Thomas de Whetlay of Wlfelay, William de Dod-
wrht. Chyeft.[3]   (*Ibid.*, No. 39).

84.   Same day. Grant by Henry de Dernele and Cecily[4] his
wife, daughter of Thomas Monk of Chyft to the same of all the
lands and tenements and reversions, with appurtenances, which
they had of the grant of Sir Thomas del Stokke, rector of the
church of Darton, and Sir Nicholas de Rylay, chaplain, within the
bounds of the vills of Chiefet and Crykelston;[5] also all the lands

[1] Seal : red wax, round, ⅞ in.; on an elaborately designed background a
shield of arms on which there is a charge, possibly a building; legend not
deciphered, much chipped.
[2] Seal : red wax, round, ¾ in.; St. Margaret standing, holding a cross in
her left hand, a palm on her left side; the serpent-like object on which she
stands is intended for a dragon; SAVNCA MARGARE.
[3] Seal : red wax, round, ⅞ in.; two figures or possibly birds facing each
other, the first word of the legend may be MATRIS ; blurred.
[4] It is clear from these deeds that she was daughter of Thomas Monk
the elder, and sister of Thomas the younger, and of Alice wife of John Pell.
She married Henry de Dernele in 1367 (see Nos. 75, 76 above). Cecily Pell,
mentioned in the preceding deeds, was her niece.
[5] See No. 76 above.

and tenements and reversions, rents and services, with appurtenances, which they had within the bounds of the vills of Sandale
and Walton by hereditary right after the death of Thomas Monk
son of Thomas Monk the elder. Same witnesses[1] and place.[2] (*Ibid.*,
No. 40).

85. Quindene of Michaelmas, 6 Richard II [1382]. Fine[3]
at Westminster before Robert Bealknapp, William de Skipwyth,
Roger de Fulthorp, and Henry Asty, justices, between John
Hewell, vicar of the church of Sandale, William Walton, chaplain,
and John Woderoue, querents, and Henry Dernele and Cecily
his wife and Thomas Berneslay and Alice his wife, deforciants, of
two messuages, eighty acres of land, twelve acres of meadow,
3s. 2d. rent, and a third part of a messuage, forty-six acres of
land, and six acres of meadow, with appurtenances in Cheuet,
Cregilston, Sandale, and Walton; the deforciants recognized the
tenements as the right of John Woderoue as those which the
querents had of the grant of the deforciants, and quitclaimed
them to him and his heirs from them and the heirs of Cecily and
Alice.[4] The querents gave 100 marks of silver. (*Ibid.*, No. 41).

86. Grant[5] by John Woderoff, John Hawell, perpetual vicar
of Sandall,[6] and Thomas Auggill, rector of the church of Elston,
to Thomas Boswill son of Sir John Boswill, knt., of all their lands
and tenements in the vills and fields of Wombewell, Derfeld,
Ryle, and Wynterset, with all lands, rents, bondages, [and] services
of all their tenants in Stanlay; also a burgage in Wakefeld formerly
belonging to William Leuersegh, with the rent of Schamells, and
all the houses formerly belonging to John de Fery in *le Brede-
bothes*; also all their lands and tenements in Cheft which had
formerly belonged to Robert Mounkes, except Halleynges, and all
their lands and tenements in the same vill and fields called Beton-
land, with a third part of all the lands and tenements called
Gryndilnoteland, with all appurtenances; also all their lands and
tenements in the vill and fields of Stoke which had formerly
belonged to William Elys, Adam Symond,[7] John Leueryk and
Cecily Mise, with Wyloghcroft called Venourland, and with a
messuage called Vikersplace, with all lands, meadows and pastures
belonging thereto; and also a burgage in Newarch situate in

<hr>

[1] Except that the fourth is given as Thomas de Staynton of Wlfelay.
[2] Two seals of red wax : (1) round, ¾ in.; a flower; legend not deciphered;
(2) broken.
[3] Two parts, joined by a tag with a seal of red wax, letter B.
[4] Possibly Alice was Cecily's daughter. Alice wife of John Pell was then
dead.
[5] Undated draft.
[6] John de Howell was inst. to the vicarage of Sandal Magna on 31 Aug.
1379, and his successor in 1393 (*Y.A.J.*, xxiv, 36).
[7] Or possibly Stymond; there is an abbreviation mark, possibly the letter
t, above.

Milnegate, with all appurtenances; to hold to him and the heirs
male of his body, with reversion to the right heirs of Sir John
Boswill, knt. (*Ibid.*, No. 46).

87. Nativity of the B.M. [Sept. 8], 1384. Grant by Edmund
Scheperd of Sandale to Sirs John de Howell, vicar of the church
of Sandale, and William de Walton, chaplain, of a third part of a
messuage which formerly belonged to Magota Bethebrok in the
vill of Cheft, and half an acre of arable land lying on Christianrode.
Witnesses, John Grenehod of Crygeleston, John Rylay of the same,
William de Dene of the same, Thomas Isaud of Cheft, William
Isaud of the same. Cheft.[1] (*Ibid.*, No. 42).

88. Sunday after St. Matthew the Apostle [Sept. 25], 1384.
Grant by Edmund Schepherd of Sandal to William de Storthes
the younger of Cheuet and Joan his wife, of all the tenements,
lands and meadows with appurtenances, which he had of the
grant and feoffment of the said Joan in the vill and territory of
Cheuet; to hold to them and the heirs of their bodies, with re-
mainder to the right heirs of Thomas Gryndelnote of Cheuet.
Witnesses, Thomas Staynton of Woluelay, John de Rylay, John
Grenhude, John Tomsone of Sandal, Thomas de Cheuet. Cheuet.
(*Ibid.*, No. 43).

89. St. Thomas the Apostle [Dec. 21], 1392. Grant by
William Monk of Rawmarch to Robert his son, his heirs and
assigns, of twelve acres of land lying in the fields of Cheuet which
had formerly belonged to Robert Monk his father. Witnesses,
John Bosseuill of Erdeslay, Thomas de Swath of Wyrkesburgh,
Thomas de Calthorn of Erdeslay, Richard Whyte of the same,
Robert Godfray of the same. Cheuet.[2] (*Ibid.*, No. 44).

90. Invention of the Cross [May 3], 1393. Grant by Robert
son of William Monk of Rawmarch to William de Sandale, chaplain, and William de Doddeworth, of the same premises [*as in the
preceding deed*]. Witnesses, John Woderof, Richard de Keuerisforth, William Pynder of Berneslay, Thomas Stephunson of
Cheuet, William his son. Cheuet.[3] (*Ibid.*, No. 45).

91. Monday after Holy Trinity, 16 Richard II[4] [May 18,

[1] Seal : white wax, round ½ in.; letter B.
[2] Seal : brown wax, round, 1⅛ in.; a winged animal standing; legend
not deciphered.
[3] Seal : red wax, round, ⅝ in.; a bird surrounded by foliage.
[4] Anno regni regis Ricardi secundi post conquestum Anglie sexto
decimo. The words *post conquestum* in the case of Richard II are unusual.
Indeed Round (*Family Origins*, p. 105) assumed that a document containing
the words was for that reason a fraud. But things which are unusual are
not necessarily impossible; and Hampson (*Medii Aevi Kalendarium*, ii, 21)
gives an example for 4 Ric. II.

1393]. Receipt by John de Annesleye, knt., from Achilles Boswell of 50s. sterling in part payment of 100s. in accordance with a bond. Annesleye. (*Ibid.*, No. 47).

92. June 12, 5 Henry IV [1404]. Receipt by John de Holme, chaplain, and William Torner, executors of the testament of Richard de Ferybrigg, chaplain, and coexecutors with John de Ferybrig, clerk, and assigns of the latter, from Achilles Bosuyll of 40s. sterling for the preceding Whitsuntide term for the farm of Monkeplace in Chyft. (*Ibid.*, No. 48).

93. June 6, 2 Henry VI [1424]. Grant by William del Droke of Sulgraue, co. Northampton, son and heir of Robert del Droke of Chete, co. York, to Adam de Mirfeld, William de Mirfeld, and Oliver de Woderoue, esqs., of three and a half acres of land with appurtenances in the vill of Chete in the north field, lying together between the land of Achilles de Bosville, esq., on one side, and that of the lord of Darcy on the other, and abutting on the pasture of Northwode, which had descended to him by hereditary right after the death of Robert his father. Witnesses, William Amyas, John Doghty, vicar of the church of Sandall, John Jakson, John Melton, Thomas Symkynson. Chete.[1] (*Ibid.*, No. 49).

94. Nativity of St. John the Baptist, 4 Henry VI [June 24, 1426]. Grant by Henry Chete to Elizabeth[2] his wife, her heirs and assigns, of all his tenement with all lands within the bounds of Chete, and appurtenances and rents. Witnesses, Achilles Boyswille, Thomas Cusworthe, William Lyghtolores, Geoffrey de Staynton, Simon de Norton. Chete. (*Ibid.*, No. 50).

95. Wednesday after the Assumption of the B.V.M., 10 Henry VI [Aug. 20, 1432]. Grant by John Smyth and Joan his wife to Thomas Smyth, their son, of a third part of a messuage built at the end of the vill of Chete, and another third part of a messuage called Margetplace lying in the middle of the vill, and fifteen acres of land and meadow with appurtenances lying in scattered lots in the fields of Chete, of which four and a half lay separately in divers parcels in an assart called Deconrode, five in *le Estfeld*, two in Chapelfeld, three in the field called Southfeld, three roods lay in Cristeanrode, and four swaths (*swatheas*) of meadow in Hardyng and two swaths in Adam Carre; to hold to him and the heirs of his body, with successive remainders to their son William and their daughter Agnes Chester and the heirs of

---

[1] Seal : red wax, small signet; not heraldic.
[2] Also written *Ezabell*.

their bodies. Witnesses, John Olyff,[1] Henry del Hill, John Bolton, William Lill, Henry Steuenson. Chete.[2] (*Ibid.*, No. 51).

96. Feb. 20, 4 Edward IV [1464-5]. Grant by John Stevynson the elder to Richard Hobkynson, chaplain, John Sprigonell, Oliver Haghe, Richard Wageor, John Hobkynson, and John Haghe, of all his messuages, lands, tenements, rents, reversions and services, with appurtenances in the vills and territories of Chete and Chapelthorpe. Witnesses, Robert Chapman, William Johnet, Thomas Blakker. Chete.[3] (*Ibid.*, No. 52).

97. Saturday before St. John the Baptist, 7 Edward IV [June 20, 1467]. Receipt by Maud Boswill, formerly wife of John Bosvill of Stoke by Newarke, from John Boswill, esq., of Chet, her son, of 5 marks for the preceding Whitsuntide term. (*Ibid.*, No. 53).

98. July 10, 3 Richard III [1485]. Quitclaim by John Smyth, brother and heir of Thomas Smyth, late of Chete, to William Bosvile of Chete, esq., of all right in a messuage with garden and croft adjacent, with appurtenances in Chete, and in all the lands and tenements in Chete which lately belonged to Thomas, late his brother.[4] (*Ibid.*, No. 54).

99. Oct. 14, 1 Henry VII [1485]. Whereas[5] Thomas Smyth late of Chete made estate to John Boswile, late of the same, esq., and his heirs, of a messuage, lands and tenements with appurtenances in Chete, and John Smyth his brother had quitclaimed to William Boswile of Chete, esq., son and heir of the said John, all his right therein, now William Boswile demised the same to John Smyth, "excepte percell therof which is depertied and assigned to too women in the name of thair hole dower therof for terme of thair lyues;" to hold for life, yielding yearly a red rose at the Nativity of St. John the Baptist if demanded, with reversion to the said William Boswile and his heirs. (*Ibid.*, No. 55).

100. Oct. 16, 21 Henry VIII [1529]. Receipt by Roger Rokley, esq., from John Nevell of Cheytt, knt., of 20*li.* in part payment of a larger sum due to him by reason of a marriage portion (*ratione maritagii*). Per me Rogerum Rokley.[6] (*Ibid.*, No. 56).

101. June 3, 1 Edward VI [1547]. Grant and feoffment by Thomas Dawnay of Cowyke, co. York, esq., and Christopher

[1] Or Clyff.
[2] Two seals, red wax : (1) a bird looking backwards; (2) letter R beneath an antique crown.
[3] Seal : red wax, small; letter W.
[4] Seal : red wax, small; letter C.
[5] In English.
[6] Seal on a tongue of the parchment : black wax, signet; letter R.

Haldenby of Haldenby, gent., at the request of dame Elizabeth Nevyll of Cheite, widow, and of Henry Nevyll, her son and heir, to the said dame Elizabeth of all their four closes with appurtenances in Cheite, namely, one called *le Crokes* of a yearly value of 33s. 4d., another called *Litle newe close*, 12s., another called *le Greate newe close*, 14s., and another called *le Greate Norwoode*, 20s.; which they lately had of the grant of the said Elizabeth and Henry; to hold for life without impeachment of waste, with remainder to Henry and Dorothy his wife and Henry's heirs. Cheite. (*sd.*) Thomas Dawnay and C.H.

Dorso : seisin delivered by [*sic*] Elizabeth Nevill and Henry Nevill to Thomas Dawnay and Christopher Haldenby, same day, in the presence of Gerard Haldenby of Cowik, gent., Robert Thornton of Cheit, clerk, Robert Sikes of the same, yeoman, Humphrey Holmes of the same, gent., John Jakson of Sokburn in the bishopric of Durham, yeoman, Robert Howit of Notton, husbandman, Richard Gill of the same, tanner, William Fyxby of the same, husbandman. (*Ibid.*, No. 57).

North Cliff (North Cave).

102. Friday after St. Nicholas [Dec. 9], 1334. Agreement[1] between Ellen formerly wife of William de Clif and Nicholas son of the said William, by which Ellen should have all the goods and chattels at York and Widyngton at the price placed on them in the inventory, except the small things found in the coffers of the said William and his chests which were devised to the said Nicholas; and she should answer from those goods to Katherine her daughter for what was devised to her in the testament of Alan (*Aleyn*) de Apelby, and also to William and Mariot her children for what belonged to them for their third part and also to the said Mariot for what was devised to her in the testament of the said William de Clif. Nicholas should have all the goods and chattels at Clif and in the coffers and chests of the said William at the price placed on them, and should pay therefrom the burial expenses of the said William, and also to Katherine de Clif and to a nun of Watton, sisters of the said William, and to Elizabeth his daughter what was devised to them in William's testament. Mutual seals to either part of the indenture.[2] Witnesses, Brother Edmund de Clif, Sir Richard de Melton, Sir Adam the chaplain. York.

Addition : And Ellen and Nicholas would pay William's debts both from the chattels belonging to the said children as from their own. (*Sir William Worsley*, North Cliff, No. 38).[3]

[1] In French.
[2] Small fragment of a seal of red wax on a tongue of the parchment.
[3] Nos. 1-37 of this series were printed in vol. vii.

103. Sunday before St. John the Baptist [June 23], 1336. Grant[1] by John de Holme of Northcliff[2] to Juliana his daughter, her heirs and assigns, of a messuage and a bovate of land which Stephen Bune had formerly held of him, with meadows, pastures, moors and marshes, and other appurtenances within the vill and without, doing to the lords of the fee the services due and rendering to the grantor for his life 7s. 6d. for all secular services at Martinmas and Whitsuntide in equal portions. Witnesses, William de Houton, Nicholas de Cliff, Richard de Santon, Thomas at the hall, William Suthiby, Richard the clerk of Santon. Northcliff. (*Ibid.*, No. 39).

104. All Saints, 15 Edward III [Nov. 1, 1341]. Grant[3] by Constance Cowyng of Northcliff to Elizabeth her daughter and Katherine, the latter's daughter, their heirs and assigns, of a toft and a selion of land with appurtenances in the vill and territory of Northcliff, the toft lying between that of Richard de Santon on one side and that formerly belonging to John de Holme on the other, and the selion lying in breadth between the land of Nicholas de Cliff on one side and that of John Talle on the other and in length from the foot of the hill (*le fotet del hill*) as far as Mardik. Witnesses, William de Houton, Richard de Santon, Nicholas de Cliff, William Secker of Cliff, William Westiby of the same. Cliff.[4] (*Ibid.*, No. 42).

105. Sunday before Michaelmas [Sept. 26], 1344. Grant[5] by William son of Henry, dwelling in Northclyff, and Alice his wife to William formerly son of John de Bagotby of Estthorp, of a yearly rent of 6s. from the toft and four acres of land in Northcliff, which he had of the grant and feoffment of the said Alice his wife before their marriage; to hold for his life of the grantor and his heirs. Witnesses, William de Houton, Nicholas de Cliff, Richard de Santon, Thomas Attehalle of Southcliff, William Southiby of the same. Southcliff. (*Ibid.*, No. 43).

106. Thursday after the Deposition of St. Cuthbert, 27 Edward III [March 21, 1352-3]. Whereas Nicholas de Northclif

[1] On the following Saturday Adam son and heir of John de Holme released and quitclaimed to Juliana his sister all right in the same; same witnesses, Southyby and Saunton so spelt; seal, yellow wax, indecipherable. (*Ibid.*, No. 40).

[2] On Thursday after Easter, 2 Edward III [April 7, 1328] he granted to William son of Nicholas de Northclyff all his land called *le Rodes* in Northclyff; witnesses, William son of Thomas de Houton, Richard de Santon, Roger a la Sale of Southclyff, William Southiby of the same, Geoffrey de Holton. (*Ibid.*, No. 41).

[3] *Cf.* No. 259 of date 1311 in vol. vii.

[4] Fragment of seal, red wax.

[5] On the following day this was inspected and confirmed by Henry son and heir of the grantor; the grantee was described as the elder; same witnesses. (*Ibid.*, No. 44).

by Santon was bound to William de Notton of Houeden in 16*li*. sterling to be paid on the feast of the Invention of the Cross, 29 Edward III [May 3, 1355], William granted that if he could freely fell, transport and sell a wood at Northclif called *le Oupwode* abutting on *le Oupgarth* towards the west, the field of Northclif towards the east, the wood formerly belonging to John de Holme towards the north, and the wood of the said Nicholas called *le Neweclos* towards the south, and also the herbage of the garden called *le Oupgarth* as inclosed by ditches, purchased from the said Nicholas, from the feast of the Invention of the Cross, 27 Edward III, up to the same feast, 29 Edward III, the said bond should be of no effect; but if William should be hindered from disposing of the said wood to his own use the bond should remain in force. Warranty of the said wood by Nicholas against the king and all men. Mutual seals to either part of the indenture.[1] Witnesses, Stephen son of Stephen de Houeden, Robert Roscelyn, Thomas de Hoperton, John Spaldington, Walter de Belleby, Walter de Brayton. Houeden. (*Ibid.*, No. 45).

107.   Sunday after Holy Trinity, 32 Edward III [June 3, 1358].   Grant by Nicholas son of William de Clif to William atte Marre, chaplain, and Thomas atte Halle of Southclif, of all his lands and tenements, and services of free tenants with all villeins and their progeny, with appurtenances in the vill and territory of Northclif, together with all his goods and chattels found in the said lands and tenements.   Witnesses, Thomas de Bentele, Simon de Heselarton, knts., Robert Danyel, John de Meus, Richard de Santon, Richard de Bolton, Richard Bernard the younger, William de Wyteby. Cliff. (*Ibid.*, No. 46).

108.   Wednesday after St. Barnabas the Apostle, 32 Edward III [June 13, 1358].   Grant by William atte Marre and Thomas atte Halle of Southclif to Nicholas son of William de Cliff for his life of all their lands, tenements, and services of free tenants. with villeins and their progeny, which they had of his grant and feoffment in the vill and territory of Northcliff, with power to Nicholas to make waste at will; with remainder after his death as to one moiety to Richard his son and Elizabeth, Richard's wife, and the heirs of their bodies, and as to the other to Katherine, Nicholas's wife, for her life with remainder to Richard and Elizabeth and the heirs of their bodies; with remainder as to both moieties, in default of issue, to Nicholas's right heirs. Witnesses, Marmaduke Conestable, Gerard Saluayn, knts., Gerard de Grymeston, Robert Danyel, John de Meus, William de Howton. Northclif. (*Ibid.*, No. 47).

[1] Fragment of seal of white wax; not deciphered.

NORTH CLIFF (NORTH CAVE)   39

109. Thursday, St. Simon and St. Jude [Oct. 28], 1372. Release and quitclaim by Juliana de Holm of Northclyf to Geoffrey de Birsay, her servant, and his heirs, of all right in a toft built on with a croft and an acre of land with appurtenances in North-clyf, which he had of her grant. Witnesses, John Tothe of Midilton, Thomas attehalle of Clyf, Matthew de Brunfleth.   Northclyf.[1] (*Ibid.*, No. 48).

110. Sunday before St. Gregory the Pope [March 7], 1377[-8]. Grant by Juliana de Holl'm, dwelling in Northclif, to Geoffrey de Birsay, her servant, his heirs and assigns, of a plot of land with appurtenances, which she had of the grant and feoffment of Richard de Besingby, son and heir of William de Besingby, as it lay in *leker*[2] of Northeclif in length between Rudhollm and the moor, and in breadth between *leker* of Adam Gous on the south side and *leker* of William Secker on the north. Witnesses, Richard de Clife, Thomas attehalle, John Seckar, Matthew de Brouneflete, William de Hirland, Richard de Birsay.   Northclife.[3]   (*Ibid.*, No. 49).

111. Tuesday after the Annunciation of the B.V.M. [March 27], 1380. Release and quitclaim by Juliana de Holm of North-clyue to Geoffrey de Bursay, her servant, his heirs and assigns, of all right in a piece of arable ground lying at the end of his croft between the land of Richard de Clyue on either side, [and] extending as far as the brow of the hill (*supercilium montis*), that is, Hulle Bree; which piece he had of her grant. Witnesses, Richard de Clyue, Thomas atte halle, John Sekker, Richard de Bursay.[4] Northclyue. (*Ibid.*, No. 50).

112. Monday, St. Hilary, 11 Richard II [Jan. 13, 1387-8]. Release and quitclaim by William de Westiby, chaplain, kinsman and heir of Constance daughter of Robert de Westiby of North-cliff, to Richard de Cliff, of all right in a toft and croft and eight acres of land with appurtenances in Northcliff, which Nicholas de Cliff his father had of the grant of the said Constance. Witnesses, Robert Conestable, knt., Gerard Saluayn, knt., William Dene of Hothom, Richard Rogerson of Neubald, Roger Fraunklayn of Wyghton, Thomas atte halle of Southcliff.   Northcliff.[5]   (*Ibid.*, No. 51).

---

[1] Seal : white wax, round, ¾ in.; a cross; legend not deciph̲

[2] The carr or water-meadow.

[3] Seal : white wax, round, ¾ in.; apparently a shield of arms, but much blurred.

[4] Seal : brown wax, round, ⅞ in.; a kneeling figure and several objects; legend not deciphered.

[5] Seal : brown wax, pointed oval, *c.* 1¼ × ⅞ in.; within a single crocketed canopy the Virgin, crowned, standing and holding the Child; below, beneath an arch, a figure in prayer; S WILL' I DE . . . . ; chipped; the place-name is not apparently Westiby.

113. Sunday, St. Barnabas the Martyr [June 11], 1394.[1] Grant[2] by Juliana de Holm of Northeclyf to Geoffrey de Birsay, his heirs and assigns, of a toft with croft adjacent and two selions of land in the vill and territory of Northclif, the former lying between the tofts and crofts formerly belonging to Thomas Daraynnes on either side, one selion lying on the south side of a certain cross in the field of the same between the land of the said Thomas on the north and that formerly belonging to Maud de Holm on the south, containing half an acre, and the other selion lying in the said field in a place called Brothland between the land of the said Thomas on the north and that of the said Maud on the south, containing three roods; with all easements, rendering yearly to the chief lords of the fee 1d. at Christmas for all services. Witnesses, Richard de Clif, Thomas athal of Southclif, Roger de Heuerigham, Thomas Marchal, William de Hireland, Henry Herui. Northclif. (*Ibid.*, No. 52).

114. Saturday after Ash Wednesday (*festum cinerum*), 1 Henry IV [March 6, 1399-1400]. Whereas John Vyle, chaplain, and Adam Gose had granted to Geoffrey de Birsay and Cecily his wife a messuage, a croft, two selions of land and a plot of land with appurtenances in Northcliff, for the term of their lives, with remainder to John de Birsay and Constance his wife and the heirs of their bodies, the said John and Constance granted that Geoffrey and Cecily should never be impleaded by them or their heirs by reason of any waste in the said tenements. Northcliff.[3] (*Ibid.*, No. 54).

115. Nov. 9, 1441, 20 Henry VI. Surrender by Constance widow of John Byrsay, in her widowhood, to Juliana one of the daughters and heirs of Geoffrey de Byrsay and to Elizabeth her sister, of the same premises [*as in the preceding deed*], which John Vile, chaplain, and Adam Gose had granted to the said Geoffrey and Cecily his wife for their lives, with remainder to the said John Byrsay and Constance his wife and the heirs of their bodies, with remainder in default of issue to Geoffrey's right heirs. She had put them in full possession by John Clerk of Santon her attorney.[4] Witnesses, John Parke of Beverley, chaplain, John Byrsay of Clyff, Thomas Snertforth of the same. North Clyff.[5] (*Ibid.*, No. 55).

---

[1] In 1394 June 11 fell on a Thursday.

[2] On Sept. 29, 1399 the grantee (Byrsay) granted these premises and also those described in No. 49 of this series to Sir John Wyle, chaplain, and Adam Gous; witnesses, Richard de Clyf, William de Eueringham, Thomas Marchall, Richard his son, William Byrsay, Henry de Gerthom; Northclyf; seal, white wax, small, not deciphered. (*Ibid.*, No. 53).

[3] Two seals, red wax; both broken.

[4] His appointment as attorney is dated the same day; John Byrsay is described as of Beverley; same seal. (*Ibid.*, No. 56).

[5] Seal: red wax, octagonal, small; a letter.

116. Nov. 10, 1441, 20 Henry VI. Grant by Juliana widow of William Boynton of Beverley, *skynner*, one of the daughters and heirs of Geoffrey de Byrsay, in her widowhood, to John Worleby of Kyngeston on Hull and Elizabeth his wife, her sister, their heirs and assigns, of the same premises, which formerly belonged to John Byrsay of Clyffe and Constance his wife. Same witnesses.[1] (*Ibid.*, No. 57).

117. Oct. 26, 1456, 35 Henry VI. Grant[2] by John Worlaby of Kyngeston on Hull to Edmund Portyngton, his heirs and assigns, of the same premises, which formerly belonged to John Birsay and Constance his wife; rendering yearly to the chief lords of the fee 1*d.* at Christmas for all secular services. Witnesses, John Holme of Bilton, esq., Thomas Etton of Kyngeston on Hull, merchant, Robert Downay of Hothom, Thomas Hert of Northclyff, John Arrowez of Newbald. Northclyff.[3] (*Ibid.*, No. 58).

118. Feb. 6, 2 Edward IV [1462-3]. Grant[4] by Edmund Portyngton of Beverley, esq., to William Gye, his heirs and assigns, of the same premises, which formerly belonged to John Worlaby; rendering yearly [*as in the preceding deed*]. Also appointment of Thomas Hert of Northcliff as attorney to deliver seisin. Witnesses, William Snartforth, John Clerkson, Robert Milles. Northcliff.[5] (*Ibid.*, No. 60).

119. April 7, 1465. Grant by William Gye of Beverley, yeoman, to Thomas Kirkman, Richard Smyth the elder, and John Syce of Beverley, chaplains, of the same premises, which formerly belonged to Edmund Portyngton; rendering yearly [*as before*]. Also appointment of Thomas Wystow of Welton as his attorney to deliver seisin. Witnesses, Sir John Snayth, prior of North-feryby,[6] Henry Lund of Southcaue, gent., Sir William Wels, vicar of Caue aforesaid,[7] Sir John Robynson and John Gryme of Beverley. Northcliff.[8] (*Ibid.*, No. 63).

120. Jan. 4, 5 Edward IV [1465-6]. Grant by Thomas Kirkman, Richard Smyth the elder, and John Syce of Beverley,

[1] Seal : red wax; broken; not heraldic.
[2] Also, same day, appointment of Edmund Mathew of Kyngeston on Hull as attorney to deliver seisin; same seal. (*Ibid.*, No. 59).
[3] Seal: red wax, small; a leaf.
[4] On the following day Gye granted the premises to Portyngton to hold for his life without impeachment of waste; witnesses, Thomas Mershall, Henry Eueryngham, Thomas Godsawe of Southcliff. (*Ibid.*, No. 61). And Portyngton appointed Thomas Hert as attorney to receive seisin. (*Ibid.*, No. 62).
[5] Seal: red wax, small; letters I and [?] D.
[6] Not mentioned in the list of priors in *V.C.H. Yorks.*, iii, 242.
[7] South Cave.
[8] Seal : red wax, small; a monogram or merchant's mark.

chaplains, to William Snayth and Ellen his wife, and William's
heirs and assigns, of the same premises, which formerly belonged
to Edmund Portyngton, and which they lately had of the grant
and feoffment of William Gye of Beverley, yeoman; rendering
yearly [*as before*].   Also appointment of William Kirkman of
Willardby as attorney to deliver seisin. Witnesses, John, prior of
Feryby, William Stakhous, William Pulton, Nicholas Kirkman,
Thomas Snayth. Beverley.[1] (*Ibid.*, No. 64).

121.   Jan. 14, 18 Edward IV [1478-9].   Grant by William
Snayth[2] of Willardby in the county of the town of Kyngeston on
Hull and Ellen his wife to William Fayrbarne and Margaret his
wife and William's heirs and assigns, of the same premises, which
formerly belonged to Edmund Portyngton, and which they lately
had of the grant and feoffment of Thomas Kyrkman, chaplain;
rendering yearly [*as before*].   Also appointment of William Dene of
Northcliff as attorney to deliver seisin. Witnesses, Thomas Madson,
Anthony Clarke, John Hert, John Swanne. Northcliff. (*Ibid.*,
No. 65).

122.   Monday after the Epiphany, 3 Henry V [Jan. 13,
1415-6].   Grant[3] by William Ermet of Northcliff and Alice his wife,
late wife of William Sekker of Northcliff, to Joan his (William
Ermet's) daughter of a toft with croft adjacent called Colplace in
the vill of Northcliff, as it lay in length and breadth between a
lane called Oughtgange on the north and the croft of Thomas
Brounflet, knt., on the south; also eleven selions of land with
appurtenances lying in the field of Northcliff; all of which Alice
and William Sekker, her late husband, had of the grant and
feoffment of John Lagg, chaplain; to hold for life, with reversion
after her death to Thomas Sekker of Northcliff, son of William
and Alice, his heirs and assigns. Witnesses, William de Cliff of
Cliff, Nicholas his son, Geoffrey Birsay of Northcliff, John his son,
Richard Pay of the same. Northcliff. (*Ibid.*, No. 66).

123.   Oct. [?],[4] 7 Edward IV [1467].   Grant by Richard
Sekkerr of North Clyff to Thomas Usflete of Holton and William

---

[1] Three seals, red wax : (1) letter T; (2) a merchant's mark; (3) a fleur-
de-lis.
[2] On Feb. 8, 19 Edward IV [1479-80], he released to William Farbarne,
husbandman, of Northe Clyf all real and personal actions which he had
against him. Northe Clyfe. Seal : red wax, small ; a castle with letters E
and ?. (*Ibid.*, No. 67).
[3] Stitched to this are two deeds giving the earlier history of the same
premises. In 1318 they were granted to Alice his daughter by Robert Westiby
of Northclif, who had them of the grant of Hawise his mother; and in 1385
they were granted to John Sekkar of Northcliff by William Westiby, chaplain, who had them by hereditary right after the death of Henry Westiby
his father.
[4] The deed is stained in places.

Snartforth of North Clyff of his capital messuage which he was then inhabiting in North Clyff, lying on either side between the tenements of Henry lord Vescy; and eight acres of land and meadow there; under the condition of fulfilling his will concerning the same. Witnesses, Robert Miles, Thomas Marschall, William Gybson, Richard Byrsay, ... Clyff. (*Ibid.*, No. 68).

124. July 4, 8 Henry VII [1493]. Grant by John Sekkerr of North Clyffe, kinsman and heir of Richard Sekkerr of the same, to William Usflete, his heirs and assigns, of a toft with a garden built on with appurtenances in the vill and territory of North Clyffe, as it lay in length and breadth between the toft of Elizabeth Vavasour of Thornton on *le hyll*, daughter and heir of Nicholas de Clyffe, on the south and the land of Hugh Morisby on the north, and abutted on the highway of the vill on the west and the wood of dame Margaret de Clyfford on the east. Also appointment of John Snarford as attorney to enter and deliver seisin. Witnesses, Thomas Usflete and John Usflete, gents., William Watson, John Taliour, Richard Hog. North Clyffe. (*Ibid.*, No. 71).

125. July 4, 8 Henry VII [1493]. This Indenture maid . . . . . bytwyx' Thomas Usflete and William Usflete of North Clyffe Gentilmen on that one partie and Raufe Legiard of Anlaby Gentilman on that odir partie wytnesseth that thiez partiez beyn agreed in maner and forme folowyng that is to saye that William Usflete son unto the foresaid Thomas schall by the grace of God wed and take to wife Alianor Twyer dowght'eley[1] unto the foresaid Raufe on this halfe[2] the fest of saynt Mich next efter the daytt heir of for the wheche mariage to be had the foresaid Raufe schall paye or make to be payed unto the foresaid William Usflete in penez and pene worth within one yeir next efter the daye of the mariage or within viij days next efter the said yeir xxx li. of lawfull mone of Inglond and of the oder partie the sayd Thomas Usflete is agreed to make and deliuer one sufficient astate in his mancion place the wheche he wonnys[3] in in North Clyffe unto the said William Usflete and Alianor Twyer to haue and to hold unto the said William and Alianor for terme of their two lyfez the rem[ainder] unto the right heirz of the said William Usflete and also yt is agreed by the said William that he on his partie schall deliuer or make to be deliuered unto the said Alianor afore the daye

[1] Daughter-in-law, *i.e.*, step-daughter. According to the ped. in *Glover's Visitation*, ed. Foster, p. 54, Ralph Legard of Anlaby married Constance Cutts and had a dau. Ellinor who married . . . Usfleet. It looks as if he married as a second wife the widow of one Twyer, and that Eleanor was her daughter, and not his. The next deed, where it is stated that Elizabeth Twyer was mother-in-law of John Usfleet, suggests that she had another dau., and that her two daus. married William and John Usfleet respectively.
[2] Side.
[3] Dwells.

of the mariage one sufficient astate for terme of life in lands and
tenements unto the yeirly valowe of xiijs. iiijd. and more ouer
yt is agreed by this present indenture that the foresaid Thomas
Usflete John Usflete and Sir Thomas Usflete parson of the parisch
church of Scorburgh that they or one of thayme schall within iiij
yeir next eftir daye of the mariage deliuer or make to be deliuered
one sufficient astate in lands and tenements unto the yeirly
valowe of xiijs. iiijd. unto the said William and Alianor for terme of
their two lifez the rem[ainder] unto the right heirz of the said
William and os by one obligacion for the more suyrte maid unto
the said William Usflete for the performance heir of more lairgely
dothe appere. In wytnesse wheir of . . . (*Ibid.*, No. 69).

126. March 4, 16 Henry VII [1500-1]. This Indenture
maid . . . . bytwyx' John Usflete Sir Th[omas] his broder on that
one partie and William Usflete their broder on that oder partie
wytnesseth that thiez partiez beyn agreid in maner and forme
folowyng that wheir diuers trauerseez is and hathe beyn bytwyx'
thiez said partiez for the howse with the apportenance wheche
Thomas Usflete fader unto thiez foresaid partiez purchased in the
feild and towne of North Clyffe, and also for the diliuere of one
obligacion wheir in the said Will[iam] Usflete sathe that the fore
named John and Sir Th[omas] his breder war bound in at the
mariage of the said Will[iam] with all oder contrauersez debaitez
and trispassez had or moued afore this daye os towchyng the
premissez to abied and fulfyll the award odir and jugement of
Mastrez Elizabeth Twyer moder in lawe unto the said John,
Robert Astyn Gentilman and Joh[n] Garthom of Fosham in and
of the tityll of the foresaid howse and odir os afore is rehirsed, for
gude peez and unite heir aftir to contenewe bytwyx' thiez said
partieez, Fyrst thiez arbitrows odirs awards jugez and demez that
the said Will[iam] Usflete schall haue unto hym and Alinore his
wife for terme of their livez the howse in North Clyffe and also
the howse wheir in theye won at makyng heir of in Newbold and
aftir their discesse the said John Usflete to haue the said howse
in Newbold to remayn unto hym his heirz for euermore, and also
it is agreid that the said Will[iam] Usflete schall make or cause
to be maid one sufficient estait in and of the howse of the Corner
next unto the said howse afore graunt in Newbald for terme of
life unto the said John and to his heirz for euermore aftir the
discesse of the said William and Alienore, and more ouer it is
agreid for the howse at North Clyffe whech the foresaid Thomas
Usflete purchased that the said Will[iam] and Alienore his wife
schall haue and inioye it for terme of their twoo lifez and yf it
fortuyn theme to haue issue then the said howse to remayn unto
the said issue and heirz for euermore, and yf it fortuyn the said
Will[iam] and Alienore to discesse without issue that then the said
John Usflete to haue the said howse in North Cliffe to hym his

heirz for euermore, and also one oder howse in the said North
Cliffe whech the said Will[iam] purchased in the said North Cliffe,
and moreouer os for the obligacion whech the said John Usflete and
his broder Sir Th[omas] was bound in unto their broder Will[iam] it
to bee cancelled with this that the said Sir Th[omas] schall paye
yeirly duryng the lyvez of the said Will[iam] and Alienore his
wife unto his broder John Usflete and his heirz vs. unto the whech
couants well and trewly to be performed and kept ouder partie
unto oder hathe setto·their sealez the daye and yeir aforerehirsed.[1]
(*Ibid.*, No. 70).

127. Quindene of Easter, 16 Henry VII [April 1501]. Fine
at Westminster between Robert Constable, serjeant at law, and
Thomas Fayrfax son of Guy Fayrfax, knt. (*militis*), querents, and
William Craythorn and Cecily his wife, deforciants, of the manor of
Northclyffe with appurtenances, also six messuages, four hundred
acres of land, twenty acres of pasture, sixty acres of meadow,
five hundred acres of wood, and 20s. rent with appurtenances in
Northclyffe; also two messuages and 3s. 4d. rent in the city of
York; the right of Robert, as premises which Robert and Thomas
had of the grant of William and Cecily; quitclaim by William and
Cecily and the latter's heirs.   Robert and Thomas gave 100*li.*
(*Ibid.*, No. 72).

128. Feb. 24, 21 Henry VIII [1529-30]. Grant by Gerard
Usflete, gent., son and heir of John Usflett, gent., lately deceased,
to Thomas Colvell of Newbauld, his heirs and assigns, of a messuage
with a croft and two selions of land containing two acres, also a
plot of land lying in *le West Carre* containing about six acres of land,
with all appurtenances in the vill and territories of Northclyff,
which had descended to him by hereditary right after the death
of his father, and in which he was then alone seised in fee simple.[2]
(*Ibid.*, No. 73).

129. March 3, 21 Henry VIII [1529-30]. Grant by the same
to Thomas Colvell, late of Newbauld, his heirs and assigns, of the
reversion of a messuage, toft, croft, two acres of land and a plot
of land called *le Carre* with all appurtenances in the vill and
territories of North Clyff, of which Thomas was than seised in
right of Eleanor his wife for the term of her life; rendering to the
chief lords 1d. at Christmas for all secular services.   Witnesses,
Anthony Langdale, esq., John Jenyson, yeoman, Robert Cotes,
Randolf Harte, John Todde, Robert Sotheron, John Wressill.
(*Ibid.*, No. 74).

[1] Seal to this part : red wax, small; a star.
[2] Seal : red wax, small : three converging lines.

130. April 20, 24 Henry VIII [1533]. Grant by John Sekker to Thomas Watson, Thomas Yates of Southclyff, John Middylton of Shipton, and Randolf Harte of Northclyff, of a toft in Northclyff, lying between the land of the college of Acaster on the south and that of James Constable on the north, one end on the west abutting on *le Wescrofte* and on the east on the highroad; also eleven selions of land in the fields of Northclyff, lying between the land of the said James and of Mungo Westerdale, except on *le Burtelandes*, where the land lay between that of the said James on either side; which selions contained about three acres; to hold to the use of the grantor and Cecily his wife for their lives and that of the survivor, with remainder to the use of the grantor's right heirs.[1] (*Ibid.*, No. 75).

131. Aug. 16, 25 Henry VIII [1533]. Release by Gerard Usflete, gent., son and heir of John Usflete, and kinsman and next heir of William Usflete, deceased, for a sum of money, to John Sekker, son and heir of Robert Sekker, deceased, of all right in a messuage with garden annexed with appurtenances in North Clyff, then in the tenure of Joan Forster, widow, which were of the inheritance of the said John.[2] (*Ibid.*, No. 76).

132. July 25, 27 Henry VIII [1535]. Grant[3] by John Sekker of North Clyff to Philip Kyddall of South Clyff, his heirs and assigns, of a toft with croft adjacent called Colplace in the vill of North Clyff and eleven selions of land[4] with appurtenances in the same; which toft and croft lay between the land of the college of Acastre on the south and that of James Constable, esq., on the north, one end on the west abutting on *le West Croft* and on the east on the highroad; also eleven selions of land in the fields of North Clyff, of which seven lay scattered (*ubique*) in the fields between the land of the said James and of Mungo Westerdale, except on *le Burtlands* and in *le lauereke marr*, and one selion by *le balk* leading to *le Whyclyff* where [the land of] James Constable lay on either side, and one little headland (*hedland*) at *le Sorowcroft heed*, with appurtenances.[5] (*Ibid.*, No. 77).

---

[1] Seal : red wax, small; letter [?] L.

[2] Seal : red wax, small ; a star.

[3] Also both parts of an indenture of sale, dated the preceding day ; both vendor and purchaser are styled "husbandman" ; all muniments were to be transferred ; the vendor was to make a lawful estate before the feast of "lammesse" [Aug. 1] next following ; the purchaser paid 6*li.* 13*s.* 4*d.*; in English. (*Ibid.*, Nos. 78 and 78A). The vendor entered into a bond in 20 marks to observe the terms of this indenture (No. 79).

[4] It is clear from the warranty clause that only one set of eleven selions was granted.

[5] Seal : small, red wax ; an animal.

133. July 22, 30 Henry VIII [1538]. Grant[1] by Philip Kyddall and Ellen his wife of Sowthclyffe to James Constable of Northclyffe, esq., his heirs and assigns, of the same premises [*as in the preceding deed*].

Dorso : possession taken on St. James's day next following [July 25] "both by the handyll of the dore and by a pece of grownde of the garth syde of the howse" in the presence of Robert Constable, Thomas Marcyall, Symonde Garthom, Robert Cotts, John Wressyll, William Perkynson, John Torner, and James Cotts son of the said Robert.[2] (*Ibid.*, No. 80).

134. March 26, 30 Henry VIII [1539]. Grant[3] by Mungo Westerdayll son and heir of Robert Westerdayll and of Anne his wife, daughter and heir of William Assyngby, deceased, for a sum of money, to James Constable of North Clyff, esq., his heirs and assigns, of all his lands and tenements, rents, reversions and services, with appurtenances in North Clyff, South Clyff, and Santon, which had descended to him by hereditary right after the death of his father or mother. (*sd.*) Mungo Wyst'dayll.[4]

Dorso : possession given on the following day by the grantor by his own hands at North Clyff, delivering the same "by the snekke of the dare[5] in the name of all the hole londs herin comprysyd," in the presence of Anthony Langdale of Santon, esq., Thomas Langdale his son, Robert Constable of Sledmer, Sander Perkynson, "the tenant of the howsse now," and William his son, Robert Cotts, Thomas Harte, James Gylbart, Thomas Euers of Northclyffe, Anthony Johnson of Howghton, Thomas [?] Garth of Sowthclyffe. (*Ibid.*, No. 83).

135. Oct. 28, 33 Henry VIII [1541]. Grant[6] by John Foulburye of Holme in Spaldingmore, gent., and Humphrey

---

[1] Also, July 24, quitclaim by the same to the same of all right therein ; same seals. (*Ibid.*, No. 81). Also, July 21, indenture of sale; all muniments to be transferred; a lawful estate to be made before the feast of "lammas"; the purchaser paid 3*li*. 6*s*. 8*d*., and would pay the same sum at the following Lady Day; in English; same seals. (*Ibid.*, No. 82).

[2] Two seals : red wax, small ; (1) letter S beneath a crown ; (2) a fleur-de-lis.

[3] Also, March 28, quitclaim by the same to the same of all right therein; same seal. (*Ibid.*, No. 84). On March 24 Ralph Eure of Fowbrygg, co. York, jun., knt., Thomas Beelby of Caton, gent., and Mungo Westerdayll of Fowbrygg, yeoman, bound themselves to James Constable in 100*li*. for Westerdayll to observe the terms of an indenture of sale of the same date; (*sd.*) Rauff Eure, Thomas Bylby, Mungo Wyst'dayll; three seals on tongues of the parchment; (1) and (3) same as to the grant, (2) letters I.B. (*Ibid.*, No. 85).

[4] Seal : red wax, round, ⅝ in.; a running deer between letters E above and P below.

[5] Latch of the door. *Cf.* the preceding deed for this example of symbolic livery of seisin.

[6] Also, 12 Nov., a quitclaim by the same; same seals. (*Ibid.*, No. 87).

Pooll of Newbalde, yeoman, for the sum of 10*li*. sterling, to James Constable of Northclyff, esq., his heirs and assigns, of a messuage built on, a croft, two selions of land, and a plot of land with appurtenances in Northclyff, the messuage and croft lying between the land of the said James on the south and that of the college of St. Andrew the Apostle of Nedderacastre on the north, and abutting on the highroad towards the west, and backwards on the common field towards the east; one selion lying on the furlong (*stadium*) called Byrkelands between the land of the said college on the south and that of the said James on the north, and the other in the north field between the lands of the same, and the plot lying in *leker* of Northclyff in length between Rudholm and the moor, and in breadth between *leker* formerly belonging to Adam Gous on the south and that formerly belonging to William Seker on the north; which premises they had jointly of the grant and feoffment of Thomas Covell late of Newbald, deceased. (*sd*.) a mark, and per me John Foulberye.[1]

Dorso : possession delivered, 13 Oct. [*sic*] in the presence of Sir Harry [?] Watson, William Buttyll, Robert Burton, Robert Cots, Ralph . . . ., [?] Oliver Hayber, priest. The deed sealed [?] 14 Dec. in Newbolde.[2] (*Ibid.*, No. 86).

Crigglestone.

136. Monday after Martinmas 46 Edward III, 1371.[3] Grant by John Dey of[4] Staynton and Alice his wife to Richard de Blacker and his heirs, of all their lands and tenements within the bounds of Blacker and a third part *del Calfrod*, with meadows, woods and other apurtenances; to hold of the chief lord of the fee, and rendering to the grantors for the ensuing fourteen[5] years 9*s*. 10*d*. at Whitsuntide and Martinmas in equal portions, with power to distrain if the rent should be in arrear for more than fifteen days. And if Richard or his heirs should hold the premises beyond nineteen years he should render 20*s*. yearly at the same terms in equal portions, with power to the grantors to distrain. Witnesses, Adam de Moselay, John de Bretton, John Kyng, John del Wyk, Robert de Chauntclere, John Grenehod. Crigeleston.[6] And if the

---

[1] Two seals of red wax : (1) a shield of arms, a hart trippant and a mullet in chief ; (2) letter A. The arms are evidently those of Fowbery of Newbald (*Glover's Visitation*, ed. Foster, p. 117).

[2] The witnesses' names are blurred and conjectural, except John Lowthorpe.

[3] Clearly a mistake in either the regnal year or the year A.D.

[4] Erroneously written as if it was 'et.'

[5] Written over an erasure; the original words may have been 'decem et novem,' which come three lines later, but in the second instance no alteration has been made ; the result is an obvious discrepancy.

[6] Fragment of seal of yellow wax.

said tenements were to be sold Richard should have the first opportunity.[1] (*Lord Allendale*, Crigglestone, No. 3).[2]

137. Sept. 20, 8 Henry VIII [1516]. Grant by Thomas Blakkerr of Blakkerhall to William Froste, Walter Bradford, Ralph Amyas, vicar of the church of Penyston, and John Frankysh, vicar of the church of Warmefeld, of his capital messuage called Blakkerhall, with all closes, meadows, lands and tenements, with appurtenances, and all other messuages, lands, tenements, burgages, meadows, woods and pastures, with appurtenances in Crygleston, Chappelthorpe, Heton, and Wakefeld, and elsewhere in co. York; to fulfil the grantor's intention expressed in a schedule annexed. (*sd.*) per me Thomam Blacker.[3]

Schedule[4] : to hold to the use of Thomas for his life; after his death the feoffees to grant to Agnes his wife a yearly rent of 4*li.*, payable at Whitsuntide and Martinmas in equal portions, in the name of all dower which she should claim or have by right, or else at their discretion to make her an estate for life of lands and tenements of the same value in lieu; and to allow her to occupy two parlours [and] one chamber called the Newwarks, built at the west end of the hall called Blakkerhall, with "one colehouse & a swynehouse to the helpyng of the seid Agnes & of hire children as long as the seid Agnes keppeth hire sole & unmaryed," and should she take a husband they were to be seised of these premises with the residue of all his other messuages [and] lands aforesaid to the use of Ralph his son and heir apparent, and his heirs.

Dorso : seisin delivered to Ralph Amyas in the name of the feoffees in the presence of John Whetley, James More, Robert Forest, vicar of the church of Sandall, Thomas Leke, Thomas [?] Ketyll. (*Ibid.*, No. 4).

Cumberworth.

138. June 6, 2 Henry VI [1424]. Grant by William Hudson to John Hudson his brother, his heirs and assigns, of all his lands and tenements, meadows, rents and services, with appurtenances in the vill and territory of Comberworth and Northorppe, which he had of the grant of the said John. Witnesses, John Byrton, esq., Thomas Goldthorppe, William Joseppe. Byrton.[5] (*Lord Allendale*, Cumberworth, No. 12).[6]

[1] 'dictus Ricardus erit propinquior quam aliquis alius.' This is added after the date. The whole document is carelessly drawn up. It is partly in the form of a grant in fee simple, and partly in that of a grant for a term of years. These last words suggest that the latter was intended.
[2] Nos. 1 and 2 of the series were printed in vol. vi.
[3] Seal : red wax, small signet; letters.
[4] In English.
[5] Seal : black wax, small; letter I beneath a crown.
[6] Nos. 1-11 of this series were printed in vol. vi.

139.   April 12, 29 Henry VI [1451]. Release by John Hudson to John Hudson son of William Hudson his brother (*fratris*) of all right in all his lands and tenements, meadows, woods and pastures, with appurtenances in the township of Cumberworth or elsewhere in co. York, which had descended to him by hereditary right. Witnesses, Ellis Byrton, Richard Storthes, Thomas Goldethorpe, William Stone, Robert Chapell.[1] (*Ibid.*, No. 13).

140.   Dec. 4, 5 Edward VI [1551]. Bond[2] by Anne Hartlyngton of Ackeworth, co. York, late widow of Roger Hartlyngton, to Thomas Wentworth of Westbretton, esq., in 20*li.* to be paid at the following Christmas. Westbretton.

Condition : if she fulfilled the terms of indentures, dated the same day, concerning the demise of her third part and dower of the messuages, lands, tenements, and all other inheritance of Roger Hartlyngton, her late husband, in Cumberworth, the bond to be void.[3] (*Ibid.*, No. 14).

Denby (Penistone).

141.   Sept. 4, 23 Elizabeth [1581]. Grant by Thomas Horne of Overcumbreworth, yeoman, to Edward Horne of Nethercumberworth, husbandman, his kinsman and next heir apparent, namely, son of Henry Horne his brother, and his heirs and assigns, of all his messuages, cottages, houses, buildings, lands, tenements and hereditaments, with appurtenances in Denbye, Hoiland and Kexburgh, in whosesoever tenure they were. Also appointment of John Bilcliff as attorney to enter and deliver seisin. (*sd.*) Thomas Horne (*mark*).

Dorso : seisin delivered, same day, in the presence of John Walker, Giles Armitage, Renald Hooll, Henry Horne. (*Lord Allendale*, Denby, No. 2).[4]

Dinnington.

142.   Sunday before St. Margaret the Virgin [July 16], 1318. Grant by John son of John son of Ralph de Dynigton to Thomas Woderoue of Totewyk and Maud his wife, their heirs or assigns, of all his arable land lying *en le Morecroftes* of Dynigton, namely,

---

[1] Seal : black wax, small; a letter.
[2] Also, same day, bond by John Hartlyngton of Ackeworth, yeoman, to the same in 10*li.*, to ensure that Wentworth should eventually receive a total of five marks in rents from the premises, if Anne should die before such a sum had been paid; seal, red wax, letters. (*Ibid.*, No. 15).
[3] Seal : red wax, small signet : letter T.
[4] No. 1 of this series, relating to Denby in Upper Whitley, was printed in vol. v.

at the high thorn (*spinam*) between the land of Robert Attehesses on the west and that of Henry le Mayr on the east, and abutting on either side on the moor of Dynington; with all easements. Witnesses, Nicholas de Dynigton, John le Yong, John ad fontem, Alan Woderoue, Henry le Mayr, William son of Adam, Thomas Westryn. Dynigton. (*Duke of Norfolk*, Misc., II, ii, No. 9).

143. Sunday before the Purification of the B.V.M., 26 Edward III [Jan. 29, 1351-2]. Grant by John Odam of Thropon' to John Caili of Dynigton, his heirs or assigns, of a fourth part of a piece of land with meadow adjacent, with appurtenances, lying in the field of Dynigton between the land formerly belonging to John le Yong on one side and that of William son of Alexander on the other. Witnesses, William Assill of Dynigton, John ad fontem of the same, John Foyer of the same, William Skyn, Robert de Lane. Dynigton.[1] (*Duke of Leeds*, Hornby Castle Muniments, Dinnington, No. 1).

144. Sunday after the Apostles Peter and Paul, 30 Edward III [July 3, 1356]. Grant by John Forman the elder of Dynigton to John Cayly of the same, his heirs or assigns, of all his lands and tenements with appurtenances in the vill and fields of Dynington. Witnesses, William de Dynington, William [?] Assil, John ad fontem, John Foyer, William Skyn, Thomas de Longden, John Mayr. Dynington.[2] (*Ibid.*, No. 2).

145. Sunday, March 4, 32 Edward III [1357-8]. Release by William de Dynigton to John Caylly of the same, his heirs or assigns, of all the service due to him from the tenements of the said John which had formerly been in the seisin of John Forman, namely the service of reaping and ploughing and all other service. Witnesses, William Assill, William Skyn, John ad fontem, John Foyer, John Mayr. Dynigton.[3] (*Ibid.*, No. 3).

146. Dec. 6, 35 Edward III [1361]. Notification by Jocelyn (*Goscelinus*) de Eywill, steward of Sir Walter de Mauny[4] in co. York, that whereas Hugh de Kyueton had held on the day he died of the said Sir Walter as of his manor of Donyngton eight bovates of land with appurtenances by the service of 23s., he had

[1] Fragment of seal of yellow wax.
[2] Seal : yellow wax, pointed oval, 1¼ × ⅞ in.; blurred.
[3] Seal : green wax, round, ⅞ in.; blurred. On the back of the deed there are writings in a contemporary hand, which may be rough notes of proceedings in a manorial court; the parchment being subsequently cut and used for this deed.
[4] The celebrated soldier, for whom see the accounts in *D.N.B.* and *Complete Peerage*, new ed. A list of his lands in Yorkshire which he held of the honour of Tickhill in right of his wife is given in the order to the escheator in Yorkshire after his death in 1372; they include lands in Dinnington and Kiveton (*Cal. Close Rolls*, 1369-74, p. 377).

received from John de Kyueton, son and heir of the said Hugh, 23s. for his relief due to the said Sir Walter after the death of Hugh from the said tenements; and acquittance of John, his heirs and executors, therefor. Kyueton. (*Ibid.*, No. 4).

147. Sunday after the Assumption of the B.V.M., 48 Edward III [Aug. 20, 1374]. Grant by Thomas de Koknay to John Odam, his heirs or assigns, of a messuage in Dinygton, lying between the messuage of John Atyewell on one side and that of John Ghill on the other, with a garden adjacent, and seven acres of land lying in different places of the field of Dynigton, with all appurtenances. Witnesses, William Schyne of Dynigton, John de Haulay, John Atywell of the same, William Ascill of the same, Thomas Bath of the same. Dynigton.[1] (*Ibid.*, No. 5).

148. Aug. 26, 7 Henry V [1419]. Grant by Richard Spynk of Tykhill and Margaret his wife to William Taylour of Dynyngton, his heirs and assigns, of all their lands and tenements with appurtenances which they had in the vill and fields of Dynyngton and held by free charter. Witnesses, William Barbur, Thomas Nelson, John Saundur, William Henreson, John Skyn. Dynyngton. (*Ibid.*, No. 6).

Doncaster.

149. Grant[2] by Hugh de Alwerdel' of Donec[astre] to Ellis (*Elie*) le Tauorner of Donec[astre], his heirs or assigns, for a sum of money given beforehand, of a yearly rent of 2s. with appurtenances in Donecastre to be taken at the four terms of the year fixed in Donecastre from the messuage in which the grantor had dwelt in Magdalene street (*vico*), lying between the land of Hugh le Cartewrith and that of Hugh del Hehnsis, of which one end abutted on the bakehouse (*forn'*) and the other on *le Aldecasteldick*; with power to distrain. Witnesses, Thomas Framfer,[3] William Turtays, Hugh de Aula, Robert de Lomby, Hugh de Kanewic, William Dussel, John Auennel, Adam Bansce, Gilbert le Carpunter, Reginald de Messingham, Ralph the clerk.[4] (*Y.A.S.*, DD 17).

[1] Seal : white wax, round, 1 in.; a shield of arms, a fess or a cross, two annulets in chief and [?] a mullet in base; legend chipped.

[2] The grantee and two witnesses witnessed No. 429 below, dated 1294, in which the first and fourth witnesses are mentioned in circumstances suggesting they were then dead. The date of this deed is therefore likely to be shortly before that year.

[3] Fraunfer on the seal to No. 429.

[4] Seal : green wax, pointed oval, 1¼ × ⅞ in.; a device; ✠ S' HVGONIS DALWA . . The last two or three letters of the name are crowded into an insufficient space.

150. Trinity Sunday [June 9], 1297. Grant by Ellis (*Elyas*) le Tauerner of Donecastre to Robert Stirton' of the same, in frank-marriage with Joan his daughter, and the heirs of their bodies, of a messuage lying in the street (*vico*) of St. Mary Magdalene in Donecastre between the grantor's own messuage on one side and that formerly belonging to Hugh the carpenter on the other; rendering yearly to the chief lord of the fee 2s. at the four terms of the year fixed in Donecastre; with reversion, in default of issue, to the grantor or his heirs or assigns. Witnesses, John son of Ellen, Nigel de Mar, Reginald de Messingham, John de Knarsburg', John de Eland, Hugh de Clayton.[1] (*Ibid.*).

Drax.

151. Thursday before Whitsuntide [May 13], 1361. Grant by Robert son of Stephen de Langrak to John Elyot, his heirs and assigns, of two acres of land with appurtenances, lying in six selions, of which four selions lay in Litylwestwod between the land of Thomas de Luddygton on one side and that of the said John on the other, and one rood lay in Norwod between the land of John de Hyllum on one side and that of John Elyot on the other, and one *laygker* lay by the land of Thomas de Luddygton. Witnesses, John Spellere of Hayles, Richard Fallays of Burth'g, John Durem of Lanehuse, William Buttelere of Langrak, Peter de Hemygburgh of Drax. Draxburgh.[2] (*Lord Allendale*, Drax, No. 23).[3]

152. Wednesday before the Apostles Peter and Paul, 11 Henry IV [June 25, 1410]. Grant by William Hudson of Langrak to Peter Hubert of Laynehouses, his heirs and assigns, of three roods of land lying in Northewode between the land of the grantee on the east and that of Robert Falas on the west, and abutting at one end on Karregote and at the other on Lampehedeland; also grant, in warranty of the said three roods, of an acre of land lying in Dunpole between the land of John Elleyote the elder on the south and that of the grantor on the north, and abutting at one end on Dennyfeld towards the east and at the other on Hookriddyng towards the west.[4] Witnesses, John atte Wodde of Langrak of the same, John Bonome of the same, John Chereholme of the same, Richard Boteler of the same, Thomas de Burton of Drax. Langrak in Drax. (*Ibid.*, No. 24).

[1] Seal : green wax, round, ¾ in.; head and shoulders of a man to the sinister; a star behind him and a cross in front; * S' ELIE LE [TAV]ERNER.
[2] Seal : yellow wax, no impression.
[3] Nos. 1-22 of this series and a deed relating to Langrick in Drax were printed in vol. vi.
[4] habendam et tenendam sibi et heredibus suis imperpetuum pro perdicione amissione seu recuperacione predicte acre terre per aliquem titulo iuris mouend' in futurum.

153. Easter Day, 3 Edward IV [April 10, 1463]. Grant by John Dekonson of Portington and Margaret his wife, to John Hubard, his heirs and assigns, of a waste toft and thirty acres and three roods of land with appurtenances lying in scattered lots in the different fields of Lanehowse and Langrake, par. Drax, of which the toft lay in Lanehowse, containing an acre of land lying between the land of the prior and convent of Drax on either side, and abutted at one end on the common way towards the south and at the other on the land of the said prior and convent towards the north; eight acres lay together between the land lately belonging to the said John Dekonson on the south and the common way called Sandhyllane on the north, and abutted at one end on Dylane towards the east and at the other on *le Yngdyke* towards the west; four acres lay together between the land lately belonging to the said John on either side, and abutted at one end on Dyelane towards the south and at the other on the land of the said John Hubarde towards the west; four acres lay together in the place called Scharpehyll between Dyelane on the east and the land lately belonging to John Fallax on the west, and abutted at one end on the common way towards the south and at the other end on the land of John Hubard towards the north; one small parcel of land called *le Grene* lay in *le Burghe* between the green (*inter grene*) of Thomas Curby on the south and the green (*le grene*) of Joan Warde late wife of Ralph Warde on the north, and abutted at one end on the water of Use towards the east and at the other on the land of John Sellarre towards the west; one rood lay in *le Thomfeld* between the land of Joan late wife of Ralph Warde on either side, and abutted at one end on the land of John Sellarr towards the south and at the other on *le Grenedyke* towards the north; half an acre lay in Thomefeld between the land of the said Joan on the east and Guttyrmere on the west, and abutted at . . . ends; one rood lay in Pagegarthe between the land of the said Joan late wife of John Fewilliam on the east and that of Richard Hubard on the west, and abutted at one end on the land of John Medylwode towards the south and at the other end on [?] the common way towards the north; three roods lay in Howshald between the land lately belonging to John Fallax on either side, and abutted at one end on the common way towards the south and at the other end on Northewod dyke towards the north; one and a half acres lay in *le Northewod* between the land lately belonging to John Fallax on the east and that lately belonging to John Bonehom on the west, and abutted at one end on the common way towards the south and at the other on Norwodedyke towards the north; three roods lay in the same field between the land of John Hubarde on the east and that of Thomas Wodde on the west, and abutted at one end on the land of Thomas Wodde towards the south and at the other on Northewode dyke towards the north; one acre lay in the same field between the land of

[*blank*] on the west and that of the prior and convent on the west [*sic*], and abutted at one end on the land lately belonging to John Fallax towards the south and at the other on Northewoddyke towards the north; one acre and one rood lay in Pagelande between the land of Thomas Buttlar on the east and Robert Feton on the west, and abutted at one end on the land of the said Thomas towards the south, and at the other on Norwode dyke towards the north; three roods lay in *le Newryddyng* between the land of Thomas Wodde on either side, and abutted at one end on Northewode dyke towards the south and at the other on the land lately belonging to John Dekonson towards the north; and seven acres lay together between the land of Thomas Wodde on the east and that of John Elyott on the west, and abutted at one end on Karregote towards the south and at the other on the land of the prior and convent and that of Robert Feton and that of Thomas Wodde towards the north. Witnesses, William Chepyngdale of Drax, John Elyott of the same, William Warde of Newland, ... of the same, John Durham of Lanehowse. Drax.[1] (*Ibid.*, No. 28).

153A. Easter Day, 5 Edward IV [April 14, 1465]. Grant by Thomas Curbye of Langrayk to Andrew Gryce, his heirs and assigns, of an acre of land with appurtenances lying in scattered lots (*diuisim*) in the fields of Langrayk, of which two selions and one balk (*meare*) lay together between the lands of John Myddylwood on the north and those of John Warde on the south, abutting on the lands of the said John Myddylwood at one end towards the east, and at the other end on a selion of land of the said acre towards the west; and one selion lay in the same field between the lands of John Warde on the east and the road leading from Langrayk towards Laynehowseys on the west, abutting at one end on the lands of the prior and convent of Drax towards the south and on the said road towards the north; and one selion lay between the lands of John Hubbard and those of John Warde on the east, and those of John Warde on the west, abutting at one end on the land of the said prior and convent towards the south and at the other end on the said road towards the north. Witnesses, John Hubbard, John Myddylwood the younger, John Durham of Laynehowseys, Thomas Hobson of Drax, Robert Fytton of Langrayk. Langrak. (*Ibid.*, No. 25).

154. April 18, 25 Henry VIII [1534]. Release[2] by John Durham of Laynhouse, co. York, to William Baxster of his right in seven and a half acres of land. Witnesses, William Nelson,

---

[1] Two tags for seals; one remains: red wax, letter W.
[2] This deed is much stained; the bounds of the parcels of acres are given, the names Claycrofts, Sandelands, Holynbusklayne being mentioned.

George Goldtwhait, Robert Warde. At Laynhouse.[1] (*Ibid.*, No. 26).

155. Oct. 4, 2 Edward VI [1548]. Grant by William Myddil-wod of Laynhouses by Drax, and Katherine his wife, to John Warde son of Randolf Warde of Langrake and Elizabeth Myddil-wod their daughter, whom John was to take as his wife, of three and a half acres of arable land lying in the field of Langrake, of which two and a half acres lay together in the place called Behynde Warde garth, between the land of Randolf Warde on either side, abutting on the land of the said Randolf towards the north, and another acre lay there in three selions by Pollard garth; to hold to them and the survivor and the heirs of Elizabeth's body, with reversion in default of issue to William Myddilwod's right heirs.[2]

Dorso : seisin delivered in the presence of Robert Doughtye, William Dent, James Thakrowe, Henry Hadaman, John Wells, Robert Thakrow. (*Ibid.*, No. 27).

North Elmsall.

156. Sunday after St. Mark the Evangelist, 13 Edward II [April 27, 1320]. Release by John son of John de Burgh to Robert le Waiur, his heirs or assigns, of all right in all the lands and tenements which John his father had had in the vill and fields of Northelmesale, Mensthorp, and Wrangbrok. Witnesses, Edmund le Botiler, John Byset, Adam Byset, Roger le Norrays, John Daungerus. Northelmesale.[3] (*Lord Allendale*, North Elmsall, No. 3).

157. The Apostles Peter and Paul [June 29], 1392. Grant by William Olyuer of Uppton to Hugh Waiour of Northelmesall, his heirs and assigns, of two roods of arable land lying in the field of Northelmesall, of which one lay at the end of the croft, one end abutting on the croft of Robert Dunnok, and the other end abutting on Hungyrhill, and the other rood lay between the land of John son of Robert of the same, one end abutting on *le Appell-gang* and the other on *le Dale*; in exchange for half an acre of land lying next the grantor's land as a gore to his profit in the same field.[4] Witnesses, John Winteworth of Northelmesall, John Flyntill of Kyrkeby, John Smyt of Helmesall, Richard Smyt of Northelmesall, John Gode of the same. Elmesall. (*Ibid.*, No. 4).

[1] Seal : red wax, small; an animal and letters.
[2] Seal : red wax, same as to the preceding deed.
[3] Seal: yellow-brown wax, round, ⅝ in.; an eagle displayed; * IE SV PRIVE.
[4] iacentem propinquiorem mihi in Goram ad proficuum meum in eadem [*sic*] campo iacent'.

158. Sunday in the second week of Lent, 1 Henry V [March 4, 1413-4]. Grant[1] by Hugh Waiour of Northelmesale to Thomas Bonewell, vicar of the church of South Kirkeby, and John de Bretton, chaplain, of a messuage in which he then dwelt, with a croft adjacent, a bovate of land and meadow called Waiour oxgang, [and] a toft with a croft lying on the west side of his said messuage in the vill and fields of Northelmesale, with all appurtenances; also the reversion of a messuage with a croft adjacent in the said vill called Murrok thyng, after the death of Richard Waiour his brother, and the reversion of all the lands and tenements which the said Richard was holding for life in the said vill, the reversion of which belonged to the grantor. Witnesses, John Wenteworth of North Elmesale, Richard Wentteworth, John atte Styghill, John Roper, Richard Bell, all of the same. North Elmesale.[2] (*Ibid.*, No. 2).

Emley.

159. May 10, 8 Edward III [1334]. Release by Adam son of Henry in le Wroo of Emelay to Thomas his brother, of all right in a messuage and one bovate of land with appurtenances in the vill and within the bounds of Emelay, which had fallen to him (Adam) by hereditary right after the death of Henry his father. Witnesses, Thomas de Cresacre, John de Wrtelay, Richard son of Haukyn de Emel', John son of Paulinus of the same, William del Storthes. Emelay. (*Lord Allendale*, Emley, No. 24).[3]

Eppleby.

160. Sept. 1, 7 Henry VI [1428]. Grant by Roger son of William Sergeant, chaplain, to Richard Pudsey, esq., his heirs and assigns, of a toft and fifteen acres of land with appurtenances in Appilby on Teese, which he and Henry Pudsey, deceased, lately had of the feoffment of Peter son of Robert Stevenson of Caldwell. (*Y.A.S.*, M[D] 161A, Eppleby, No. 1).

Fearby.

161. Saturday after St. William the Bishop and Confessor, ...[4] Grant by John . . . . beke of Fegherby to William Papioy of Helay, his heirs and assigns, of a toft lying . . . . of

[1] For a deed in 1418 relating to the same premises (No. 1 of this series) see vol. vi, No. 241.
[2] Seal : red wax; round, *c.* ⅛ in.; an animal; the word PRIVE occurs in the legend; broken.
[3] Nos. 1-23 of this series were printed in vols. v and vi.
[4] The document is torn in several places. The date ends in . . . . *essimo secundo.* The writing suggests the first half of the fourteenth century.

Fegherby between the toft of the lord of Newyll[1] on the east and the toft *Caprone* on the west, and an acre of land in the north field of Fegherby between the land of the lord of Neuell on either side; with appurtenances; to hold of the chief [? lords]. Witnesses, Ranulf . . . . ., knt., Alan de Staflay, Geoffrey Bucktroyte, John de Burght of Sutton, Stephen Marchall of Fegherby, Thomas . . . . of the same. Fegherby.[2] (*Duke of Norfolk*, Misc., II, i, No. 12).

Flockton.

162. Notification to the archbishop of York and the chapter of St. Peter by Jordan de Flocketon of his grant to God and the monks of St. Mary of Byland (*Bellande*) of a sufficient way for them, their men, beasts and necessaries, through his land from their forge of Bentley as far as Deneby, and of common fully throughout all his land of Floketon for all their beasts of Deneby; in perpetual alms, free from all terrene service and secular exaction, for the health of his soul and of all his ancestors and heirs; rendering yearly to him and his heirs 2s. for all services, 12d. at Whitsuntide and 12d. at Martinmas. Witnesses, Thomas de Horburi, Adam son of Philip, Thomas de Thornet[on], Reinald the clerk of Bradef[ord], Simon de Ferseleia, Henry Scottus of Pugkesey, Thomas Scottus of Neut[on]. (*Lord Allendale*, Flockton, No. 60).[3]

163. Grant by Ingram (*Ingeram*) son of Adam de Kyrkeby to Peter son of Adam de Floketona, his heirs or assign, except religious men, lords of the fee, and Jews, for homage and service and a mark of silver given beforehand in the name of recognition, of a bovate of land with appurtenances in the vill of Floket[on], with buildings placed thereon, which Adam the grantee's father had formerly held of the fee of Alexander de Neuill; to hold of the grantor and his heirs, with liberties, commons and easements in the vill of Floketon and without, belonging thereto; paying yearly 12d. of silver, at the Assumption of the B.M. 6d. and at Martinmas 6d., for all service, saving forinsec service.[4] Witnesses,[5] Sir Ralph de Horbiri, Sir Thomas of the same, William de Floket[on], John de Batel', John de Deneby, Henry de Kyrkeby, Adam son of

---

[1] *i.e.* Neville.

[2] Seal : red wax, oval, ⅞ × 1⅟₁₆ in.; within a geometrical panel the standing figure of a female saint, crowned; legend not deciphered.

[3] Nos. 1-38 of this series were printed in vol. v; Nos. 39-84 are printed here. There is another example of the present charter among the Byland charters in the British Museum; see vol. vi, No. 248. The first two witnesses suggest a date early in the 13th cent.; for the Horbury family see *Y.A.J.*, xxvi, pp. 334 *et seq.*

[4] The sealing clause runs : in huius uero rei testimonium presentem *paginam* sigilli mei apposicione roboraui.

[5] For the witnesses *cf.* vol. v, No. 132; the date is in the middle of the 13th cent.

Ellis, Henry son of Simon, Adam de Leptona, Matthew de Leptona.[1] (*Ibid.*, No. 62).

164. Grant by John de Bateley to John son of Adam del Cote, his heirs or assigns, for homage and service and a sum of money given beforehand, of all the croft in the territory of Floketon which Thomas Gerland had formerly held, and also all the moiety of the toft which John de Horbyri had formerly held, as they lay together between the land of Adam son of Emma on the east and the highroad on the west; to hold of the grantor and his heirs, with all liberties, commons and easements within the vill of Floketon and without, belonging thereto; rendering yearly 1*d*. at the feast of All Saints for all services. Witnesses, Sir Ralph de Horbir', Sir John his son, Michael de Floketona, Henry de Kirkeby, Peter son of Lucy de Floketona, William son of Robert of the same, Henry son of Adam of the same, Adam de Houirhalle. (*Ibid.*, No. 61).

165. Grant by Richard son of William de Ovenden, dwelling in Thornyll, to Henry son of Robert de Floketona, and his heirs or assigns, of four acres of land with appurtenances in the field of Floketon lying by Stockebrygge between the land of Sir John son of Ralph de Horebyry on one side and that of William del Sike on the other, for a sum of money given beforehand; to hold of the grantor, rendering yearly 1*d*. of silver at Christmas for all secular service. Witnesses, Sir John de Horebyr', Sir Richard de Thornyll,[2] knts., master Gilbert de Bingeley, Adam son of Peter de Floketona, Michael de Floketona, William del Sike.[3] (*Ibid.*, No. 39).

166. Quitclaim by Adam son of Martin de Overfloketona to William son of Ingramy de Kyrkeby, of a yearly rent of 1*d*., which William was wont to pay him for an acre of land lying on *le Kylnestedes* and Schollegge. Witnesses, William son of Robert, Henry son of Tylle, Adam del Cote of Floketon, Hugh son of Emma, Henry de Hotona. (*Ibid.*, No. 40).

167. Michaelmas [Sept. 29], 1294. Grant by Adam son of Martin de Floketon to Richard son of Jose de Wakefeld, his heirs or assigns, of a moiety of an acre of land within the bounds of Floketon, lying in Scolegge between the land of Adam son of Andrew on one side and that of John Fox on the other, and abutting

---

[1] Seal: green wax, pointed oval, $1\frac{3}{8} \times 1\frac{1}{4}$ in.; a scroll device within a bordure; ☩ SIGIL' . INGERA[M] : DE . KIRK :
[2] He was head of the Thornhill family in the period *c*. 1250–90 (*Y.A.J.*, xxix, 295).
[3] Seal : green wax, round, $1\frac{1}{4}$ in., a floral device; ☩ SI[G : RI]CARDI : DE : . . . . . N ; chipped.

at one end on the wood of Kyrkeby and at the other on the common
moor of Floketon; for a sum of money given beforehand; with all
easements belonging thereto; rendering yearly to the grantor and
his heirs a rose at the Nativity of St. John the Baptist for all
secular services.[1] Warranty against all men and women. Witnesses, Michael de Floketon, William Ingramis de Kyrkeby, John
of the same, Thomas de Floketon, Robert de Horbyr', clerk.[2]
(*Ibid.*, No. 66).

168. Wednesday, the Decollation of St. John the Baptist
[Aug. 29], 1296. Grant by Adam son of Martin de Ouerfloketona
to William son of Ingramy de Kerkeby, his heirs or assigns, of an
acre of land in the field of Floketon, as it lay in the following
parcels, namely, three roods (*perticat'*) between the land of Michael
de Floketona on one side and that of Richard Cusyn on the other,
and one rood between [the land of . . . .][3] Cussyn on one side and
that of Thomas Tagun on the other; with all appurtenances and
profits for [a sum of money given beforehand]; [rendering] yearly
to the lord of the fee 1*d.* at Whitsuntide for all secular service.
Witnesses, ... de Floketona, Henry del Wodehous, Henry
de Hotona, Adam del Cote, William son of Robert, Adam son of
Richard. Kyrkeby. (*Ibid.*, No. 68).

169. Wednesday after St. John the Baptist [June 26], 1297.
Grant by Richard son of Jose de Wakefeud to William son of
Ingramy de Kyrkeby, his heirs or assigns, of all right in the assart
called Hynggebrigge within the bounds of Floketon with its
appurtenances and profits, lying between the territory of Crowes-
chathe and the moor of Floketon, with a ditch round it, for a sum
of money given beforehand. Witnesses, Henry del Wodehous',
Henry de Hotona, Adam del Kote, William son of Robert, Adam
son of Richard de Floketona. Floketon. (*Ibid.*, No. 41).

170. Monday in Easter week [March 27], 1307. Grant by
Simon del Grene of Floketon to Henry his son, his heirs or assigns,
of a messuage with buildings thereon in the vill of Floketon, except
the portion which he had earlier granted to Isabel, Sybil, and
Margery his daughters for building on; also the croft lying on
either side of the messuage and abutting at the south end on the
moor of Floketon, and at the north end on *le Freredik*, and lying
between the lands of Baldwin le Tyeys on either side, namely
towards the east and west; this messuage and croft he had of the

[1] The tenendum clause does not specify that the land was to be held of
the chief lord; but such, no doubt, was the case after the statute of *Quia
Emptores* in 1290. The wording shows a transition stage before the new rules
were perhaps universally understood; see the Introduction to vol. vii on
the effect of the statute.
[2] Fragment of seal of yellow wax.
[3] A large tear in the middle of the deed.

grant of Margery daughter of Henry son of Christiana; to hold
with easements belonging to so much land. Witnesses, Baldwin le
Tyeis, William Ingrais, William de Floket', William le Soyngur,
William son of Peter, Adam del Cote, John son of William, John
de Foxholes. Floketon. (*Ibid.*, No. 59).

171. Sunday after the Exaltation of the Cross, 1 Edward
II [Sept. 17, 1307]. Grant by Henry de Bingelay to Adam son of
Adam son of Andrew de Floketon,[1] his heirs or assigns, for a sum
of money given beforehand, of a moiety of all the assart with
appurtenances called *le Caluwerod* within the bounds of Floketon,
as it lay in length and breadth between the moor of Floketon and
the field of Croweschaye, inclosed (*vallatur*) everywhere with
bounds and ditches; with all liberties and easements, doing the
forinsec service as much as belonged to so much land for all services.
Witnesses, Henry de Hoton, William son of Michael de Floket[on],
William son of Peter of the same, John son of William, Robert
the clerk. Floketon.[2] (*Ibid.*, No. 63).

172. Thursday after the Epiphany [Jan. 11], 1307[-8].
Grant by Simon del Grene of Ouerfloketon, with the consent of
his heir, to his three daughters Sybil, the other Sybil, and Margery,
their heirs or assigns, of a messuage with appurtenances in the
vill of Ouerfloketon, lying within the bounds of his tenement on
the north (*borientale*) side; and an acre of land with appurtenances
in the territory of the same, as it lay between the land of Sir John
de Horbyr' on the west and that of Thomas Tagon of Floketon
on the east, and abutted on *le Sordolis* and extended in length
as far as the dike (*foueam*) of Floketon; for a sum of money given
beforehand; to hold of the grantor and his heirs,[3] with all easements within the vill of Floketon and without; rendering yearly
to him for the messuage a rose at the Nativity of St. John the
Baptist, and to Adam son of Peter de Floketon for the acre ½*d.*
of silver at Easter for all secular service. Witnesses, William son
of Michael de Floketon, William son of Peter of the same, Henry
son of Robert of the same, Michael of the upper hall, Adam del
Cote, John del Syk, John·son of William son of Robert, Henry de
Biglay, Richard Scappenca', Adam son of Andrew, Adam Cussin.
Floketon. (*Ibid.*, No. 73).

173. Tuesday after St. Peter ad vincula [Aug. 3], 1311.
Grant by John son of Adam de Ouerfloketon to Richard le Schap-

---

[1] On July 17, 11 Edward II [1317] the grantee granted back and quitclaimed to the grantor the same moiety; witnesses, Baldwin le Tyeis, William
son of Michael de Floketon, William son of Peter of the same, William son
of Robert of the same, Robert de Horbyr', clerk ; Floketon. (*Ibid.*, No. 64).
[2] Seal : brown wax, oval, ⅝ × ½ in.; a man's head to the sinister; legend
not deciphered.
[3] This is unusual after *Quia Emptores*.

peman of the same, his heirs or assigns, of an acre and three roods of land as they lay in parcels in the fields of Floketon, namely, an acre lying in the place called *le Moycrot* in four parcels, and three roods lying in the place called *le Thwychel* between the land of Baldwin le Thyes on the west and that of John the miller on the other side; for a sum of money given beforehand; with all easements within the bounds of Floketon and without. Witnesses, William son of Michael de Floketon, William son of Peter, Adam del Cote, John del Sik, John son of William, William Ingrays. Floketon. (*Ibid.*, No. 69).

174. Sunday after the Nativity of St. John the Baptist, 9 Edward II [June 27, 1316]. Grant by Henry son of Simon de la Grene of Floketon to John his brother, his heirs and assigns, of a messuage with buildings and all the croft adjacent on either side, with appurtenances, as it lay in breadth between the lands of Baldwin le Tyeis on either side, and abutted in length at one end on the moor of Floketon and at the other on *le Freredik*; which premises he formerly had of the grant of Simon his father; for a sum of money given beforehand; with all easements. Witnesses, William son of Michael de Floketon, William son of Peter of the same, William son of Robert of the same, Adam son of William Ingrais, Adam del Cote of Floketon, Adam Cosyn of the same, Richard le Mercer of the same. Floketon. (*Ibid.*, No. 71).

175. Sunday, the octave of Easter [April 10], 1317. Grant by John son of Simon del Grene of Floketon to Henry the miller of Emelay, his heirs and assigns, for a sum of money given beforehand, of all the messuage with buildings and the croft adjacent on either side, as it lay in breadth between the lands of Baldwin le Tyeys on either side, and abutted at one end towards the south on Floketonbrok in length and at the other end towards the north on *le Freredyk*; which premises he formerly had of the grant of Henry his brother in the vill and within the bounds of Floketon; with all easements. Witnesses, Baldwin le Tyeis, William son of Michael de Floketon, William son of Peter of the same, William son of Robert of the same, Adam del Cote of the same, Robert de Horbyr', clerk. Floketon.[1] (*Ibid.*, No. 72).

176. Sunday before St. Margaret [July 15], 1319. Grant by Alice formerly wife of John Panal, in her widowhood, to John de Metheley, his heirs and assigns, of 4*d.* yearly rent from a messuage and three acres of land with appurtenances in Flokton, as they lay between the land of Maud daughter of Michael de Flokton on the west, and the land formerly belonging to John le Heuwer on the east; with reliefs and escheats and appurtenances into whosesoever hands the messuage and three acres should fall;

[1] Seal : yellow-brown wax, round, ⅜ in.; an eagle displayed; * PRIVE SV.

to be paid in equal portions at Martinmas and Whitsuntide. Witnesses, John de Thornhill, Nicholas de Wortlay, Jordan Deney, William son of Peter de Flokton, Adam del Cote of the same, Michael del Ouerhall, John del Syke. Thornhill. (*Ibid.*, No. 65).

177. Whit Monday [May 19], 1320. Release by Alice daughter of Adam son of Christopher de Ouerflocketon to Henry Bingelay of Flocketon of all right in two acres of land with the messuage which Adam her father had granted her, with appurtenances and profits, for a sum of money given beforehand. Witnesses, William son of Michael de Flocketon, William son of Peter of the same, Adam del Cote, John del Syke, Adam Ingramy, clerk. Flocketon. (*Ibid.*, No. 67).

178. Sunday after St. John of Beverley, 15 Edward II [May 9, 1322]. Grant by Margery daughter of Simon de la Grene of Floketon, in her pure virginity and lawful power, to Henry the miller of Emelay, his heirs and assigns, of two thirds (*partes*) of an acre of land with appurtenances in the field of Ouerfloketon, which acre the said Simon formerly granted to Isabel and Sybil, her sisters, and to her, of which one third lay in length and breadth between the land of Baldwin le Tyeis on the west and the third part of the acre which William son of Peter de Floketon had of the grant of Sybil her sister on the east, and the other third lay between that third part on the west and the land formerly belonging to Thomas Tagon of Floketon on the east; for a sum of money given beforehand; with all easements. Witnesses, Baldwin le Tyeis, Adam Ingrays, William son of Michael de Floket', William son of Robert of the same, Adam del Cote of the same, John son of John the miller of the same. Floket[on].[1] (*Ibid.*, No. 70).

179. Nov. 10, 1322. Grant by John son of Thomas Tagun of Floketon to Adam del Cote of the same and Sybil his wife, the survivor and their heirs, of half an acre and half a rood of land lying together in the field of Floketon in a place called *Le Fordoles*, between the land of John son of John the miller on one side and that of Thomas son of Adam on the other, abutting at one end on *le Freredik* and at the other on *le Haueding'* by the road of Floketon; also quitclaim of all right in the land with appurtenances called *Hyngebrigg'* within the bounds of Floketon, whether in rent or service. Witnesses, Baldwin le Tyeis, William son of Michael de Floketon, Adam Ingra[m]ys of Kyrkeby, William son of Peter de Floket', John del Syk of the same, Michael de Aula of the same, Robert de Horbyr', clerk. Floketon. (*Ibid.*, No. 42).

---

[1] Seal : greenish-brown wax, oval, *c*. 1¼ × ⅞ in.; a fleur-de-lis ; chipped round the edge.

180. Monday before the Conversion of St. Paul, 9 Edward III [Jan. 22, 1335-6]. Release by John son of John de Pokelyngton to John de Metheley of Thornhill, of all right in all the lands and tenements which the said John [de Metheley] had of the grant of Alice widow of John de Panal within the bounds of Flokton; for a sum of money given beforehand. Witnesses, William de Byrton, John de Shelveley, the younger, William son of Michael de Flokton, William son of Peter, Robert le Graunt, Adam del Cote, all of the same, John del Syk. Thornhill. (*Ibid.*, No. 44).

181. Thursday after the octave of the Translation of St. Thomas of Canterbury, 12 Edward III [July 16, 1338]. Release by Nicholas de Worttelay, knt., to John son of William son of Peter de Flocton, of all right in all the lands, tenements, messuages, buildings, meadows, plains, feedings, pastures, woods, rents and services which John had purchased of Henry Irnehard in the vill and fields of Ovir Flocton, and which John de Horbir', formerly knt., had earlier sold to German Filcock of Wakefeld. Witnesses, Adam de Hopton, John de Methelay, William de Flocton, William son of Peter, Robert le Graunt. Worttelay. (*Ibid.*, No. 49).

182. Monday after St. Andrew the Apostle [Dec. 3], 1341. Quitclaim by William son of Peter de Flokton to John his son and Agnes the latter's wife, and John's heirs, of all right in all the lands and tenements with appurtenances which formerly belonged to John son of Adam son of Peter within the bounds of Flokton; and all his property of goods and chattels which he then had in the said lands or tenements. Witnesses, John de Metheley of Thornhill, John de Amyas of Schitlington, William de Flokton, Edmund de Emlay, Michael del Overhalle, John del Syk, Robert le Graunt. Flokton. (*Ibid.*, No. 45).

183. Saturday, St. John the Apostle and Evangelist [Dec. 27], 1343. Grant by Robert le Graunt of Flokton to John son of William son of Peter de Flokton and William his son, their heirs and assigns, of his toft with adjacent croft in the said vill called Holsyk, containing one and a half acres of land and meadow, and an acre of land lying in *le Shortgrenes* between the land of Robert del Grene on the west and that formerly of Adam son of Martin on the east, and an acre of land lying on *le Toftes* between the land of Henry son of William son of Peter on the west and that of Robert the cobbler (*sutoris*) on the east; together with all easements. Witnesses, John de Methelay of Thornhill, Henry son of William son of Peter, Edmund de Flokton, John del Syk, Henry de Whetelay, clerk. Flokton. (*Ibid.*, No. 46).

184. Sunday before the Nativity of St. John the Baptist, 19 Edward III [June 18, 1345]. Grant by Thomas de Mydelham

to John son of William Perkynson of Flokton and William his son, their heirs and assigns, of a messuage, with its buildings and adjacent croft, and five and a half acres of land and meadow with appurtenances in Flokton, of which two and a half acres lay in a place called Kylnestede, half an acre and half a rood lay in the said place, one acre in Skoleegge in two plots, half an acre in Skoleeggeker, half an acre of meadow in the same, and half an acre and half a rood in *le Fordoles* by *le Freredik*. Witnesses, John de Methelay, William de Flokton, John son of William de Flokton, Edmund de Flokton, John son of John the miller. Flokton. (*Ibid.*, No. 43).

185. Thursday before St. Hilary, 20 Edward III [Jan. 11, 1346-7]. Grant by Richard son of Robert le Graunt of Flokton to John son of William Perkynson and John his son, their heirs and assigns, of a moiety of the toft formerly belonging to Baldwin Tyes, with all the lands and meadows, which the grantor had of the grant of Robert le Graunt his father, as they lay in the territory of Flokton. Witnesses, John de Amyas, William de Flokton, William de Birton, Edmund de Flokton, Henry son of Peter. Flokton. (*Ibid.*, No. 50).

186. Friday, Michaelmas [Sept. 29], 1357. Grant[1] by William de Castelford of Wakefeld to John son of William Perkynson of Flocton, of 8s. yearly rent from his tenants in Flocton, namely, John [?] Tull 2s., John Leue, John de Sharneston and Robert de Flocton 2s., Michael del Syke 2s. 4d., the said Robert de Flokton 16d., John Tagon 3d., John del Cote 1d.; to be taken in equal portions at Whitsuntide and Martinmas. Witnesses, Henry de Flocton, William de Kerkeby, Edmund de Flocton, John de Kerkeby. Flocton. (*Ibid.*, No. 58).

187. Sunday before Christmas [Dec. 24], 1368. Grant by Henry son of John Milner of Flocton[2] to John son of John Milner of Flocton, *nayler*, and Denise his wife, of all his messuages, lands and tenements in Flocton, which he had of the grant of the said John;[3] with meadows, woods and other appurtenances; to hold for their lives and that of the survivor, with successive remainders to John their son and the heirs of his body, to William their son and the heirs of his body, and to the heirs and assigns of the said John son of John Milner. Witnesses, John de Amyas, William de

---

[1] Also, Sunday after the Conception of the B.M. [Dec. 11], 1362, release by the same to the same of all right in the same rent; witnesses, William de Kerkby, John de Kerkby, Richard de Rocley; Flocton. (*Ibid.*, No. 74).

[2] Written Flotton.

[3] This grant had been made on the preceding day; same witnesses, except that Robert de Flocton occurs instead of John del Cote; seal blurred. (*Ibid.*, No. 76).

Kirkeby, John de Bretton, John Perkynson, John del Cote, Michael del Syke. Flocton.[1] (*Ibid.*, No. 75).

188. Monday after St. Edmund the King [Nov. 22], 1378. Indenture witnessing that although Robert Jacson of Flocton and Edmund de Flocton had enfeoffed Henry del Syke of Flocton in a plot of land in Flocton called Eddyngrode, as appeared by Robert's charter and Edmund's quitclaim,[2] Henry granted that whenever Edmund should pay to him, his heirs or assigns, ten marks sterling the charter, quitclaim, and seisin should have no effect. Mutual seals. Witnesses, John de Amyas the elder, John de Amyas the younger, William de Kirkeby, John Perkynson, John son of Edmund de Flocton. Flocton.[3] (*Ibid.*, No. 77).

189. Eve of Peter and Paul [June 28], 1379. Grant by John son of Adam de Bynglay to Robert de Roklay and Adam de Worldworth, chaplain, of his messuage in Flocton, with a toft and croft containing two acres of land lying between the tenement of John Perkyn on one side and the messuage of Thomas Soignour on the other. Witnesses, John Amyas the elder, John Amyas the younger, William de Kyrkeby, Robert Jacson of Flocton, John Perkyn of the same. Flocton. (*Ibid.*, No. 79).

190. Monday, the morrow of Holy Trinity, namely May 22, 1381.[4] Grant by Agnes daughter of Robert son of Richard de Boland, widow of Thomas son of Adam de Wodhous, to William son of Adam of the same, his heirs and assigns, of all the lands and tenements, feedings, pastures, mines (*mynuras*) and meadows, with appurtenances in Overflocton which had formerly belonged to Thomas Tagon, and which the grantor had of the grant and feoffment of Sir John Mychel, chaplain, and John Waynwryght, brother of the said Thomas her husband. Witnesses, John Perkyn of Flocton, Robert Jakson and John Mylner of the same, Henry del Syc, Henry Jakson of Emlay. Flocton. (*Ibid.*, No. 51).

191. June 4, 1406. Grant by William son of Adam Alman of Emlay to Robert son of Robert de Rokelay, knt., and William Fynche, chaplain, of a messuage and thirteen acres of land, and all the meadows, woods, and pastures belonging thereto with appurtenances in Flocton, which messuage was situated between the tenement of Henry del Syke on the west and that of Henry Milner

---

[1] Seal : yellow-brown wax, broken and blurred.
[2] A charter, not quitclaim, of Edmund granting the same plot to Robert Jacson is dated Easter, 49 Edward III [April 22, 1375]; witnesses, John Amyas the elder, John Amyas the younger, John de Kyrkeby, Edmund de Flocton, John Parkynson; seal : red wax, round, $\frac{13}{16}$ in.; a hare courant; legend, a motto, not deciphered. (*Ibid.*, No. 78).
[3] Seal : yellow wax; blurred, not heraldic.
[4] Trinity Sunday fell on June 9 in 1381; but on May 21 in 1391.

of Emlay on the east. Witnesses, William de Dronsfeld, knt., John FitzWilliam, Richard de Keresforth of Barneslay, Henry del Syke of Flocton, John de Whetelay of Emlay. Flocton.[1] (*Ibid.*, No. 47).

192. Nov. 12, 1407. Release by Robert son of Robert de Rokeley, knt. (*militis*), and William Fynche, chaplain, to William son of Adam Allman of Emlay of all right in the same premises [*as in the previous deed*]; which they lately had of the grant and feoffment of the said William. Witnesses, Henry Syke of Flokton, William Dykson, John Hauley, Henry Wright, William Grenehous of the same. Flokton.[2] (*Ibid.*, No. 53).

193. July 24, 31 Henry VI [1453]. Grant[3] by Isabel Cliderowe of Ledes, sister of John Flokton, late of Calais (*Calesia*) to Brian Beston, esq., his heirs and assigns, of all her messuages, lands and tenements with appurtenances, which had lately belonged to John her brother in Flokton. Witnesses, John Clayton, Thomas Dicson, John del Sikes, William Houley, Adam Alot.[4] (*Ibid.*, No. 82).

194. July 1, 9 Edward IV [1469]. Grant by Richard Dicson of Ouer Flocton to Richard Wentworth, esq., his heirs and assigns, of all his lands and tenements, meadows, feedings and pastures, with appurtenances in Ouer Flocton, which had descended to him by hereditary right after the death of John Dicson his brother. Also appointment of John Bretton and Thomas Clerk as attorneys to enter and deliver seisin. Witnesses, John Bedfforth, John Jacson the younger, Thomas Mooke. Ouer Flocton. (*Ibid.*, No. 80).

195. Oct. 12, 17 Edward IV [1477]. Release by John Dycson son of Thomas Dycson, late of Nederflokton, to Richard Wyntworth of Westbretton, esq., of all right in a messuage with appurtenances lying in Overflokton, which Thomas his father, together with Sir Thomas Sayvile, knt., and Thomas Clayton, lately had of the grant and feoffment of William Dycson, late of Overflokton. (*Ibid.*, No. 48).

[1] Seal : black wax; device of a cross and square.
[2] Two seals : (1) a cinquefoil ; (2) letter W beneath an antique crown.
[3] Also, Aug. 1, same year, bond by Isabel and William Cliderow her son to Brian Beyston, esq., in 20 marks sterling to be paid at Christmas to ensure their keeping him indemnified against the heirs of John Flokton, and to ensure a release to him by John Clyderow, chaplain, son of Isabel, of all right in the same premises within the ensuing two years ; same seal, broken. (*Ibid.*, No. 83).
[4] Seal : red wax ; signet, a bird with wings displayed ; broken.

196. Oct. 21, 17 Edward IV [1477]. Grant[1] by Thomas Dicson of London, son and heir of William Dicson, late of Derby, to Thomas son of Randolf Smyth of Monkebretton, his heirs and assigns, of all his lands and tenements, meadows, woods and pastures, rents and services, with appurtenances within the township of Flocton. Witnesses, William Turneley, John Wodde, John Dicson. Flocton.[2] (*Ibid.*, No. 52).

197. Dec. 12, 17 Edward IV [1477]. Grant by Thomas son of Randolf Smyth of Monkebretton to Richard Wenteworth of Westbretton, esq., his heirs and assigns, of all his lands and tenements, meadows, woods and pastures, rents and services, with appurtenances within the township of Flocton, which he had of the grant and feoffment of Thomas Dycson of London. Witnesses, Richard Keresforth of Bernesley, John Page, Thomas Ceu. Flocton. (*Ibid.*, No. 54).

198. 1506. Grant by William son and heir of William Allman, late of Overfflokton to Christopher Dyghton of West Byrton, his heirs and assigns, of a messuage [*as in* vol. v, No. 158]. Witnesses, Richard Wyntworth of West Byrton, esq., John Wodroff of Wollay, esq., John Wheytley, John Warde, John Staynton, William Tomlynson of the same. Overfflokton.[3] (*Ibid.*, No. 56).[4]

199. June 3, 6 Henry VIII [1514]. Indenture[5] by which Thomas Rokley, knt., demised to John Spenser his mill in Floctun with the house and croft lying beside it; to occupy the said millhouse and croft to John, Alice his wife, and Edward Dicsun and Margaret his wife; after John's death Edward and Margaret to occupy half or the whole with Alice as they should agree; from the following Martinmas for a term of twenty-three years, paying 17s. yearly, half at Martinmas and half at Whitsuntide; the lessees to uphold and repair the mill with "thack and morter," and to do other repairs "as it wyl serue them" during the term. Mutual seals.[6] (*Ibid.*, No. 84).

200. May 31, 23 Henry VIII [1531]. Indenture[7] between Roger Rokley, esq. and Richard Ellys and Jennet his wife, by which Roger demised to Richard and Jennet "and to one of thayr chyldur" a watermill with appurtenances called Flokton mylne, from Martinmas next following for a term of twenty years, paying

---

[1] Quitclaim printed in vol. v, No. 157.
[2] Seal : red wax, letter T.
[3] Seal : yellow wax, small, a rose.
[4] No. 55 is a quitclaim by Christopher Dyghton to Richard Wentworth, Nov. 2, 1482, corresponding to the grant printed in vol. v, No. 158.
[5] In English.
[6] Missing from a tongue.
[7] In English.

17*s.* yearly, equally at Whitsuntide and Martinmas; the lessees to maintain the mill with Roger's timber. (*sd.*) Rog' Rokley.[1]

Dorso : "provydyd allway that the withinnamyd Jennett shall keyp her solle[2] or ells her parte of the present leys to be voyd." (*Ibid.*, No. 57).

201. Dec. 20, 37 Henry VIII [1545]. Sale by John Dighton, late of Notton, yeoman, to Robert Popeley of Wollay Morehowse, gent., of a messuage, a garden, a croft and all other closes belonging to the messuage, with appurtenances in Overflokton, in the several tenures of Henry Williamson and William Williamson his father; and also another messuage, a garden, a croft and all other lands, meadows and pastures, with appurtenances in the same, in the tenure of Edmund Moldeson. Witnesses, Robert Gledhill, Henry Williamson, Edmund Molsone. (*sd.*) John Dyghtton.[3]

Dorso : seisin delivered in the presence of Humphrey Beamount, John Webster, Henry Williamson, Edmund Molson. (*Ibid.*, No. 81).

Gildingwells.

202. Grant and sale by Hugh the forester of Lettewell to Richard de Ottelai, his heirs and assigns,[4] of 14*d.* of his rent which Ranulf son of Roger de Gildanwell was wont to render to him for his messuage and land which he was holding of him in Gildanwell; rendering yearly to the grantor and his heirs 2*d.* at the four terms fixed in the soke of Tikehil, at each term $\frac{1}{2}$*d.*, for all services. For this sale Richard gave him a mark of silver in his great need. Witnesses, Ralph Selvayn, Walter de Wlfthuait, John his son, Peter de Lettewell, Thomas de Lindric, John son of Joseph, Benet de Trumflet, William the mason (*cimentario*). (*Duke of Leeds*, Hornby Castle Muniments, Gildingwells, No. 1).

Girrick (Skelton).

203. Demise by Sir Walter Fauconberg, knt., lord of Skelton[5] in Cleueland, to John son of Hugh de Grenerig, his wife and heirs, of a messuage and two bovates of land with appurtenances in the vill and fields of Grenerig,[6] namely, the messuage

[1] Fragment of a seal with letter R.
[2] *i.e.* sole in her widowhood.
[3] Fragment of seal of red wax.
[4] et cui assignare voluerit.
[5] *Slelton*, MS.
[6] Medieval form of Girrick, now a hamlet in Great Moorsholm, par. Skelton in Cleveland.

which William de Flathowe formerly held; to hold of the demisor, his heirs or assigns, from Whitsuntide, 1361 for a term of twenty years, rendering yearly 8s. at Martinmas and Whitsuntide, and doing suit at two chief courts in the year; the demisee to do no waste, but to leave the premises in good state or better by the view of lawful men. Mutual seals to either part of the indenture.[1] Witnesses, Roger son of Peter, William son of Sybil, Simon son of Hugh, William de Mersk, Roger de Woldale. (*Duke of Norfolk, Misc.*, II, i, No. 13).

Gomersal.

204. St. Laurence the Martyr, 26 Henry VI [Aug. 10, 1448]. Demise[2] by John, duke of Norfolk, John Talbot, knt., and Oliver Mirfeld, esq., to William Popelay of all their lands and tenements, rents and services, with appurtenances in the vills and territories of Gomersall, Heccundwyke, Birstall and Clerkheton, for a term of twenty years, rendering yearly to John, duke of Norfolk, a pound of pepper at Christmas.[3] (*Duke of Norfolk*, Box x, No. 101).

Gowdall (Snaith).

204A. Oct. 20, 17 Henry VI [1438]. Release by John de Goldale of Goldale to John Fechshere of Goldall, of all right in 16d. of a yearly rent of 20d. which he had paid him from a messuage in Goldale.[4] (*Lord Allendale*, Gowdall, No. 1).

Grimston.

205. Charter[5] of William de Mala Palude, canon of York, stating that whereas William son of Herbert had brought a writ of right against the dean and chapter of York, complaining that the grantor had deforced him of half a carucate of land in Grimeston[6] which he claimed to hold by hereditary right of the grantor and his successors as canons, the dispute had been settled as follows: that he (the grantor) had recognized two bovates of the said half carucate to the said William (son of Herbert), and had

[1] Seal: white wax, round, *c.* 1⅛ in.; a shield of arms, a lion rampant (Fauconberg); chipped, and legend indecipherable.
[2] This deed can be compared with No. 289 in vol. vii, issued on the same day.
[3] Two seals of red wax; one an armorial signet, blurred.
[4] Seal: red wax, small, letter A.
[5] For the full text and description of the seal, together with some notes, see Appendix I; illustrated in the Frontispiece.
[6] It is uncertain with which Grimston this can be identified; see the notes.

put him in seisin thereof in the presence of the dean and chapter by rod and staff, and had taken his homage in their presence, to hold to him and his heirs, with all free appurtenances within the vill and without, of the grantor and his successors as canons, rendering yearly for all service and exaction 3s. 2d., namely 19d. at Whitsuntide and 19d. at Martinmas; and that the said William (son of Herbert) had restored the other two bovates, namely those which Richard had held; and that William son of Herbert had granted for life to Beatrice, the grantor's mother, one of the former bovates, rendering yearly 2s. 2d., half at Whitsuntide and half at Martinmas, with reversion after her death to the said William son of Herbert. Seal. Witnesses, Simon the dean, Hamo the treasurer, Adam de Torner, archdeacon of York, William, archdeacon of Nottingham [and others named]. (Y.A.S., M^D 152).

Grimthorpe (Great Givendale).

206. March 26, 2 Richard III [1485]. Grant,[1] indented, by Ralph, lord de Graystok and Wemme, to William Potman, clerk, Edmund Hastyngs, knt., Robert Sheffeld, Thomas Pole and Edmund Thwayts, of the site of his manor of Grymthorpe and all the messuages contained and situate therein, and all the lands, tenements, closes, meadows and pastures with appurtenances in Grymthorpe, in the tenure of Thomas Richardson, farmer thereof, together with the water-mill there; also the lordships and manors of Thornton and Thirntoft and all the lands and tenements in Thornton, Thirntoft, Hoton and Teryngton, with appurtenances in co. York. Also appointment of Robert Peke and John Todd as joint attorneys to enter and deliver seisin.[2] (Duke of Norfolk, Misc., II, iv, No. 12).

Guisborough.

207. Friday before the Nativity of St. John the Baptist [June 19], 1338. Grant by Sir John de Faucumberge of Skelton to Robert, prior of Giseburn, and the convent that they and their successors could cut in part or in whole all the wood growing then or in the future in the close called le Swaytiheued in Giseburn, as inclosed by a dike and the stream called Swynstibek, and carry it therefrom; also grant of common of pasture for their cattle in the said close, and of all other things to be done there for their convenience. Sir John and his heirs would not pasture the close with his own cattle nor take any profit of wood or pasture, and the prior and convent could impark any of his cattle unless they entered by default of fencing. The prior and convent could make

[1] Also the counterpart of the indenture; same seal (No. 13).
[2] Seal: red wax, round, ⅝ in.; a fleur-de-lis.

and repair ditches and hedges as often as should be necessary, provided that any wild beasts of Sir John could enter, the ground of the close with hunting rights being saved to him and his heirs. Mutual seals (common seal of the chapter) to either part of the indenture. Giseburn in Clyueland. (*Duke of Norfolk*, Misc., II, ii, No. 26).

Ibackness.

208. Friday after[1] the Nativity of St. John the Baptist, 11 Richard II [June 1387 or 1388]. Grant by William Lorimer' of Whitteby and Joan his wife, formerly daughter of Herbert de Hastyngs, to Walter de Selby and his wife,[2] of that part of the land which had belonged to John de Swerdby[3] for life [in] Broksay;[4] rendering yearly 12*s*. 4*d*.[5] in equal portions at Whitsuntide and Martinmas; to hold for the life of the said Joan. Power to distrain if the rent should be in arrear for forty days. Mutual seals to either part of the indenture.[6] Whitteby. (*Lord Derwent*).

209. Feb. 21, 6 Edward IV [1466-7]. Grant by Henry Langdale of Ebirston in Pikerynglithe, gent., to John Selby the elder of Bidilsdayn,[7] co. Northumberland, gent., his heirs and assigns, of all his lands and tenements with appurtenances in the vill, fields and territories of Brokkissay within the lordship of Haknes, co. York. Witnesses, Edmund Hastings, knt., John Hastings, esq., John Selby the younger, gent., William Saretryn, yeoman, John Colson, yeoman, Peter Lawnde, Thomas Lawnde, husbandmen. Brokkissay.[8]

210. March 3, 34 Henry VIII [1542-3]. Release by Christopher Seggefeld and Alice his wife, one of the daughters and heirs of John Fowforth, William Cowper and Beatrice his wife, one of the daughters of Richard Ellershawe, and Emota Ellersh[a]we, another daughter and heir of the said Richard, to Robert Snype, their kinsman, of all right in a third part of a tenement or toft and croft with appurtenances in Haknes lying there in a street (*vico*) called Estgate, with all the croft, namely one *le bought acecia*, one acre of land, and half an acre of land and wood lying between Thirlsay and Mayehede on either side of the water. Witnesses, William Procter of Haknes, gent., John Appilby, bailiff there, Richard Kyldale, John Wassande.

[1] Possibly 'before'; obscured beneath a stain. The date is therefore either June 28, 1387 or June 19, 1388.
[2] *et uxori sue* inserted above the line.
[3] *de Swerdby* inserted above the line.
[4] Broxa, par. Hackness.
[5] *et quatuor denarios* inserted above the line.
[6] Missing to this part.
[7] Biddlestone.
[8] Seal: red wax, round, ¾ in.; a shield of arms within a geometrical border; rubbed and legend obscured.

Ibaddlesey.

211. Grant by Peter de Perdeuile of Hausai to Simon de Camelesford, his heirs or assigns, except men of religion (*preter Relligionem*), for his homage and service, of all the south part of his land of Swinehache in the territory of Hausai,[1] namely, all the land lying between the old dike (*fossatum*) of Swinehache and the rood which had belonged to Adam; to hold of the grantor and his heirs, rendering yearly 9*d*. for all service, half at Whitsuntide and half at Martinmas. Witnesses, Thomas de Pouelington, John de Hecke, Henry de Goudale, Hugh his brother, Geoffrey son of Lewin, Hugh his brother, Henry de Wridelesford, Alan de Hausai.[2] (*The Hon. Mrs. Stopford*).

West Ibaddlesey.

212. Grant by John Lokoc of Vesthausay to William de Camlesforthe of Vesthausay, his heirs or assigns,[3] of a long headland (*foreram*) of land in the west field of Hausay Vest, lying between the land of the said vill on the south and that of Robert le Neuile on the north, one end abutting on the land of John Alan and the other on that of the same man; for a sum of money given beforehand; to hold of the grantor and his heirs or assigns, with all easements within the vill of Vesthausay and without, rendering yearly ½*d*. at Christmas for all secular services, customs and demands, tallages and suits of court. Witnesses, Sir Peter de Hausay, Roger de Behale of Hausay Vest, John de Vridelesforthe of the same, Robert de Camlesforthe of the same, Richard [?] Alri, Robert Neuile, John Balkoc of Middle Hausay (*Hausay media*).[4] (*The Hon. Mrs. Stopford*).

213. Grant[5] by Roger de Wridelesford to Sir Miles de Stapelton, his chief lord, his heirs and assigns, of fourteen roods (*perticatas*) of land in Suallai with appurtenances in Westh' in exchange for fourteen roods of land in Gillepighel with appurtenances in the same vill; also quitclaim of all right in all the lands

[1] Haddlesey. This deed and the next are earlier than *Quia Emptores*, 1290. John Balcoc of Middle Haddlesey, the last witness to No. 212, made an agreement with Sir Miles Basset in 1268 (*Y.A.J.*, xvi, 92); and three of those named in No. 212 occur as tenants in West Haddlesey in an extent made there in 1280 (*Yorks. Inq.*, i, 209).

[2] Seal: brown wax, pointed oval, *c*. 1¼ × 1 in. when perfect; a fleur-de-lis; ✠ S' PETRI FI . . . . . IL; chipped.

[3] In the tenendum clause the phrase is 'and to whomsoever he should wish to assign, sell or bequeath it.'

[4] Seal: brown wax, pointed oval, *c*. 1½ × ⅞ in.; an animal, probably a lion, courant along the major axis; ✱ S' IOH'IS LO . . . . . . E. E.; chipped.

[5] All the witnesses except Basset occur as witnesses to a grant by Robert de Camelsford to Sir Miles de Stapelton of land in West Hathelesey, dated 14 Jan. 1308-9 (*Y.A.J.*, xvi, 93).

and tenements of Sir Miles in Suallai, Asshelay, Suallaiker and Le Holme with appurtenances in the same vill, and leave to him to hold them inclosed in severalty by the construction of fixed bounds, so that if the grantor's beasts should enter through default of fencing they should be driven out without being imparked. Mutual seals to either part of the indenture. Witnesses, Sirs Adam Deueruigham,[1] Richard de Berlay, knts., John de Lasci of Gaitford, Walter Basset, John de Birne.[2] (*Duke of Norfolk*, Box x, No. 79).

Great Hatfield.

214. Christmas, 1264. Indenture between Walter de Faucumberge, lord of Rise, and William formerly son of Gilbert de Munceaus, by which Walter demised to William or his assigns the custody of all the land of the son and heir of John de Munceaus with appurtenances in the territory of Est Hatfeld, with the mill and villeins and their services, for a term of ten years; to hold of Walter and his heirs, until he had taken ten crops therefrom; rendering yearly 9 marks, 3s. 1d., half at Whitsuntide and half at Martinmas, for all services, saving to Walter a third part belonging to Lucy, mother of the said heir, if she should die within the term. Power to Walter to give or sell the custody within the term, saving to William the crop and expenditure thereon for the year in which such gift or sale might be made, and saving to him (William) the messuage in which his mother had formerly dwelt for the remainder of the term and one year after at a yearly rent of 4s. William to maintain the buildings in as good a state as he should receive them. Mutual seals; and for better security William found for Walter these sureties (*fideiussores*), namely Sir James de Mora, Bernard de Araines, John son of Walter de Witorwic, and Hugh ad Aulam, who granted to Walter that he could distrain (*constringere*) them by their movable and immovable goods if William should fail in any term, until William gave full satisfaction, and who also affixed their seals, a penalty of 40s. to be paid to the countess of Albemarle if William should fail in any term. Witnesses, Sir Henry de Faucumberge, Sir Simon Withik, knts., Sir William de Cauerle, Peter de Faucumberge, Walter de Faucumberge of Apeltun, William de Withik, Stephen de Hastorp, Peter the marshal (*Marscallo*), John the clerk.[3] (*Duke of Norfolk*, Misc., II, ii, No. 1).

Hemsworth.

215. June 20, 31 Henry VIII [1539]. Appointment by William FitzWilliam, esq., of [*blank*] as attorney to receive on his

[1] De Everingham.

[2] Endorsed in a medieval hand: carta Rogeri de Wrydelesforth. Sq'llay juxta Westhathelsay.

[3] Five tags for seals.

behalf the attornment of [*blank*] Wortley, esq., for the manor of Hymmysworth with appurtenances of which the latter was seised in his demesne as of fee tail, the reversion or remainder thereof having been lately granted to the said William, his heirs and assigns, by Thomas Wentworth, knt. (*sd.*) by me Wylliam Fytz-Wylliam.[1] (*Lord Allendale*, Hemsworth, No. 1).

Ihull.

216. March 25, 4 Henry V [1416]. Grant by Hugh de Clyderowe of Kyngeston on Hull to Richard de Popelay and Henry de Clyderowe of all his goods and chattels on this side of and beyond the sea, living or dead, movable and immovable, with all things due to him (*debitis meis*) wherever found. Witnesses, Robert Shakell, mayor of Hull, John de Aldewyke, bailiff of the same, Thomas Segefeld of Kyngeston on Hull, Robert the parochial chaplain of the chapel of Hull, Richard de Scoles. Hull.[2] (*Lord Allendale*, Hull, No. 1).

Ihunmanby.

217. Gift[3] by Gilbert de Gant to Peter de le Stane, for his homage and service, of four carucates and two and a half bovates of land in Hundemanebi with all appurtenances within the vill and without, in meadows and feedings, waters, paths and all easements belonging to the land; of which Ralph de Nitherafne had held three bovates, Ralph son of Walter two, John del Hyl two, William son of Walter one, Robert Danz two, Gerard Child two, Simon Danz two, John son of Authen two, Everard de Fonte one, Hugh son of Godwin one, Richard son of Walter one, Walter Nout one, Albert son of Authen two, Agnes the widow one, William son of Authen one, Ralph son of Gosse two, Stephen son of Duva[4] two, Thomas the smith one, Geoffrey the carpenter one, Henry son of Kay one, Stephen de Fonte one, Richard Noel one, Geoffrey de la More one, Walter son of Arnald a half, with tofts and crofts belonging to the land. Also gift of a toft which Ralph de Nitherafne had held, and one which Ralph son of Walter had held, three crofts which John del Hyl had held, and others (one each) which Henry Pep, Arnald the parker (*parcator*), Simon Danz, Robert Renibute, Freissant, Anna, William Trittling, Sigerithe, Hisegot, Richard the smith, Geoffrey the butler (*pincerna*), Geoffrey son of Authen, Huelina the widow, Robert Charles, Gerard son of Ingolf,

---

[1] Seal of red wax; traces of the impression of a signet, an eagle.
[2] Fragment of seal of red wax.
[3] dedi et hac presenti carta mea confirmaui.
[4] filius Duue.

William le Taillur, Orm,[1] and Albert Bray had held; and one where the guild-meeting (*gilda*) was wont to be; and others (one each) which Alger and Walter [?] Maugeri[2] had held. To hold to him and his heirs of the donor and his heirs, freely and quit from all service, doing the forinsec service as much as belonged to a third part of a knight's fee. Witnesses, Ellis (*Eliseo*), prior of Bridligtona,[3] Stephen de Gant, Reginald de Gant, John de Melsa, Peter de Melsa, Henry de Folketona, Ralph de Nouilla, Walter de Sancto Laudo, Roger son of Malger.[4] (*Duke of Norfolk*, Misc., II, i, No. 22).

Cold Ingleby (Stainton).

218. Grant by Roger Lohareng of Engelbi to Samson the Jew, son of Samuel, and his heirs, of a bovate of land in Engelbi[5] with a toft and croft and all appurtenances within the vill and without, which Walter son of Merevin had held of the grantor for 4*s.* yearly; to hold with 4*s.* rent of the grantor and his heirs for service and for 4 marks of silver given to the grantor; doing the forinsec service for one bovate where six carucates of land made the service of half a knight's fee; with leave to the grantee to give or sell the land and rent of 4*s.* to anyone, clerk or lay, saving the forinsec service. Witnesses, Robert de Maltebi, Walter de Stainesbi, Richard de Hilton', Roger de Hilton', Thomas de Eggesclif, Roger de Schutherschelf, Ralph de Vado, William de Braidewat, Ylger de Kiltona, Alan de Wiltona, Stephen de Rosel, Robert de Normanbi, Richard Loste, Roger de Stainesbi, William de Stainesbi, Raven de Engelbi, Wada de Engelbi, John de Rungton', William son of Brictmer of Jarum, William le Waid', Simon Joie, Walter son of Herbert of York, Robert the archbishop,

[1] Ormus.

[2] Blurred; possibly Maugeri (son of Malger); but this name is spelt Malgeri in the list of witnesses.

[3] An Ellis (*Helyas*) occurs as prior of Bridlington, 1199-1202; and the next known prior occurs in 1218 (*V.C.H. Yorks.*, iii, 204). Stephen de Gant, the second witness, was probably the donor's brother who witnessed a charter of the donor in the late 12th cent., and who issued a charter to Drax priory early in the 13th cent. (*E.Y.C.*, vi, pp. 150-1).

[4] Through a slit is a double strand, about 10½ in. long and ¼ in. broad, of a light-brown woven material, with traces of pink, tied in a knot, doubtless contemporary; this has probably carried a seal, now missing.

[5] The name of the grantor proves the identification as Cold Ingleby, medieval forms of which included Engleby-Lorenge (*V.C.H., N.R.*, ii, 296; Eng. Place-Name Soc., *N.R. Yorks.*, p. 170). William Loreng gave 3 bovates of land in Caldengleby to Guisborough priory (*Chartulary*, i, 96); and Robert de Pothou and William Loereng were parties to a fine of 3 bovates in Engelby in 1218 (*Yorks. Fines*, 1218-31, p. 5).
The handwriting of the present document suggests the twelfth century, and the witness Ilger de Kilton appears to have died *c.* 1190 (*Y.A.J.*, xxxiv, 309).

William de Lundon', Stephen Engelram, Robert Pothau, Walter Pothau.[1] (*Duke of Norfolk*, Misc. II, i, No. 7).

Irton (Seamer).

219. Grant by William son of William de Yrthon to William his son, his heirs or assigns, of a toft in the vill of Yrthon, which toft he had of the grant of Richard son of Maud de Yrthon, lying in breadth between the toft which John de Wathsand formerly granted to Idonea his daughter on the west and the meadow called Thorpeneg . . e on the east, and in length from the common street (*vico*) of Yrton and abutting on Litelholm; with all easements within the vill of Yrthon and without; the assigns to exclude any house of religion and Jews; rendering yearly to the grantor and his heirs or assigns 1*d*. at Christmas for all secular service. Witnesses, William, lord of Athon, Thomas de . . lakebi,[2] John his son, Robert de Roston, William de Fisburn, John Russel of Yrthon, Richard de Wathsand of the same, Rikeman Franciscus of the same. (*Duke of Leeds*, Hornby Castle Muniments, Irton, No. 1).

220. Grant by John son of William de Irton to John son of Thomas of the same and Hawise his wife, their heirs and assigns, of three selions of arable land lying in the vill of Irton on the south[3] and Buksondik on the north, and in breadth between the toft of Walter son of William on the west and the land of the said John son of Thomas on the east; to hold of the chief lord of the fee, with appurtenances. Witnesses, Henry de Fisseburn, William Barde of Ossegodby, John de Kilwarby, John Gelle of Aton, Richard Palmer of the same, Robert de la [?] Pancrace of Semer, William Russell. (*Ibid.*, No. 2).

221. Grant by Henry de Fiseburn to William son of William de Irtona, and Maud his wife, and William's heirs,[4] of a bovate of land with appurtenances in Irton by Semer, namely, the bovate which lay between the land of the said William on one side and that of John son of William de Irtona on the other, and which he had of the grant of Thomas de Irtona in the same [vill]; with the meadow and all things belonging both in demesne and lordship; to hold of the chief lords of the fee. Witnesses, Robert de Wyherum, William Barde, John Morin, John Cresaker, William Russel, John de Wykham, John son of Thomas de Irton, William [?] Ruchet'. (*Ibid.*, No. 3).

[1] Seal: green wax, round, 1⅜ in.; an animal passant to the dexter; [✠] SIGILLVM ROGERI LOHERENG. Slightly chipped at the edge.
[2] The document is in bad condition.
[3] Possibly *in longitudine* and the bounds on the south are omitted.
[4] Also his assigns, in the tenendum clause.

222. May 4, 38 Edward III [1364]. Appointment by William de Neuport, parson of the church of Spofford, and Henry de Percy, the esquire (*valectus*), of Robert de Burton, rector of the church of Lekynfeld, and Robert de Malton as attorneys to receive seisin on their behalf of a messuage and six bovates of land with appurtenances in Irton by Semere, which messuage John Cleruaux of Croft had granted them by his general charter. Spofford.[1] (*Ibid.*, No. 4).

223. Nov. 15, 41 Edward III [1367]. Grant by Thomas de Shirborne and William de Neuby, chaplains, to Sirs William de Swynflet, archdeacon of Norwich, and John de Akom, rector of the church of Almanbiry, of all their land which they had of the grant of John son of Richard son of Simon de Irton, namely, the toft with the croft lying in the vill of Irton in breadth between the toft formerly belonging to Thomas Dust towards the east and that of the hospital of St. John of Jerusalem towards the west, and in length from the common street (*vico*) of Irton towards the south as far as the land formerly belonging to William Fraunceis towards the north; and the toft with the croft lying in the vill of Irton between the toft formerly belonging to John Tochet on one side and that formerly belonging to Thomas Dust on the other, and in length [*as before*]; also the toft with the curtilage and croft adjacent with appurtenances which they had of the grant of the said John son of Richard son of Simon de Irton; with buildings and appurtenances. Witnesses, Sir John de Irton, chaplain, Robert Brouse, John Nelson, Stephen Baty, John Bulmere of Aton. Semer.[2] (*Ibid.*, No. 5).

224. Sunday on which *Quasi modo geniti* is sung, namely, the last day of March, 1394.[3] Quitclaim by Hugh Moresom to Robert de Roderham of all right in a messuage, five tofts, five bovates of land, and one and a half acres of meadow called Wardebryel, with appurtenances in the vill and territory of Irton by Semer in Pykrynglyth; also in thirty cart-loads (*carectat'*) of turves to be taken and dug in Hoton Ker; with all rents, homages and services of tenants both free and villein, as contained in a charter of John de Neuby and Agnes his wife made to the said Hugh and Robert. Witnesses, Robert de Unkleby, Robert de Malton, John de Cotom, Robert Bard, Thomas de Kylwordeby. Semer. (*Ibid.*, No. 6).

---

[1] Seal on a tongue of the parchment: red wax, round or oval, *c.* ⅞ in.; a gem, a human head to the sinister; legend indecipherable; badly chipped. Another tongue for a seal, now missing.

[2] Two tags for seals; one remains: red wax, round, ⅞ in.; a stag's head cabossed; legend indecipherable.

[3] Probably so, but the beginning of what seems to be *nonagesimo* is obscured.

225. Monday after the Purification of the B.V.M., 1 Henry V [Feb. 5, 1413-4]. Release by William de Chambre of Thueng, son and heir of Agnes widow of John de Neuby of Irton, to Thomas Hebson of Irton and Idonea his wife and the heirs of their bodies, of all right in those bovates of land and the cottage [and] waste with *le Bryell* with appurtenances in the vill and territory of Irton, which they had of the grant of the said Agnes. Witnesses, John Sparow of le Northstede by Scharburgh, John Rotse of Semer, Thomas de Kelk of the same, William Baty of Irton, William Danby of Scharburgh, *barkar*. Irton.[1] (*Ibid.*, No. 7).

226. Feb. 3, 4 Edward IV [1464-5]. Grant at fee-farm[2] by John Cowpelande, late of London, baker, to Robert Cosyn of Fyuelay, his heirs and assigns, of two tofts and two crofts and one bovate of land with appurtenances in Irton by Semar, which had lately belonged to Thomas Mathew of Semar, deceased, and which had descended to the grantor by hereditary right by the death of William Coupelande his father, as they lay together between the land belonging to the chantry of Semar on the east and that of the lord of Semar on the west, and between the highway towards the north and the common of Irton towards the south; rendering yearly to the grantor, his heirs and assigns, 4*d.* of silver if demanded at Whitsuntide and Martinmas in equal portions. Mutual seals.[3] Witnesses, Robert Perkynson, vicar of Semar, Henry Jenkynson, John Forthe, John Andrew, John Werner. Irton. (*Ibid.*, No. 8).

227. St. Edmund the King, 8 Henry VII [Nov. 22, 1492]. Grant by Alice Mery, daughter and one of the heirs of Thomas Depdale of Scardeburgh, lately deceased, to William Mery her husband and the heirs of their bodies, of a messuage and two bovates of land with appurtenances in the vill and field of Irton, which had descended to her by hereditary right. Witnesses, Thomas Edmondson, Thomas Hoppar, William Birkeby of Irton.[4] (*Ibid.*, No. 10).

228. Sept. 24, 20 Henry VIII [1528]. Grant[5] by Robert

[1] Seal: red wax, round, ¾ in.; a stag's head cabossed, a cross between its horns; * IESVS MERCI.

[2] Also, same day, place and witnesses, grant in fee simple by the same to the same and Joan his wife of the same premises. (*Ibid.*, No. 9).

[3] Seal: yellow-brown wax; signet; letter J.

[4] Seal: red wax; small signet upside down on the tag; letter R beneath an antique crown.

[5] Also, same day, indenture of sale in English; Mery described as of Flett in Holland, Lincs., barker, and Grave of Houeden, Yorks.; the premises consisted of "half a meisse, half a close" in Yrton and two oxgangs of land in the field of the same, sometime "Depdaill lands," late in the holding of William Hutton of Irton, and a waste ground in Ayton, late in the holding of Alan Harper; consideration, 6*li.* besides 4*li.* 6*s.* 8*d.* received from Hutton beforehand; mutual seals; same witnesses, Preston and Tenaunt described as gentlemen; seal, red wax, letters AP interlaced. (*Ibid.*, No. 11A).

Mery, late of Brompton, to William Grave, his heirs and assigns, for a sum of money paid beforehand, of all his lands and tenements, rents, reversions and services, with appurtenances in the vills and territories of Yrton and Aiton. Also appointment of Roger Grave and Ralph Stubbs as joint attorneys to enter and deliver seisin. Witnesses, Edward Edgouer, auditor, Arthur Preston, Robert Tenaunt, Robert Bikerstath, Leonard Myres. Topclyf.

Dorso : possession taken at Yrton, Sept. 27, in the presence of Ralph Stobs, Christopher Bottere, Thomas Bridkerk, Thomas Smythe, Richard Bottere, Martin Godyer, Thomas Bollerd. (*Ibid.*, No. 11).

229. Oct. 31, 23 Henry VIII [1531]. Letters patent exemplifying that Martin Goodyere, Thomas Goodyere and Nicholas Trowghton in the king's court before his justices at Westminster impleaded Thomas Cooke concerning a moiety of a moiety of three messuages, fourteen bovates of land and 12*d.* rent with appurtenances in Yrton and Thwyng by the king's writ of entry sur disseisin in the post, the record of which was as follows. At Westminster before Robert Norwiche, knt., and his fellow justices of the Bench, Michaelmas term, 23 Henry VIII [1531], the plaintiffs by James Fox, their attorney, sought the premises as their right and inheritance, in which the defendant had no entry except after the disseisin which Hugh Hunt[1] unjustly made; they said that they were seised in demesne by taking explees. The defendant by William Danby, his attorney, vouched Thomas Chapman to warranty, who denied the disseisin, but afterwards made default. The plaintiffs recovered seisin. Witness, R. Norwiche at Westminster. Seal *ad brevia in Banco predicto.*[2] (*Ibid.*, No. 12).

230. Dec. 14, 29 Henry VIII [1537]. Indenture[3] by which William Couny and Alice his wife of Hornsebeke, co. York, *laborers*, bargained and sold to Robert Wod of Fylay and his heirs two cottages, two crofts and one oxgang of land with appurtenances lying in the town and fields of Irton near Semer in Pikeringlith; for 4*li.* sterling, namely at the following Christmas 13*s.* 4*d.*, at the Nativity of St. John the Baptist 13*s.* 4*d.*, and so yearly at the same feasts until the sum was fully paid; the payments to be made in the house of Richard Atkynson at Fyley, whoever was inhabiting it. Mutual seals.[4]

[1] A fictitious person. This is a common recovery. Chapman, presumably an official of the court, was the common vouchee.

[2] Only a portion remains in black wax; but it is evidently the seal of the Court of Common Pleas (*B.M. Cat. of Seals*, No. 895). At the foot of the deed is the name Jenom.

[3] In English.

[4] Red wax: blurred impression; initials.

Dorso : per me John Buckelay, *recevyr* of Holdernes, per me Richard Cowerd, priest, Robert Ledley, *baley* of Dekeryng, Richard Smart of Horsebek, Richard Atkynson of Filey. Received Jan. 2 in part payment 13*s.* 4*d.* Received at the feast of St. John the Baptist last past 13*s.* 4*d.* Richard Akenson, Robert Stenson, William [?] Topden. Paid to William Counyn 3*li.* 14*s.* 4*d.*[1] (*Ibid.*, No. 13).

231. March 2, 33 Henry VIII [1541-2]. Release[2] by William Percye of Scardebrough, son and heir of Thomas Percye of Scardebrough, lately deceased, to Ralph Dowslaynd of Rudston, of all right in all the messuage, barn, toft and garden, and one bovate of arable land with appurtenances lying in the vill and fields of Irton and Ayton; the messuage lay from the highway towards the north as far as the highway towards the south. Witnesses, Sir John Job, clerk, John Stubbs of Ayton, Bedell[3] of Rudston, Thomas Dale of Semer.

Dorso :[4] possession delivered, March 3, in the presence of William Bridekirke, Edward Claye, Robert Bedell, Robert Russell, Martin Gudyere, Thomas Bridekirke, Thomas Smith, Thomas Gudyere, Thomas Stubbs, George Smith, John Jobson, Christopher Buttre, Robert Douslay, Edmund Buttre, Thomas Dunslay, Ralph Gudyere, William Gudiere. (*Ibid.*, No. 14).

232. Oct. 12, 1570. Will and testament of Robert Dowson of Yrton, par. Seamer. To be buried in the churchyard of Seamer. To Elizabeth Dowson his wife his house in Yrton with all things belonging thereto, for her life with remainder to Richard Hawser and his heirs. Residue of his goods and chattels to his wife, sole executrix. Witnesses, Charles Cant, John Dixon, John Hoton, Thomas Goston, John Cant.

Annexed : Proved before the dean of the deanery of Dickering, and administration granted by Richard Percye, LL.B., commissary and receiver-general of Edmund [Grindal], abp. of York. York, May 3, 1571. Seal of his office.[5] (*Ibid.*, No. 15).

Ikilnwick Percy.

233. Thursday after the three weeks of Easter, 10 Edward III [April 25, 1336]. Whereas[6] John de Kyllyngwyk was bound1 in 200 marks of silver to William de Moubray, clerk, by a recog-

---

1 The last entry is in a different hand.
2 Copy on paper in a seventeenth-century hand; 'copia vera' at the foot.
3 No Christian name given.
4 As stated in the copy.
5 Only a fragment of a seal of black wax remains.
6 In French.

nizance made in the Common Bench on the previous day, to be paid at Michaelmas, 1336, William granted that if John enfeoffed before that date Thomas his elder brother and Margaret daughter of Geoffrey de Rosselles in 10 marks worth of land and rent, namely 100s. worth of land of which John then had the fee simple, and 2½ marks worth of what he should choose in Kyllyngwyk,[1] [to hold] to them and the heirs of their bodies, paying a rose yearly for all services, and if John did not alienate in fee simple or fee tail any land which he then had in demesne or reversion except to Thomas and Margaret, then the bond should be null and void; otherwise it should remain in force. Mutual seals to either part of the indenture.[2] York. (*Bradford Public Libraries*, Misc. MSS.).

South Kirkby.

234. Michaelmas [Sept. 29], 1378. Demise by John de Flynthill of Kyrkeby to John son of Thomas de Scollay, his heirs and assigns, for a sum of money given beforehand, of four and a half acres of land with the meadow adjacent and appurtenances, lying in the field of Kyrkeby in the place called *le Northryddyng*; to hold from Michaelmas, 1378 for a term of twenty years. Witnesses, John de Wyntworth of Northelmesall, Thomas de Skelbrok, William Smyt of Southelmesall, John his brother, William Trigot of Kyrkeby, Adam de Stokhyng of the same. Kyrkeby. (*Lord Allendale*, South Kirkby, No. 2).[3]

235. Morrow of St. John the Baptist [June 25], 1407. Grant by John Joynour of Southkyrkeby to John Dughty and Adam Wryght of the same, their heirs or assigns, of an acre of land and half a rood lying in the south field of Southkirby between the land of John Jakson on the west and that of John Perrot on the east, which he formerly had of the feoffment of John de Stockyng, chaplain; rendering yearly to the chief lord a rose on St. John Baptist's day, if demanded, for all services. Witnesses, John Flynthill of Southkirkby, William Dyconson, Edward Howat, John Bynglay, William Perott, John Jacson. Southkirby. (*Sir Thomas Pilkington*).

[1] The place is not easy to identify; but in 1339 and 1345 a Thomas de Killyngwyk and Margaret his wife occur in fines; and the place from which he took his name was Kyllyngwyk near Pocklington (*Yorks. Fines, 1327-47*, p. 178). This suggests that the present deed refers to the same place.

[2] Seal: dark green wax, round, ⅞ in.; a device; motto not deciphered. Endorsed: Irr[otulatur] in Banco rotulo primo de cartis et proteccionibus de termino Pasche anno regni regis E. tercii a conquestu decimo.

[3] No. 1 of this series was printed in vol. vi.

Leeds.

236. April 1, 36 Henry VIII [1545]. Receipt by William Killingbecke of Waikfelde, *boechar*, son and heir of Thomas Killingbecke late of Leeds, deceased, from John Killingbecke of Leeds, of certain sums of money to the value of 60*li.* in full payment for all his burgages, messuages, tenements, cottages, meadows, pastures, lands, woods or underwoods which he had lately sold to the said John, his heirs and assigns, as they were situate and built on within the vill and parish of Leeds; and quitclaim therein. Witnesses, John Godson, John Myllgaytt, Henry Wayde, Christopher Kyllingbecke, Thomas Sheffelld. (*Lord Allendale*, Leeds, No. 1).

Lintborpe (Middlesbrough).

237. Friday before St. Ambrose the Bishop, 16 Edward II [April 1, 1323]. Agreement to last for the life of the feoffee witnessing that John de Fawkenberg, lord of Sceltona, granted to William de Gaytrigg his plot of land with half an acre belonging thereto in the vill and territory of Leuigthorp', with his fishery in the water of Teys opposite the place called *le Fawkenbergenese*; with all appurtenances and easements; rendering yearly to the grantor and his heirs a salmon in Lent for all service. Mutual seals to either part of the indenture. Witnesses, Robert de Steynesby, Robert de Martona, Robert de Clifland, Robert de Waxsand, Robert de Thormotby, Robert the clerk. Scelton.[1] (*Duke of Norfolk*, Misc., II, ii, No. 13).

Markington.

238. May 16, 1322. Grant by Agnes daughter of Reginald de Merkyngton to Thomas son of Simon de Galghagh of Merkyngton, his heirs and assigns, of a rood of land with appurtenances lying at Mouskeld between the land of the grantee on one side and that of the monk at the gate of Fountains on the other in the field of Merkyngton. Witnesses, John Litester, John de Bradeley,[2] John Giliot, William Foghel, Roger de Galway, Richard Rachard, John de Didens', clerk. Merkyngton. (*W. M. Staveley, esq.*, Markington, No. 1).

239. 11 Kal. May [April 21], 1335, 9 Edward [III]. Grant by Adam de Garton, chaplain, of Aldefeld to Thomas de Galhaghe, dwelling in Aldefeld Northous and Eleanor the latter's daughter of the toft with croft adjacent in Merkington between Fontaynes-

[1] Seal: red wax, round, ⅜ in.; an object possibly a dolphin; * WARE MEN O MAN (no divisions between the letters.
[2] Or Brodeley.

gate on one side and the toft of William Fugel' on the other; and four and a half acres of land and five parcels of meadow in different places in the territory of Merkington and Ingerthorpe, of which half an acre of land lay by Fonteynesgate on the east, one rood by the land of John de Merkington on the west, half a rood at Milnepolacreheued, half a rood on Langlay, one rood abutting on the wood of Nicholas de Burton, one rood in Formby, one rood at Muskeld, one and a half roods in Bottis, one rood on Layrlandes, one rood in Scharstykes, half a rood in Esselandes, half a rood of land and meadow on Wynesword, one rood on Laytholfur, one rood on Tendelesheued, one rood on Gaselandes, one rood of land and meadow at Kerpot, one parcel of meadow in Rysedales, one parcel in Mikeldale, one parcel in Lynedale lying everywhere throughout the meadow of Sir Andrew de Merkingfeld, one parcel in Mykelker by the meadow of Richard de Southend, and one parcel in Hundeker by the meadow formerly belonging to Richard de Southend, and half an acre of land of which one rood lay at Eldmoderacre between the land which William de Bere was holding on one side and that which Robert the reeve had held on the other, one rood at Muskeld between the land of the said Thomas de Galhaghe on one side and that of the monk at the gate of Fountains on the other in the field of Merkington, and one rood on Deen between the land of the said William de Bere on one side and that which Robert the reeve had held on the other; to hold to Thomas for life and Eleanor and the heirs of her body, with reversion, in default of issue, to Thomas, his heirs or assigns. Witnesses, Sir Andrew de Merkingfeld, knt., William de Bere, William de Merkington, John Gyliot, William de Aldefeld. Merkington. (*Ibid.*, No. 2).

240. Saturday before St. Bartholomew [Aug. 22], 1366. Appointment by Eleanor widow of William Mason of North-staynlay of William son of Thomas de Neuby as attorney to deliver seisin to Thomas de Neuby of all her lands, tenements and meadows in the vills of Merkynton and Ingerthorp in accordance with her charter. Merkynton.[1] (*Ibid.*, No. 3).

Marske (Cleveland).

241. Grant by Walter de Faucumberg', lord of Skelton, to Henry Marescall and Beatrice his wife of Mersk, for their lives and that of the survivor, of an acre of land lying in the place called Gyldehuseflatte on the south side by the tenement which William son of John de Mersk was holding of the grantor by

---

[1] Seal: brown wax, round, ¾ in.; a shield of arms, a bend between two charges; rubbed and legend not deciphered. This is the same seal as to No. 290 below; and there is nothing to show that it was the seal of the grantor in either case.

charter (*per scriptum*) in the vill of Mersk; to hold of the grantor and his heirs, with all easements within the vill of Mersk and without, rendering yearly 8*s*. at Whitsuntide and Martinmas in equal portions, and sixteen boon-works in the autumn when required by the reeve of Mersk. Mutual seals to either part of the indenture. Witnesses, John de Fontibus, then steward, Cuthbert Capun, Matthew de Aunay, Hugh Pykwastel of Skelton, William son of John de Mersk. And Henry and Beatrice would do during their lives two attendances (*venues*)[1] at the grantor's court of Mersk, namely at the courts immediately after Michaelmas and Easter. (*Duke of Norfolk*, Misc. II, i, No. 18).

242. Sunday in Christmas week [Dec. 29], 1331. Grant by William Brindboys of Mersk to Hugh son of Richard styled (*dicti*) Tholesun, his heirs and assigns, of three and a half acres of land with appurtenances in Mersk, of which one and a half acres lay in Ouercatteflatte, one and a half acres in Nethercatteflatte, and half an acre at Ryehill in *le Slak*; doing to the chief lords the services due, and rendering yearly to the grantor and his heirs a grain of pepper at Christmas. Witnesses, Sir Robert Capoun, knt., Matthew Daunay, Nicholas de Hoperton, John de Fontibus the younger, William Skotte of Mersk. Mersk. (*Ibid.*, II, ii, No. 20).

243. Monday before the Translation of St. Thomas the Martyr, 35 Edward III [July 5, 1361]. Grant by Walter de Faucomberg, lord of Skelton, to Sir Richard Bewner, chaplain, his heirs and assigns, of a bovate of land with appurtenances in Mersk, which William son of Roger de Redker, his villein (*natiuus*), had acquired from John de Funtayns; with easements. Witnesses, John de Fulthorp, John de Toucotes, James de Towcotes, Nicholas Rosels, Thomas Benes of Cotu.'[2] Mersk.[3] (*Ibid.*, II, iii, No. 9).

244. April 12, 43 Edward III [1369]. Grant by Roger Lascels to Roger son of Sir Walter de Faucomberge and the heirs of his body of all his lands and tenements with appurtenances which he had of the feoffment of the said Sir Walter in the vill and territory of Merske in Cliueland; with remainder in default of issue to the right heirs of Sir Walter. Witnesses, John Percy of Kyldale, John Gower of Sexhowe, James de Toucotes, William de Lackynby, John Capon. Skelton in Cliueland.[4] (*Ibid.*, II, iii, No. 13).

---

[1] The document is otherwise in Latin.
[2] Cotun or Cotum, mod. Coatham.
[3] Seal : red wax, round, 1¼ in.; a shield of arms, a lion rampant; SIGILLVM WALT[ERI] . . . . . .; chipped.
[4] Fragments of seal of red wax.

245. Saturday before St. George the Martyr, 43 Edward III [April 21, 1369]. Grant by Roger de Faucomberge, son of Sir Walter de Faucomberge, lord of Skelton in Clyueland, to Sir Thomas de Faucomberge and Constance his wife and Thomas's heirs, of all his lands and tenements with appurtenances which he had of the feoffment of Sir Roger Lascell', knt., in the vill and territory of Mersk in Clyuel[and]; rendering for Roger's life 40s. of silver yearly at Whitsuntide and Martinmas in equal portions; with power to distrain if the rent should be fifteen days in arrear, and to enter if the rent should be [?][1] days in arrear. Mutual seals to either part of the indenture. Witnesses, John de Hurworth, prior of Gyseburne, John de Fulthorp, John Gower of Faiceby, James de Toucotes, John Capon. Mersk in Clyuel[and].[2] (*Ibid.*, II, iii, No. 14).

246. Aug. 1, 5 Henry VI [1427]. Quitclaim by Edmund Hastynges, knt., to William Neuyll, knt., lord de Faucomberge, of all right in all his lands and tenements in Mersk, Ridker and Uplethom in Cliueland called Downayland; and ratification of his estate therein. Witnesses, Christopher Boynton, Robert Lambton, James Toucotes, John Denton, Thomas Wharrom, William Fulthorpe.[3] (*Ibid.*, II, iv, No. 4).

Masbrougb (Rotherbam).

247. Sunday after the Nativity of St. John the Baptist [July 1], 1347. Grant by William de Bradelay and Agnes his wife to Christiana called Litester of Roderham, for her life, of three selions of arable land with appurtenances lying scattered (*discontinue*) in the field of Markesburgh between *les Fletes*, as contained in the charter made to them; which selions they had of her grant and feoffment. Witnesses, John son of John de Mappels, Hugh Pouay, Simon Litester, John Menewot, Thomas de Hartelay. Roderham. (*Duke of Leeds*, Hornby Castle Muniments, Masbrough, No. 1).

Newby (Stokesley).

248. Sunday before St. Margaret the Virgin, 11 Edward III [July 13, 1337]. Grant by Silla widow of William Pother to John son of Adam le Keu of Neuby and Alice her daughter of

[1] *quindecim* again, evidently in error.
[2] Seal on a tongue of the parchment; red wax, round, *c.* 1 in.; within an elaborately interlaced geometrical pattern, triangular in shape, a bird looking back with a flower in its beak; legend chipped; S F IOH' DE VER . . . .
[3] Seal: red wax; small signet; a dog passant in front of a tree.

two bovates of land, and a moiety of a messuage, croft adjacent and all her meadow in Skelton Kerre on the south, with appurtenances in Neuby[1], which had belonged to Thomas du Boys, together with the other moiety and two other bovates of land; to hold to them and the heirs of their bodies, rendering during the grantor's life 26s. of silver at Whitsuntide and Martinmas in equal portions; with power to distrain if the rent should be in arrear; with remainder, in default of issue, to the heirs of Alice's body, and reversion to the grantor and her heirs. Mutual seals to either part of the indenture.[2] Witnesses, Robert del How, Thomas Sturmy, Roger de Neuby, Thomas son of Roger. Neuby. (*Duke of Norfolk*, Misc., II, ii, No. 25).

249. Nov. 8, 16 Henry VI [1437]. Grant by Roger Cotom and Richard Utley of Gyseburn in Clyueland to Joan widow of John Langwath, of a tenement and two bovates of land with appurtenances in Neuby in Clyueland, in the tenure of John Cornford; to hold for life without impeachment of waste, with successive remainders in tail to Thomas Atkynson, Nicholas his brother, and Alice wife of John Nykson, their sister, and remainder to the right heirs of John Langwath. Witnesses, John Denton, John Boynton, Richard Wurseley, John Thweyng, esqs., Thomas Graveson, Robert del Hall. Gyseburn.[3] (*Ibid.*, II, iv, No. 7).

Newland (Drax).

250. Saturday before the Annunciation of the B.V.M., 7 Henry V [March 18, 1418-9].[4] Grant[5] by John de Steton of Neuland and Maud his wife to William Benland, his heirs and assigns, of a messuage in Neuland containing six acres of land, lying between the land formerly belonging to William Crubane on the west and that of John Williamson on the east, and abutting at one end on Thwartergate towards the north, and at the other as far as the river Ayer towards the west. Witnesses, Henry Warde, Thomas Warde, William Rede, William Thomson, William son of John Houeden of Neuland. Neuland.[6] (*Lord Allendale*, Newland, No. 1).

251. Christmas Day, 17 Henry VI [Dec. 25, 1438]. Grant by William Beynland of Neuland on Ayer' to John Ward of the

---

[1] Probably Newby, par. Stokesley, which is certainly the identification of the next document from the same collection.

[2] Seal: brown wax, round, ⅜ in.; blurred, not heraldic.

[3] One seal remains; red wax; letter R; broken.

[4] Actually March 18 fell in 6 Henry V; but this appears to be intended, as the deed is certainly earlier than the deed in the following note.

[5] Also, Tuesday before Easter [April 11, 1419], same year and place, grant by the grantee to the grantors for the term of their lives of the same premises; same witnesses, except the last, Thomson being described as of Neuland in Drax; seal: brown wax, a letter, chipped. (*Ibid.*, No. 2).

[6] Seal: brown wax, small; letters.

same, son of John Ward, his heirs and assigns, of an acre of arable land lying in *le Midilfeld* of Neuland, between the land of Robert Ward towards the east and that of the said Robert towards the west, and abutting on the land of the said Robert towards the south and that of the said John Ward towards the north. Witnesses, John Turnour, Robert Ward of Neuland, William Houeden of the same. Neuland on Ayer.'[1] (*Ibid.*, No. 3).

Notton.

252.   Christmas Day, 9 Richard II [Dec. 25, 1385]. Demise by Sir Philip Darcy, lord de Menyll, to John Maunsel and Joan his wife of a messuage and a bovate of land with appurtenances in Notton, which William Forester had earlier held; to hold for their lives and that of the survivor according to the custom of the manor by the services due, rendering to him and his heirs 8s. 6d. at Whitsuntide and Martinmas in equal portions. John and Joan to repair the messuage, and at the end of the term to leave it in as good state as when they received it. Mutual seals to either part of the indenture.[2] Knayth. (*Duke of Norfolk*, Misc., II, iii, No. 15).

Potto.

253.   Grant by Nicholas de Menyll to Robert de Pothowe and his heirs of the meadow called *le Littelenge* in the territory of Pothowe, which he had of the gift of Stephen Louerd of Pothowe, containing five acres and half a rood; to hold of the grantor and his heirs, rendering 1d. yearly at Christmas for all services. Witnesses, Sir John de Menyll of Rungeton, Sir William de Rosell, Sir Robert de Scotherskelf, knts., John de Menyl of Midelton, Robert Gouer of Feyceby, Hugh de Hilton, Thomas de Semer.[3] (*Duke of Norfolk*, Misc., II, i, No. 6).

254.   Grant and quitclaim by Richard . . . . ward of Pothowe to Sir Nicholas de Meynill, lord of . . . . lton,[4] his heirs and assigns, of a toft with croft and half a bovate of arable land in the vill and territory of Pothowe, with appurtenances in the vill and without; which toft with the croft lay in length and breadth between those of Sir John de P[? othowe], knt., on one side and the grantor's chief messuage on the other; and the half

---

[1] Seal: yellow wax, round, ⅝ in.; a floral device; legend not deciphered.
[2] Seal: red wax, round, ¼ in.; letter W beneath an antique crown.
[3] Seal: green wax, round, 1 in.; within a cusped border a shield of arms, a chief and three bars gemelles; SIGILLVM NICHOLAI DE MEN . . . . The Meinill arms were *azure, two* (*or three*) *bars gemelles and a chief or* (*Knights of Edw. I*, Harl. Soc.).
[4] Doubtless some spelling of Whorlton.

bovate lay in length and breadth throughout the whole field of Pothowe between the land of Robert del Howe on one side and that of Emma Leuedy, the grantor's mother, on the other. Witnesses, Sir John de Meynill of Rungton', Sir Robert Gower, Sir Robert de Scotherskelf, knts., Stephen de Gowton', Geoffrey Leuedyman, Thomas de [?N]othayth. (*Ibid.*, II, i, No. 14).

255. Grant by Alice formerly wife of Hugh Apesceg' of Weruilton, in her free widowhood and lawful power, to Agnes her daughter, her heirs or to whom she should wish to give, assign, sell or bequeath it, of a bovate of land in the vill of Pothou, lying on the south of the two bovates which she (Alice) had by hereditary right in the vill, by the land of Robert de Pothou; with all easements within the vill and without; to hold of the grantor and her heirs, rendering yearly 6*d.* at Easter for all services. Witnesses, Sir Robert de Meynil, Sir John de la Mare, Alan de Pothou, Robert his brother, John de Gouton, Robert Guer, Robert de Schothereskelf', Alan his brother, Roger Sturmi, Stephen son[1] of Roger de Pothou, Robert son of Wimina,[2] Ingram de Pothou. (*Ibid.*, II, i, No. 19).

Pudsey.

256. Grant by Simon son of Robert de Oulecotes to John the miller of Podd[esey],[3] his heirs or assigns, of a rood of land in *le Brotes*, except the meadow at the end of the rood on the east, lying by the house of the grantee on the north and the land of William le Wayt next on the north; for a sum of money given beforehand; with all easements within the vill of Podd[esey] and without; doing the service due to the lords of the fee. Witnesses, Hugh de Wodhall, John of the same, William son of Roger, John the clerk, Robert son of Simon. (*Bradford Public Libraries*, Misc. MSS.).

257. St. John the Baptist, 13 Edward III [June 24, 1339]. Indenture between Alice le Rede of Podesey and Walter de otheley[4] witnessing that, if Alice paid Walter 20s. of silver at the Nativity of St. John the Baptist in the tenth year after this indenture at Podesey, the charter of feoffment which Walter had from her in respect of a toft and house with a rood of land in Podesey should be void; otherwise the charter should hold good,

---

[1] Apparently *filio*, but the word is not very clear.
[2] filio Wimine (or) Wimme.
[3] He issued an undated charter, *c.* 1308, to which three of those witnessing the present charter were witnesses (*Calverley Charters*, Thoresby Soc., p. 82).
[4] Probably Rotheley, a name which frequently occurs in *Calverley Charters*, and which represents the place-name Rodley.

and Walter bound himself to pay Alice, her heirs or assigns, 20s. at the end of the said term. Witnesses, John de Morley, Robert le Rede of Podesey, John [de][1] Birle, William Alayn, Simon Alayn, William de Tirsale, John de Bercroft, William Attewelle.[2] (*Ibid.*).

Ravenfielð.

258. Sunday after St. Hilary [Jan. 18], 1337[-8]. Grant by Richard son of Nicholas (*Necolay*) de Frisbi to Robert his son, his heirs and assigns, of a toft formerly belonging to Andrew le Pinder, lying between the toft of Sir Thomas de Sanddebi on one side and that of Thomas Boyssewile on the other, and thirteen and a half acres of land in the fields of Rauenfild, namely, ten and a half acres of the bovate formerly belonging to John Baye and two acres of the land formerly belonging to Reginald son of Ralph the forester, lying in different places, namely, two acres in *le Oldfild*, one and a half at Marioriasik, three roods at Setkoppehill, half an acre in *le Crokidlandes*, one and a half acres in *le Brekes* by Hilleclif, an acre at Stonewonge, two at Castelwelleing, half an acre on Celdehanwe, one and a half at Suninebrigge, one on *le Suggehill*, half in Smalwode, half at the head of the vill, and a rood at Horscroft. Witnesses, William Bacon of Rauenfild, Robert Alon of the same, Thomas Bacon, clerk. Rauenfild. (*Duke of Norfolk*, Misc., II, ii, No. 23).

259. Sept. 20, 7 Henry VI [1428]. Indenture between Hugh de Ranfeld on one part and Richard Tallour of Malteby and Emma his wife on the other, witnessing that whereas Hugh had granted to them two messuages and twenty acres of land with appurtenances in the vill and fields of Ranfeld, paying him 8 marks sterling at Easter and the Assumption of the B.M. in equal portions, they now willed that if they failed in the payment Hugh could enter the premises; they also granted to him for life a chamber as an easement with free entry and exit. Witnesses, William de Hoton, Robert Cusworth, Henry Boswell, John Barbot, William Nelson. Ranfeld.[3] (*Ibid.*, II, iv, No. 5).

Reðcar.

260. Grant by Joan daughter of Godfrey de Hoge, in her free power and virginity, to Sir Peter de Brus,[4] his heirs or assigns,

---

[1] Torn.

[2] Fragment of seal of red wax.

[3] Seal: red wax, small; a shield with the letters IH; broken.

[4] Probably Peter de Brus III, who died in 1272; see the note to no. 331 below.

of all the land which she had in Redker of the gift of Godfrey her father, with all appurtenances; in exchange for twelve and a half acres of land and half a rood which he (Sir Peter) had given to her, her heirs or assigns, in Huplyum,[1] as contained in a charter issued to them. Witnesses, Sir Walter de Perci, Sir Robert Engram, Sir Berard (sic) de Fontibus, Sir Robert de Muncell', Sir William Engram, Alan the clerk, Alan de Parco, Robert de Thormodebi, John de Tofecoster. (Duke of Norfolk. Misc., II, i, No. 5).

Richmond.

261.   Grant[2] and quitclaim by Simon de Aske [dwelling] in Richm[und] to John de Westwyke, merchant and Ellen his wife, their heirs and assigns, of an acre of land, one and a half roods and ten perches (virgatas) in the field of Richm[und] called le Galthefeld, of which an acre and ten perches lay between the land of the grantee which he had from Miles on one side and the land of Alan de Ullesou on the other, and three butts containing one and a half roods lay between the land of the hospital of St. Nicholas and that of the said Alan; to hold of the lords of the castle of Rich[mund] as other burgesses held, with all easements within the vill and without; rendering yearly to the grantor and his heirs a root of ginger at Christmas for all services. Warranty against all men and women. Witnesses, Thomas son of Geoffrey, William de Bogg', William le Blunt, Roger de Elligton, Oliver son of John, John son of Peter.[3] (Duke of Leeds, Hornby Castle Muniments, Richmond, No. 1).

262.   Grant by Simon de Aske [dwelling] in Richemund to John de Westewike [dwelling] in the same and Ellen his wife, their heirs or assigns, of three acres of land in the field of Richemund, namely, a selion abutting on Aylwardegarth, two selions lying at the well (fontem) of the Franciscans (fratrum minorum) on the west, three selions on Hydirscul suth, a selion at Haguurmlandis, two selions at Godholis, two selions in le Langebanck, with two selions lying under them, extending from Swale as far as le Myre, two selions in Staynodale, and twenty perches in length in the east selion of the grantor's land by Hauirkeldsike and two feet and sixteen feet in breadth; all of which land lay between the land of Thomas de Thorpe on the west and that of Alan de Ullesou on the east; to hold of the earl of Richmond and his heirs, as other burgesses held, with all easements within the vill and

---

[1] Upleatham.

[2] Also another example of this grant; variations in spelling, William de Bowis, Roger de Ellingtona; same seal, brown wax, the legend is probably S' SIMONIS DE ASKE; not armorial. (Ibid., No. 1A).

[3] Seal: yellow wax, pointed oval; chipped; the first part of the legend is S' SIMONIS.

without; rendering yearly to the grantor and his heirs ½d. of silver at Christmas for all secular services. Witnesses, Thomas son of Geoffrey, William de Bowis, William le Blunt, John son of Richard, Eudo de le Bayl, Walter le seler, Thomas de Thorpe, Oliver son of John, clerk.[1] (*Ibid.*, No. 2).

263. Grant by Ellen widow of John de Westwyk, formerly dwelling (*manentis*) in the vill of Richemund, to Cecily her daughter, her heirs or assigns, of all the burgage with appurtenances in the vill of Richemund lying on *le Walkergrene* between the burgage of William de Munckeby on one side and the burgage of Nicholas Chube on the other; and all the land which the said John de Westwyk formerly had in the territory of Richemund of the grant of Simon de Ask and Miles son of Onorius de Richemund, except two acres of land of which one selion lay in *les Haggewrmelandes*, and two selions on the west side of the well of the Franciscans (*fratrum minorum*) and abutted on *le mire*, and three selions lay under *le Aldequarel*, and one selion lay above *le Aldequarel*; to hold of the lords of the castle of Richemund as other burgesses held, with all easements within the vill and without, doing to the community of the vill of Richemund what other burgesses did. Witnesses, Thomas son of Geoffrey, William de Bouws, John son of Peter, Robert del Grene, Peter del Hille.[2] (*Ibid.*, No. 3).

264. Nativity of the B.M. [Sept. 8], 1297. Release by Ymania widow of Simon de Ask of Richemund, in her widowhood, to Peter son of John de Westwick, his heirs or assigns, of the third part falling to her of all the lands which the said John de Westwick had of the gift or sale of Simon de Ask, formerly her husband, with all appurtenances. Witnesses, Thomas son of Geoffrey, Bernard de Hertford, Thomas de Munckton, then reeves of Richemund, Nicholas of York of Richemund, Adam de sancto Martino, Oliver son of John of the same, William de Bogg' of the same, William styled (*dicto*) de Ask, John son of Peter of the same. Richemund. (*Ibid.*, No. 4).

265. Trinity Sunday [June 6], 1316. Grant by William de Ask and Amice his wife, dwelling in Richemund, to Josiana widow of Peter son of Henry de Richemund, her heirs or assigns, of all their messuage with appurtenances in Richemund in the street (*vico*) called Neubigging, which lay by the west gate between the messuage of Adam the goldsmith on one side and that of the grantee on the other; in exchange for her messuage which lay between the messuage of Acrisius de Skelton on one side and that of Thomas Fauxide on the other in the vill of Richemund in the

---

[1] Same seal as to the preceding deed; brown wax.

[2] Seal: green wax, round, ⅞ in.; an eagle displayed; ✠ S' IOHIS CAPELL'I.

said street; with all easements within the vill and without. Mutual seals. Witnesses, Richard de Huddeswell, Peter del Hill, John son of Eudo, William son of Henry, Peter son of Thomas de Richem[und]. Richemund. (*Ibid.*, No. 5).

266. St. Dunstan the Bishop [May 19], 1318. Grant by Thomas de Thorp, dwelling in the vill of Richemund, to John son of Peter de Richemund, his heirs or assigns, of an acre and a rood of land with appurtenances in the territory of Richemund, of which an acre lay beyond Aslabeck between the land of Adam de Bouws on the east and that formerly belonging to Geoffrey Carias on the west, and a rood lay behind Aylewardegarth between the land of Adam de Bouws on the east and that formerly belonging to Geoffrey Carias on the west; to hold of the lords of the castle of Richemund as other burgesses held similar lands, with all easements within the vill of Richemund and without, doing to the community of the vill what other burgesses did. Warranty for himself and his heirs and all his capital messuage in Richemund into whosesoever hands it should fall. Witnesses, Richard de Hudeswelle, Peter del Hille, Peter son of Thomas, Adam de Bouws, John son of Eudo, William Randeman, Alan the clerk. Richemund.[1] (*Ibid.*, No. 8).

267. Friday the morrow of St. Matthew the Apostle and Evangelist [Sept. 22], 1318. Grant by Thomas de Thorp dwelling in Richemund to John son of Peter de Richemund, his heirs or assigns, of two acres and three and a half roods of land with appurtenances in the territory of Richemund; of which one acre lay in *le Galoufeld* between the land of Adam de Boughes on the east and that formerly belonging to Geoffrey Carias on the west, and abutted on *le Galoudick* on the west of the gallows (*furcarum*), one acre and one rood lay beyond Aslabeck, one and a half roods lay beyond Gillinggat, and one rood lay behind Aylewardegarth between the lands of Adam de Boughes on the east and those formerly belonging to Geoffrey Carias on the west; to hold of the lords of the castle of Richemund, with all easements within the vill and without, doing to the community of the vill what other burgesses did for so much land. Witnesses, Richard de Huddeswell, Peter del Hill, Peter son of Thomas, Adam de Boughes, John son of Eudo, William Randeman, John son of Stephen. Richemund.[2] (*Ibid.*, No. 6).

268. Friday after the octave of St. Matthew the Apostle [Sept. 29], 1318. Grant by Thomas de Thorp dwelling in Richmund to Geoffrey de Munketon and Josiana his wife, their heirs or

[1] Seal: white wax, pointed oval, $1\frac{1}{4} \times \frac{3}{4}$ in.; a hawk over a nest; legend not deciphered.
[2] Same seal as to the preceding deed; blurred.

assigns, of a selion of land with appurtenances in the territory of Richmund, lying under Neubigging between the land of the grantees on one side and that of Adam de Boughes on the other; to hold of the lords of the castle of Richmund, doing to the community of the vill the appropriate service for so much land. Witnesses, John son of Peter, Richard de Hudeswell, Peter del Hill, Peter son of Thomas, John son of Eudo, Roger Brese, John de Ellerton. Richmund. (*Ibid.*, No. 7).

269. Friday after the Conversion of St. Paul the Apostle [Jan. 30], 1399[-1400]. Grant[1] by John de Langelethorpe of Richmund, merchant, and Katherine his wife to Nicholas de Blackeburne of Richmund, merchant, his heirs and assigns, of five acres of arable land and meadow in the fields of the vill of Richmund, namely, two and a half acres in *le Galofelde* between the land of Maud Randeman on the east and that of Thomas de Gayhtfurht of Rypon on the west, one and a half acres in *le Westfeld* on the west side of *le Faluebanke* between the land of John de Burgh on the east and that of the earl of Westmerlande on the west, lying in two selions from *le Muredyke* as far as *le banke* of Swale, and one acre lay in *le Bluntesike* between the land of John de Burgh on the east and that of Roger Bennoke on the west; with all appurtenances. Witnesses, Nicholas Tanner, William Frubber, Thomas Forster, Hugh Clergineht, Henry de Topeclyft, John Clergineht the younger, Thomas de Mallum. Richmund.[2] (*Ibid.*, No. 9).

270. Aug. 8, 1426, 4 Henry VI. Grant by Henry Ravenswath, chaplain, to John Wyott of York, chaplain, and John Yoman of York, *bower*, of all the acres of land and meadow within the territories of Richemond and Huddeswell, which he lately had of the grant and feoffment of Thomas Mallom of Richemond and Agnes his wife. Witnesses, William Fraunk, John Clereionett, Thomas Mallom. Richemond.[3] (*Ibid.*, No. 11).

271. [Aug. 20, 1539]. This indenture mayd the xx^{tl} day of Auguste in the thirty and one yeres of the reynge of oure souerand lord Kynge Henry the eght Betwixt Rauff Gower of

---

[1] On Friday after St. Luke the Evangelist [Oct. 24], 1393 the grantors had been granted the same premises by Alan Stroude of Richmond and Joan his wife; precisely the same descriptions, except that the earl of Westmerlande is called lord le Nevill; witnesses, ..., ... de Clesby, Nicholas de Blakeburne, Henry de Topeclyfe, John de Garthesdalle, Hugh Clergineht; at Richmund; two seals of green wax, one having letter I; the deed is torn in places. (*Ibid.*, No. 10).

[2] Two tags for seals: one remains, red wax; letter W.

[3] Seal: red wax, round, ⅞ in.; a shield of arms, six fusils in bend between six annulets; S . ELT . . . . S . IOTE in black letter; chipped at the bottom. The last word suggests it may have been the seal of John Wyott, but no corroborative evidence for the arms is available.

Rychemond mercer wythin the coynteye of Yorke of that one partye and the bayliffs & burgesses of the sayd towne of that other partye Wyttenessyth that qwere as the sayd Rauff hathe by leisse for twenty and one yeres the house late of the gray frears of Rychmond wyth all the singler approttenances aswell wythin the wauls as the towne for xxxjs. viiid.[1] yerely rente painge to the kynge oure soueringe lorde or to his assigners at suche times as in the sayd leisse dothe espesyfye shewe and mayke mencon the said Rauff Gower of his sencere and mere mynd hayth gevyn and grantyd and by thes presens geffs and grants to the sayd bayliffs & burgesses to the use of the sayd towne all his strenthe tytle clame or entrest that he hathe in the sayd frearrege wyth the approttenance aforesayd in as ample and large maner as he hathe takyn it apon the kynge oure sayd souerand lord or of his ryght honorable chanceler of the agmentacion as by same leisse sealyd wyth the seall of the same offece more planely wyll appere To haue and to hold the same leisse to the sayd bayliffs and burgesses of the aforesaid towne durynge the sayd yeres to the use aforesayd without any interupcion or lattyn of the sayd Rauff or any other in his name hereafter Provydyt allvay that the sayd bayliffs & burgesses shalbe bownd in XLli. sterlynge by thare ded oblygatory to dyscharge and aqwyte the sayd Rauff his heires excutors and assigners aganste oure sayd souerand lord his heires executors and assigners of and for suche payments or anuall rent and other things as the sayd Rauff is bownd fore in the leisse durynge the sayd yeres In wyttenes qwhere of the sayd Rauff Gower hayth to the one partye of thes indentors remanynge wyth the sayd bayliffs & burgesses hayth setto his seall and the same bayliffs & burgesses to the other partye remanynge wyth the sayd Rauff hayth setto the comyn seall of the sayd towne of Rychmond the day and yere abouff sayd.[2] (*Richmond Corporation*).

Rimington.

272. Grant by John de Bolton to Nicholas de Bolton and the heirs of his body of ten acres of land with all the meadow adjacent, with appurtenances in Rimyngton, lying in a culture called Martintoftes;[3] rendering yearly a rose at the Nativity of St. John the Baptist, and doing homage and service; with reversion to the grantor in default of issue. Mutual seals to either part of the indenture.[4] Witnesses, Richard Tempest, Edmund Maunsel, William de Roucestre, Alan de Bolton, Henry de Rymyngton, Simon de Pathenal', John his brother. (*Y.A.S.*, M^D 161A, No. 1).

[1] viijd. inserted above the line.
[2] Seal: red wax, lozenge-shaped, small and broken; a merchant's mark.
[3] A large number of documents relating to Rimington are pd. in *Pudsay Deeds*; and in several the name Martintofts occurs.
[4] Seal: dark green wax, round, ¾ in.; a hare riding a dog.

273. Thursday after St. Leonard, 30 Edward I [Nov. 8, 1302]. Grant by John son of John de Boulton to William Baudewyn of Rymington, his heirs or assigns, of all his lands and tenements in the vill and territory of Rymington, namely, a messuage and half a carucate of land with appurtenances; to hold of the grantor and his heirs,[1] with all liberties and easements within the vill and without, by the services due therefrom, namely, homage and forinsec service as much as belonged to so much land and an arrow at Whitsuntide. Mutual seals to either part of the indenture.[2] Witnesses, William de Roucestre, Henry de Rymington, Robert and William his brothers, Alan de Boulton, Hugh Gillemyn. Rymington. (*Ibid.*, No. 2).

Ripon.

274. Sale[3] by Margaret widow of Robert the smith of Massham, in her widowhood and lawful power, to Robert Chykin of Rypona, his heirs or assigns, for a sum of money given beforehand, of the burgage with appurtenances in Rypona in the street (*vico*) of All Saints, lying between the burgage of John de Ebor' and that of John de Panahal; with all liberties and easements within the vill of Rypona and without belonging thereto; rendering yearly to the archbishop of York and his successors 4*d.*, half at Whitsuntide and half at Martinmas, and doing forinsec service as much as belonged. Witnesses, Sir John de Thoucotys, bailiff of Rypon, John de Ebor', Robert Dispenser, Walter de Routhekyfe, William Campanar', Bernard de Suaynby, Geoffrey Euerard, John de Panhal, Walter le Dulbur. (*W. M. Staveley, esq.*, Ripon, No. 1).

275. Sale by John de Lanum in his great need to Robert de Hilton, clerk, his heirs or assigns, of part of his toft and croft in the vill of Ripon, containing fifty feet in breadth both at one end and the other and the same length as the toft and croft;[4] which part lay between his house and the toft which had belonged to Hubert the carpenter; to hold of the grantor and his heirs, rendering yearly 2*d.*, namely 1*d.* at Whitsuntide and 1*d.* at Martinmas, for all services; with all easements within the vill and without. For this Robert had given him 30*s.* sterling. Witnesses, William de

---

[1] This is unusual as the date is after the statute of *Quia Emptores*, 1290.

[2] Seal: dark brown wax, pointed oval, 1 1/16 × 5/8 in.; a hawk preying over a nest; * S' : W'LLELMI . BAVDWYN; fine impression.

[3] In a hand which suggests the middle part of the thirteenth century. John de Tocotes, bailiff of Ripon, witnessed a charter dated 1258 (*Fountains Chartulary*, p. 544).

[4] et per totam longitudinem tam in tofto quam in crofto.

Widin'd,[1] steward of the archbishop, Peter de . . . ., . . . Ward,
. . . . newyc, Ralph de Neuby, Roger de Eueston, Nicholas de
. . . ., Walter de Hilton, Robert de Stouwa, Geoffrey
de . . . .[2] (*Ibid.*, No. 2).

276. Release and confirmation by Stephen son of Peter
de Skelton to John called Frere of Rypon, merchant, his heirs or
assigns, for a sum of money given beforehand in his need, of all
right in four acres and a rood of land of which Eda daughter of
Roger, his niece, had enfeoffed the said John and confirmed by her
charter. Witnesses, Sirs Simon Warde, Geoffrey de [He]wich,[3]
knts., Thomas Abboth, Thomas son of Simon, Robert F . . . .
(*Ibid.*, No. 3).

277. Wednesday before St. Gregory the Pope [March 10],
1282[-3]. Sale and quitclaim by Robert Bacheler to John Frer,
for a sum of money given beforehand in his need, of 2*s.* yearly rent
which he was wont to take from the burgage in Rypon which
William Wuyt was holding, lying between the land of John de
Ebor' and that of John Scute, and of all right in the said burgage;
to hold to him, his heirs or assigns. Witnesses, William Costentyn,
Bernard de Suaynby, Walter Dulbur, John de Ebor', Stephen
Chykin, Richard de Roderham, Richard Scoticus, Adam the
marshal (*marscallo*), William Yol, William Wuyt. (*Ibid.*, No. 4).

278. Sunday after St. Dunstan the Bishop [May 23], 1305.
At Whitsuntide, 1305,[4] this agreement was made between Diana
daughter of William Chartres of Ripon, Alexander de la More of
Pontefract and Katherine his wife, Isolda, Margery and Isabel,
daughters of the said William Chartres, and Helewise his widow
on one part, and John Fyncgale on the other, by which the
former demised to the latter a burgage with appurtenances in the
vill of Ripon in the market-place between the burgage of John
Barry on one side and that which had belonged to Aunger de
Rypon on the other; with all easements, for a term of sixteen
years. John and his heirs to maintain the burgage in walls (*muris
et parietibus*) and roof at their own cost, and to leave it in as good
state or better; and should he or his heirs build anything anew in
the said burgage within the term they would take it away with

---

[1] Evidently Sir William de Widindon or Widington (and other
spellings), who frequently occurs in the *Register* of abp. Gray. He occurs in
1226 (*Reg. Gray*, pp. 221, 223) and in 1241 and 1246 (*ibid.*, pp. 191, 195, 202).
He was the archbishop's steward in 1252 (*ibid.*, p. 268; and *cf.* pp. 192*n*, 286).

[2] Badly torn at the bottom, and several witnesses are missing. There
appears to be no date.

[3] Torn; but very probably *Hewich*. Sir Simon Warde and Sir Geoffrey
de Hewick constantly occur together in charters; *e.g. Fountains Chartulary*,
pp. 189, 255, 300, 329, 581, 708, 862, three of which bear the dates 1279,
1286 and 1293 respectively.

[4] Whitsunday was on June 6.

them at the end of the term, or else the demisors should pay all the costs thereof according to the view of lawful men. Mutual seals to either part of the indenture. Witnesses, Adam de Lairthorpe, Adam Arnys, bailiffs of Pontefract, Thomas Scot of the same, William le Vauasour of Ripon, William de Swirewode of the same, William de Clutherum of the same, and John Frere of the same. Pontefract.[1] (*Ibid.*, No. 5).

279. Wednesday before St. William the Bishop [June 7], 1307. Release by Robert de Crakhale of Rypon, baker, to Aunger son of John [Fre]re[2] of Rypon, his heirs and assigns, of all right in the messuage with appurtenances lying in *le Westegat* in the vill of Rypon between that of Robert called Gretheman on the west and that of William de Schirwode on the east, with all appurtenances. Witnesses, Richard de Stowe, Roger de Cloutherum, Nicholas Huberd, William de Schirwode, Robert de Schirwode, John the fuller (*Fullone*), Hugh de Skalton. Rypon.[3] (*Ibid.*, No. 6).

280. Friday, St. James the Apostle [July 25], 1309. Quitclaim by Stephen son of Stephen Chyken of Ripon to Hugh de Thesdale, clerk, and Juliana his wife, their heirs and assigns, of all right in a messuage with appurtenances in Alhalghegate in Ripon, which they had of the grant of Stephen his father. Witnesses, Richard de Stowe, Roger de Cloutherum, William de Shirewode, Hugh de Skalton, Aunger Frere, William de Ponteburg, clerk, Peter de Malton. Ripon. (*Ibid.*, No. 7).

281. Saturday, St. Bartholomew the Apostle [Aug. 24], 1314, 8 Edward II. Grant by Roger de Ledeston of York, tanner, and Constance his wife to master Hugh de Tesedale, clerk, his heirs and assigns, of all their land with a certain burgage as they lay in Berfotgate in Ripon, in length from the high street in front as far as the land of Anger Frere behind, and in breadth between the land of the said Anger on one side and that which had belonged to William Litster on the other; with appurtenances. Witnesses, Nicholas Huberd, William his son, Anger Frere, William de Selby, Peter de Malton, Richard Aldreth, Richard Barry, Roger Herman. Ripon. (*Ibid.*, No. 8).

282. Wednesday after St. Cuthbert [March 23], 1316[-7]. Demise by Aunger Frer of Rypon to Ellen Marchall of Rypon, her heirs and assigns, of a messuage in Staynbryggate in Rypon, lying between the messuage of Robert de Clutherum on one side and that of Richard Aldreth on the other; to hold of the grantor

---

[1] Seven slits for tags.
[2] Torn.
[3] Seal : red wax, round, ⅝ in.; a hawk preying over an animal. Endorsed in a medieval hand : Inq^r quis tenet istud [?] mes[uagium] in Westgate.

and his heirs, rendering yearly 4s. at Whitsuntide and Martinmas in equal portions, and doing to the chief lord of the fee the services due. Agreement that if the messuage should be sold or alienated by Ellen or her heirs a sale to others should not be lawful before refusal by Aunger or his heirs at an amount which it would be worth to anyone else. Mutual seals to either part of the indenture. Witnesses, Adam Caperoun, William the dyer, Richard Aldreth, Richard de Brounhous, Roger de Kirtelyngton. Rypon. (*Ibid.*, No. 9).

283. Monday after St. Luke the Evangelist [Oct. 20], 1320. Grant by John le Warenner of Stodeleyroger to Aunger Frere of Ripon, his heirs and assigns, of a plot of land with appurtenances in Allehaleghgate in Ripon, abutting on the garden of the grantee on one side and on the tenement of Robert Torald, chaplain, in breadth on the east, and extending in length from the archbishop's garden as far as the grantor's garden. Witnesses, Thomas de Eyuill, bailiff of Ripon, William de Ponte Burgi, William de Shirwod, William de Cluthorum, John de Didensale, clerk. Ripon. (*Ibid.*, No. 10).

284. October 9, 1324. Release by Isolda widow of Robert Frere to Aunger Frere of Ripon and his heirs of all right in the messuage with appurtenances which she had for life between the messuage of William del Bank on one side and that formerly belonging to Nicholas Stele on the other in Westegate in Ripon. Witnesses, Thomas Dring, bailiff of Ripon, John le Warenner, John Hubert, William Hubert, Richard de Tanefeld, Adam de Scotton, Bernard Gille. Ripon.[1] (*Ibid.*, No. 11).

285. Friday after St. William of York the Archbishop [June 9], 1340. Grant by Aunger Frer of Rypon to Alan de Schirwod of Rypon, his heirs and assigns, of his three burgages lying in the vill of Rypon, namely, the one in which he was dwelling opposite *le Cornehill* and two next on either side of the first one; also all his lands and tenements, rents and services which he had in the vills of Bondegat and Skelton by Rypon. Witnesses, John de Clotherum, bailiff of the liberty of Rypon, Roger de Clotherum, Adam de Scotton, John Schirwod, Richard de Stow. Rypon. (*Ibid.*, No. 12).

286. 6 Kal. March, 16 Edward III[2] [Feb. 24, 1341-2]. Indenture witnessing that although Aunger Frere of Ripon had granted to John his eldest son a yearly rent of 20 marks from his tenements in Ripon, it was agreed that if Aunger made no

[1] Endorsed in a contemporary hand: Aquietancia Isolde de Hauldfeld de domo in Westgat. And in a later hand: Inq^r quis tenet.
[2] et regni sui Franc' tercio.

alienation or sale of the tenements or any part thereof, whether in doors (*ostibus*) or in windows or in other timbers or trees belonging thereto the said grant should be of no effect; but if he did, then the grant should remain in force. Mutual seals. Ripon.[1] (*Ibid.*, No. 13).[2]

287.   May 4, 1344. Demise by John son of Aunger Frere of Ripon to Joan his mother of four acres and one rood of land in the field of Bondegate which he had of the grant of Aunger Frere his father, as they lay in different places in the field; for the term of her life, rendering yearly a rose at the feast of St. John the Baptist. Mutual seals to either part of the indenture. Witnesses, John de Shirwod, Robert Colstane, Robert Warener, John Malson. Ripon. (*Ibid.*, No. 14).

288.   Thursday before the Decollation of St. John the Baptist [Aug. 25], 1345. Grant by Sir Adam de Bondegat of Ripon, chaplain, and Sir John de Monketon, chaplain, to Ivo Furnyuall of Rypon, butcher, for his life of a burgage with appurtenances in Rypon in the meat-market (*macella*) lying between the burgage formerly belonging to William Willyboy on one side and that of Nicholas Hubert the elder on the other; which burgage they had of the feoffment of the said Ivo; with appurtenances. Witnesses, Richard de Tanfeld, Thomas Scott, John Tauerner, William June, Richard Bondeson, William Aldadamsone, John Frere, clerk. Ripon. (*Ibid.*,No. 15).

289.   Thursday, St. Mary Magdalene [July 22], 1350. Grant by John Euerwak of Rypon to Sir John de Walkyngham, perpetual vicar of the church of St. Wilfrid of Rypon, his heirs and assigns, of a messuage in the street (*vico*) called Westgat in Rypon, which he had of the grant[3] of Aunger Frere and which lay between the messuage of Alice del Bank on one side and that of Nicholas Stele on the other; with appurtenances. Witnesses, John de Cloutherom, Roger de Cloutherom, John de Schirewode, Richard de Tanfeld, Richard de Stow. Rypon. (*Ibid.*, No. 16).

290.   St. Matthias the Apostle, 11 Richard II [Feb. 24, 1387-8]. Grant by Richard de Sunnyng of Rypon to John de Kelyngale, vicar of Kyrkebystephane, Robert de Doreham, John de Dene and John del Keld, chaplains, dwelling in Rypon, of two burgages in Rypon with appurtenances, lying together between the burgage formerly belonging to Bernard Wrygth on one side

---

[1] Seal: red wax; possibly a bird over a nest; rubbed and legend indecipherable.

[2] Also the counterpart (No. 13A); oval seal of red wax; a standing figure between two objects; legend mostly chipped away.

[3] ex dono et dimissione.

and that of Robert de Halomschire on the other towards *le Cornehyll* in length. Witnesses, John Ward, knt., Richard de Rychemond, John de Berwyk. Rypon.[1] (*Ibid.*, No. 17).

291.   Sept. 13, 1390.   Release by John de Kelyngall, vicar of the church of Kyrkebystephane, Robert de Doreham, John de Dene and John del Keld, chaplains, to Richard de Sunnyng of Rypon of all right in two burgages with appurtenances in Rypon in *le Merketstede* towards *le Cornehyll* which they had of the grant of the said Richard. Rypon.[2] (*Ibid.*, No. 18).

292.   The Purification of the B.V.M., 11 Henry VI [Feb. 2, 1432-3].   Grant by John Dall son of John Dall of Ripon to William Toon of Ripon, his heirs and assigns, of all his lands and tenements, rents and services, barn, dovecot and garden in the vill and territory of Ripon, which had descended to him after the death of John Dall his father. Witnesses, John Whixley the elder, Robert Snaith, William Frankish, Robert Tauerner, John Donnyng. Ripon.[3] (*Ibid.*, No. 19).

293.   May 22, 24 Henry VI [1446].   Grant by Richard Tone of Rypon to John Rande of Rypon, his heirs and assigns, of a messuage and his two cottages with appurtenances lying between the tenement of the vicars of the collegiate church of Ripon on the south in the street (*vico*) called Staynbriggate in the vill of Ripon and the tenement lately belonging to John Dall lying there on *le corner* on the north in the said street, which he lately had of the feoffment of William Tone his brother. Witnesses, John Walworthe, William Frankys, John Percyvale, Philip Glouer, Richard Wyrell. Rypon.[4] (*Ibid.*, No. 20).

294.   May 25, 24 Henry VI [1446].   Grant[5] by William Tone of Thorpe, son and heir of William Tone of Rypon lately deceased, to John Rande of Rypon, his heirs and assigns, of all his lands and tenements with appurtenances lying between the tenement of

[1] Seal: red wax, round, ¾ in.; a shield of arms, a bend between two charges; legend not deciphered.   This is the same seal as to No. 240 above.
[2] Four seals of red wax: (1) Madonna and Child beneath a canopy; (2) a fleur-de-lis; (3) two compartments beneath a canopy; in one a standing Saint, the right hand figure broken away; the legend contains the word AVE; (4) a boar beneath a tree.
[3] Seal: red wax, oval, letter W beneath an antique crown.
[4] Seal: red wax, round, ½ in.; letter R.
[5] Also, May 29, release by the same to the same of all right in the same; witnesses, John Walworthe, John Kendale, John Percyvale, Philip Glouer, John Doggeson; same seal on a tongue of the parchment. (*Ibid.*, No. 22).
Also, June 1, bond by Richard Tone of Rypon and William Tone of Thorpe to the same in 20*h.* payable at the following feast of St. Lawrence if they brought any plea against him in respect of the messuage, two cottages, other lands or rent of 4*d.* (*Ibid.*, No. 23).

the vicars of the collegiate church of Rypon on the south in the street (*vico*) called Staynbriggate in the vill of Rypon and the tenement lately belonging to Robert Morpathe deceased, chaplain of the chantry in the chapel of the B.M. within the said church, on the west in the street called Alhaloughgate in the said vill; also a yearly rent of 4*d*. from a tenement lately belonging to the said Robert in the said street of Alhaloughgate. Witnesses, John Walworthe, William Frankys, John Percyvale, Thomas Hert, Philip Glouer, John Doggeson, Richard Wyrell. Rypon.[1] (*Ibid.*, No. 21).

295. Copy of Court roll. Military court held at Ripon, Monday after the Deposition of St. Wilfrid, 6 Edward IV [Oct. 13, 1466]. Dame Elizabeth Arthyngton in her widowhood came and surrendered to the lord two waste cottages and a barn (*orium*) built with garden adjacent, lying in Blossomgatehende and three acres of land lying on *le Benehill* with appurtenances in Ripon to the use of Thomas Glasyn, his heirs and assigns; fine for entry, 5*s*. (*Ibid.*, No. 24).

296. Copy of Court roll. Military court held at Ripon, Monday the morrow of the first Sunday after Easter (*in crastino dominice in Albis*), 9 Henry VII [April 7, 1494]. Miles Doo, son and heir of Ralph Doo lately deceased, came and surrendered to Roger Milnes and Joan his wife and Roger's heirs all his right in two waste cottages, a barn built with garden adjacent in Ploxomgate and three acres of land in Benehill with appurtenances in Ripon, lately belonging to the said Ralph. Roger and Joan gave 12*d*. as a fine for the release and having it enrolled. (*Ibid.*, No. 25).

297. Jan. 20, 16 Henry VII [1500-1]. Release by John Rande of Kyngeston on Hull, *marchaunt*, to Robert Kettilwell of Ripon, *barker*, and John Kettilwell, his son and heir apparent, of all right in a burgage with appurtenances in Ripon, in the tenure of Robert Taillour, which they lately had of the feoffment of the said John Rande and of which they were lawfully seised. (*Ibid.*, No. 26).

298. Nov. 4, 18 Henry VII [1502]. Bond by John Rande of Kyngiston on Hulle, *merchant* in co. York *yoman*, to Robert Ketylwell of Ripon, *tanner* in co. York *yoman*, in 40*li*. to be paid at the following Martinmas, if he should bring any claim against Ketylwell in a court of law concerning lands and tenements lying together in Ripon in Stanbriggate and Alhalowgate, which Rande had of the feoffment of William Neleson, merchant of York.[2] (*Ibid.*, No. 27).

---

[1] Seal: red wax, round, ½ in.; letter W.
[2] Fragment of seal on a tongue of the parchment.

299. Copy of Court roll. Military court held at Ripon, April 19, 22 Henry VII [1507]. Whereas at the military court held at Ripon, July 11, 6 Henry VII [1491] John Hardcastell of Patheley brigg and Margaret his wife came and surrendered into the hand of the lord two waste cottages, a barn built with garden adjacent in Ploxomgate and three acres of land in Benehill with appurtenances in Ripon, lately belonging to Ralph Doo, to the use of Roger Milnes and Joan his wife and Roger's heirs, now Roger was dead; and Thomas Milnes, chaplain, came to the court and sought to be admitted to the reversion of the said premises (the cottages no longer waste but built) after the death of Joan; the reversion was granted to him; fine [blank]; admittance and fealty. (Ibid., No. 28).

300. Nov. 16, 5 Henry VIII [1513]. Release by John Brone of Rypon, son of John Brone of Nortstanley, yeoman, to Miles Staueley of Ripon parke, gent., of all actions both real and personal.[1] (Ibid., No. 29).

301. Dec. 7, 1516, 3rd year of his translation. Grant[2] by Thomas [Wolsey], cardinal priest of the title of St. Cecilia, archbishop of York, primate of England, legate of the apostolic see, and chancellor of England to Miles Staveley and John Staveley his son, his household servants, of the office of parker of his park of Rypon and the custody thereof, appointing them wardens thereof, for their lives and that of the survivor, to serve the office personally or by deputy, taking yearly the accustomed wages (vadia) and fees from the issues of his manor or lordship of Rypon by the hands of the receiver, farmer, bailiff or reeve at Easter and Michaelmas in equal portions. In his hospice near Westminster.[3] (Ibid., No. 30).

302. Oct. 19, 1525. Letters patent of Thomas [Wolsey], cardinal priest of the title of St. Cecilia, archbishop of York, legate de latere, primate and chancellor of England, bishop of Durham, and perpetual commendatory of the exempt monastery of St. Alban's, granting to Thomas Staveley the office of the custody of his warren and woods of Walkershawe, Aldewike and Dipegill near his vill of Ripon, and appointing the said Thomas warden thereof for life, to serve the office personally or by deputy, having the wages (vadia), fees, payments (regarda), commodities

---

[1] Seal on a tongue of the parchment: red wax, broken; a bird.

[2] This grant was copied into a notification issued by Brian, the dean, and the chapter of York, inspecting and ratifying and confirming its terms so far as it affected them, on March 26, 1517; in the chapter-house; fragment of seal remains; same enrolments. (Ibid., No. 31)

[3] At the foot: irrotulatur per me Ricardum Ayscoughe audit[orem]. And also: irrotulatur coram Thoma Burgoyn' audit[ore].

and profits belonging thereto, together with his livery of the suit of his yeomen.[1] In his house near Westminster.[2] (*Ibid.*, No. 32).

303. April 24, 14 Henry VIII [1522]. Indenture[3] witnessing that whereas William Norwod and Isabel his wife were seised in demesne as of fee of a burgage in Ripon lying in the horsefair and of a tenement and two oxgangs of land with appurtenances in Copydhewyk, and died seised thereof, and the premises descended to Agnes Ouerend and Margaret Coundall as their daughters and heirs, and after their death as to one moiety to William Ouerend as son and heir of Agnes, and after his death to Thomas Ouerend as his brother and heir, and as to the other moiety to Thomas Coundall as son and heir of Margaret, and whereas Thomas Ouerend enfeoffed Roland Wylson and his heirs of one moiety of the burgage and surrendered a moiety of the premises in Copydhewyk to the use of the said Roland and his heirs, it was agreed that partition of the premises between the said Roland and Thomas Coundall should be made as follows : Roland to have the whole of the burgage and Thomas to have the premises in Copydhewyk; and as the burgage was greater in value by 6s. 8d. yearly Roland had paid 4li. 6s. 8d. to Thomas. Mutual seals.

Dorso : witnesses to sealing, John Staueley, gent., Richard Batty, bailiff, Roger Glew, William Robson, Robert Staueley, William Lane, Nicholas Yakson, Christopher Clytherome. (*Ibid.*, No. 33).

304. Feb. 9, 22 Henry VIII [1530-1]. Grant[4] by Robert Kettilwell the elder of Ripon, *tanner*, to William Kettilwell his son, his heirs and assigns, of a burgage with appurtenances lying in Ripon in a street (*vico*) called Alhalogate between the tenement of Ranulf Pigote, knt., on the east and that of William Brigham on the west, in the tenure of Miles Baynbrige. Also appointment of Richard Gowithwate and Thomas Hude as joint attorneys to enter and deliver seisin. Witnesses, Sir John Halle, John Rawe, William Askewith, John Burnet.

Dorso : seisin delivered by Richard Gowithwate and Thomas Hude, Feb. 12, in the presence of William Kay, sub-bailiff, Christopher Strikland, Roger Gillowe, John Jacson. (*Ibid.*, No. 34).

305. March 28, 22 Henry VIII [1530-1]. Grant[5] by William

---

[1] una cum liberata nostra de secta valectorum nostrorum.

[2] At the foot: irrotulatur per me Ricardum Ayscoughe audit[orem].

[3] In English.

[4] Also, same day, release by the same to the same of all right therein; same witnesses, seal on a tongue of the parchment, red wax, letters RK. (*Ibid*, No. 35).

[5] Also, same day, release by the same to the same of all right therein; same witnesses, Mylnes and Askwyth so spelt. (*Ibid.*, No. 37).

Kettilwell of Ripon, *tanner*,[1] for a sum of money paid beforehand, to John Staueley of Ripon parke, gent., his heirs and assigns, of a burgage with appurtenances lying in Ripon in a street (*vico*) called Alhalowgate between the tenement of Ranulf Pigote, knt., on the east and that of William Brigham on the west, in the tenure of Miles Baynbrige. Also appointment of Antony Uckerbe and Christopher Derenbruke as joint attorneys to take and deliver seisin. Witnesses,[2] Sir Thomas Milnes, Reginald (*Ranuldo*) Braithwait, Robert Heryson, William Askwith.[3]

Dorso : seisin delivered by Antony Uckerby and Christopher Derenbruke, April 10, in the presence of John Seill, John Wenpeny, Richard Broune, Roger Gelow, Richard Broune, jun., Robert Gelow, Reginald Gelow, jun., Christopher Seill, jun. (*Ibid.*, No. 36).

306. Aug. 4, 31 Henry VIII [1539]. Sale by Robert Myddilton of Ripon, yeoman, to Marmaduke Middylton his son, for 20*li.*, of two barns and a close with appurtenances, lying at the exit [of] *le Horsfaer* in Ripon, in the tenure of Henry Norton, esq. and Thomas Williamson. Also appointment of Richard Burne and Thomas Barker as joint attorneys to enter, and take and deliver seisin.[4]

Dorso : seisin delivered, Aug. 7, in the presence of William Daill, William Browne, Thomas Hilton, Thomas Burton, Thomas Teppyng, William Setyll. Enrolled, Dec. 12, before John Pulleyn, one of the king's justices of the peace etc. in W.R., Yorks., and Henry Brome, clerk of the peace. Examined by them. Also signature of Thomas Hylton below Wyll. Day[?]lle (mark). (*Ibid.*, No. 38).

307. June 7, 32 Henry VIII [1540]. Grant by William Wandesford, gent., one of the sons of Thomas Wandesford, esq., late while he lived of Kirklyngton, for 38*li.* 4*s.* 2*d.* sterling paid beforehand, to John Staveley of Riponparke, gent., of two messuages or burgages with appurtenances lying in Ripon in a place commonly called *le olde merketsteyd*, of a yearly value of 26*s.* 8*d.*, in the tenure of William Robson, yeoman; to hold to the use of John and his assigns for the term of the natural life of the grantor. Also appointment of Anthony Uckerbe and Christopher Darnebrooke of Ripon, yeomen, as joint attorneys to enter and deliver seisin. (*sd.*) By me Wyllam Wandysforde.

---

[1] This is almost certainly the word, now partly obscured by a stain.
[2] Testibus videlicet sigillacione domini Thome Milnes, Ranuldo Braithwait . . . .
[3] Broken seal of red wax; probably a merchant's mark.
[4] Seal: greenish-brown wax; small; letter W.

Dorso : sealed, June 8, in the presence of Henry Cogyll of Rychemond, merchant, Roger Wylson of Gaytsforde, yeoman, Richard Atkynson, Ald' Smyth, Robert Meesse of Bondgayte by Ripon. Memorandum of livery of seisin, June 20, by the attorneys in the presence of Ninian Pulleyn, gent., John Middilton, William Dykson, Thomas Rege, Robert Lambert, Christopher Wailles, William Browne. (*Ibid.*, No. 39).

308. April 2, 5 Edward VI [1551]. Bond by Anthony Frankishe of Ripon, gent., to Simon Helmesley of Ripon, in 10 marks.

Dorso : condition[1] that if Simon, his heirs and assigns, should have and hold a messuage or burgage with appurtenances in *horsfaire* in Ripon which he had lately purchased of Anthony, and if Anthony delivered to him the charters and muniments relating thereto before the following Michaelmas, the bond should be void.[2] (*Ibid.*, No. 40).

Rise.

309. Sale and quitclaim (*vendidi, concessi et . . . . quietumclamaui*) by Robert le Vauassur of Ryse to Walter de Faukenberg'[3] of a bovate of land with appurtenances and easements in the territory of Ryse,[4] with free entries and exits, in feedings, meadows [*etc.*], which the vendor's mother had had in dower; to hold to him and his heirs or assigns of the vendor and his heirs, rendering yearly a rose at the Nativity of St. John the Baptist for all secular service. And if the vendor died before the death of his wife he willed that his heirs should make up to her her dower in respect of the said bovate from the land appropriated to them in inheritance.[5] For this sale and quitclaim Walter gave him 5 marks sterling beforehand. Warranty against all men and women. Witnesses, Sirs William the Constable, Sayer de Sutton, Henry de Faukenberg', knts., Robert de Hylton, Herbert de Sancto Quintino, John de Surdeual, Roger de Dol, William de Witheton,

[1] In English.

[2] Seal on a tongue of the parchment. red wax, small; a fleur-de-lis.

[3] Comparing this deed with No 342 below it may be assumed that he was Walter son of Sir Peter de Fauconberg. Walter's career from 1254 until his death in 1304 is given in *Complete Peerage*, new ed., v, 268. It is likely that the dates of the two deeds are nearer the middle than the end of the 13th cent. John de Surdeval, who witnessed both, occurs in 1252 (*Yorks. Fines*, 1246-72, p. 88).

[4] sicut se extendit in longitudine et latitudine ex omni parte territorii eiusdem uille.

[5] Et si contingat me ante obitum uxoris mee uiam uniuerse carnis ingredi volo et concedo quod heredes mei dicte uxori mee dotem suam de predicta bouata terre perficiant de terra hereditarie sibi appropriata.

Richard the marshal (*marscallo*).[1] (*Duke of Norfolk*, Misc., II, i, No. 11).

310. Friday after the Nativity of the B.V.M. [Sept. 11], 1366. Grant by Thomas Fauconberg, son and heir of Sir Walter de Fauconberg, deceased, formerly lord of Skelton in Clyueland, to dame Isabel de Fauconberg,[2] her heirs and assigns, of Robert son of Juliana, his villein (*natiuum*) of Hornsebek, dwelling in Skareburgh, with all his goods and chattels and sequel; also, for her life, all the estate which she had had or had in the manors of Ryse in Holdernesse, Wythornwyk and Estbrun, with appurtenances and all the advowson of the church and chantry of Ryse, and also in a third part of the manors of Skelton and Mersk in Clyueland with appurtenances, which she was holding in the name of dower by assignment made to her in the king's chancery and delivered to her by the escheator; and quitclaim to her during her life; and release of all actions against her by reason of waste or trespass in the said manors which she was holding or had had in custody by reason of the grantor's minority. Witnesses, Sirs John Bygott, William de Sancto Quintino, knts., Roger de Fulthorp, John de Malteby, William de Lackenby.[3] Skelton.[4] (*Ibid.*, II, iii, No. 11).

Long Riston.

311. Grant[5] by Peter de Routh, chaplain, to Alan Lygeard and Beatrice his wife of all the messuage and two bovates of land with all the *forland* and all his other lands and tenements with appurtenances, which he had of the grant of the said Alan in the vill and territory of Riston in[6] Holdernesse; to hold to them and the heirs of their bodies lawfully begotten, of the chief lords of the fee; with remainder in default of issue to the right heirs of Alan. Witnesses, Sir Peter de Nuttyll, knt., Robert Hildyerd,

[1] Fragment of seal of dark green wax, a floral device; S'ROBERT
. . . .
[2] Second wife of Sir Walter; dau. of Sir Roger Bigod of Settrington; dower was ordered to be assigned to her on Feb. 10, 1362-3; she lived to 1401 (*Complete Peerage*, new ed , v, pp. 274-5).
[3] Capital L written as ll.
[4] Seal : red wax, round, 15/16 in.; within a traceried border a shield of arms suspended from a tree, a lion rampant; SIGIL' THOME FACVMBERGE in black letter. The deed has an endorsement: Irr[otulatur] in dorso claus' cancellar' regis E. tercii mense Octobr' anno regni sui quadragesimo. See *Cal. Close Rolls*, 1364-68, p. 295 Isabel's dower gave rise to disputes with Thomas, her step-son; see *ibid.*, p 310, which gives a general undertaking by her made before the Chancellor on Nov 4, 1366, including the annulment of the present deed.
[5] This and the following four charters are not originals, but copies on a single piece of parchment in a fifteenth-century hand.
[6] *de*, MS.

Thomas Warde of Arnall, William Whityk, Peter Milner of Riston,
John Ulbright of[1] Gemelyng.   Riston.   (*J. M. Spencer-Stanhope,
esq.*).

312.   Monday[2] the morrow of St. John the Baptist [June 25],
1360.   Grant by Alan Lygeard, son and heir of John Lygeard of
Riston in Holdernesse, to Thomas de Wythornwyk, Richard de
Hedon, and William de Frothyngham of the same premises [*as
in the previous deed*] with rents, reversions and services and all
appurtenances which he then had in the vill and territory of Riston
in Holdernesse.   Witnesses, Robert Lorymer, John Hyldyerd,
William Whityk, John de Wathesande, Peter Mylner of Riston.
Riston in Hold[ernesse].

313.   Tuesday before St. Peter ad vincula [July 28], 1360.
Release by John Lygeard, chaplain, to the same of all right in the
same premises, which had formerly belonged to John Ligeard his
uncle.   Witnesses, John de Gouxhill, Thomas de Mapilton, John
Cance, John de Bilton, Peter Milner of Riston.   Riston in Holdernesse.

314.   Thursday after All Saints, 15 Richard II [Nov. 2,
1391].   Release by Alan Ligeard, son and heir of John Ligearde of
Riston in Holdernesse, to the same (Thomas, Richard and William)
of all right in all the lands and tenements, rents, reversions and
services with appurtenances which they had of his feoffment in
Riston in Holdernesse.   Witnesses, Ralph de Lellay, John de
Redenesse, William Constable, Richard Rolleston, William Coett,
Robert Rolleston.   Riston in Holdernesse.

315.   Monday after the Epiphany, 21 Richard II [Jan. 7,
1397-8].   Release by Beatrice widow of Alan Ligeard of Riston
in Holdernesse to Richard de Hedon and William de Frothyngham
of all right in the same lands [*etc.*] which they had of the feoffment
of Alan Lygeard her husband.   Witnesses, John Roos of Routh,
Peter de Routh of the same, John Redenesse, William Constable,
Richard de Rolleston, William Coett, Robert Rolleston.   Riston
in Holdernesse.

Sandal Magna.

316.   May 12, 3 Edward IV [1463].   Grant by George
Frankysch' of Warmefeld to Laurence Newall, late of the parish of
Halifax, his heirs and assigns, of a parcel of land with appurtenances containing in length fifty-two ells and in breadth at the
east end twenty-four ells and at the west end twenty-two ells,

---

[1] *ad de*, MS.
[2] In 1360 June 25 fell on a Thursday.

which parcel lay between the high street of the vill of Sandayll on the east and the land of the grantor on the west, and between the messuage of the grantee on the south and the croft of the grantor on the north, in the vill and territory of Sandayll; rendering yearly 12*d.* of silver at Whitsuntide and Martinmas in equal portions for all other secular services; with power to distrain in the grantee's messuage if the rent should be a month in arrear. Mutual seals to either part of the indenture.[1] Witnesses, John Shagh, Thomas Shagh, John Hobkynson. Sandayll. (*Bradford Public Libraries*, Misc. MSS.).

Seamer (Scarborough).

317. Dec. 22, 1538, 30 Henry VIII. Indenture[2] by which Henry Davell, abbot of the monastery of St. Peter and Hilda of Whitby, and the convent demised to William Lokwode, town clerk of Scarburgh, and Thomas Dale of Semer, yeoman, all their parsonage of Semer with all fruits, profits [*etc.*], with the tithe-lathe[3] and tenements and appurtenances belonging thereto; to hold from the feast of St. Mark next following for a term of forty-one years, paying yearly 30 quarters "whete able and clene dight and wyndowede" delivered in "the garnars of the seid monastery of Whitby with the measure and busshell of the seid monastery now being," and also 82 quarters "barly malte" delivered as before at two terms by even portions, namely at "Estur"[4] and the Nativity of St. John the Baptist; power to distrain if the rent should be in arrear for twenty days, and to re-enter if it should be in arrear for forty days; the lessees to pay all charges except "the kings dismes," and to repair the lathe and tenements at their own cost except great timber. Mutual seals of the convent and the lessees.[5] In the "chapitur house of Whitby."[6] (*Duke of Leeds*, Hornby Castle Muniments, Seamer, No. 1).

[1] Fragment of seal of red wax.
[2] In English.
[3] Tithe-barn.
[4] Easter.
[5] Seal : black wax, the *ad causas* seal of Whitby Abbey. Counterseal: oval, *c.* 1⅝ × 1¼ in.; standing figure of St. Hilda. These two seals are described in *The Seals of the Religious Houses of Yorkshire* (*Archæologia*, lxxviii, 33-4), where the first is illustrated. These impressions are rubbed, but their identity is clear. They were used as seal and counterseal on a lease of Jan. 10, 1538-9 (*Y.A.J.*, xvii, 43*n*); the last words of the legend of the seal are clearly AD CAS, and not MONAS.
[6] At the foot : ex[r] per Walterum Hendle; and on the fold: irro[tulatu]r per Hugon' Fuller audit[orem]; followed by a signature not deciphered. The document has an endorsement: The tythe (*sic*) of Semer personage was let for 41: years for xxx quarters of wheat and lxxxii quarters of barlie malte. Also in another hand : Dale [the name of the second lessee].

318. Jan. 5, 38 Henry VIII [1546-7]. Grant by Henry Kelke of Semar, son and heir of Thomas Kelke of the same, lately deceased, to Charles Caunntte,[1] his heirs and assigns, of all his messuage with a garden, little close, great close, and a meadow called Hudhills and Wicks adjacent between the land of the king, formerly belonging to the earl of Northumberland, towards the west and that of Alexander Stockdell towards the east, the south end abutting on the land of the king towards the south and on *lee Marre* towards the north; to hold of the grantor and his heirs from the following Lady Day for a term of ten years, rendering yearly to the king 9s. 8d. for all other services, with reversion to the grantor. Witnesses, William Benson, bailiff of Scardebroughe, William Allatson of Semer, clerk, Thomas Dale, Nicholas Trowghton. Semar.[2] (*Ibid.*, No. 2).

319. Nov. 26, 1 Edward VI [1547]. Grant[3] by the same to the same[4] of all his great close, commonly called Kelke grett closse, which he had in the vill of Semar, lying between the grantor's land towards the east and west, the south end abutting on Westflatt, and the north end on *le Marr'*; with appurtenances; to hold of the chief lords of the fee. Witnesses, William Goston, Edmund Hayton, Richard Cottham, Thomas Allatson, William Fysshe. Semar.

Dorso : seisin delivered, same day, in the presence of William Gosston, Robert Pott, Edmund Hayton, Richard Cottham, Thomas Allatson, William Fysshe, Thomas Sanderson, Thomas Hastyngs, Thomas Thompson, Christopher Baxter, William Allatson, Thomas Candler, William Monkman, Thomas Lofftus, Ralph Thompson. (*Ibid.*, No. 3).

320. Dec. 6, 2 James I [1604]. Indenture[5] between Sir John Thornburgh of Leckford, co. Southampton, knt., Edward Gate of

[1] Doubtless the Charles Cant who occurs in No. 232 above.
[2] Seal : red wax, small; letter I.
[3] Also, Nov. 23 same year, indenture of sale in English; Cauntte described as of Semer, yeoman; for the reversion of the same close which Cauntte had in mortgage with all other lands and tenements of Kelke in Semer for ten years; consideration, 6*li.* 13s. 4d; witnesses, Christopher Midleton, clerk and vicar of Ryghton, John Marshall of Hirton, George Smyth, Thomas Dale, William Goston, Robert Pott, Edmund Hayton, Richard Cottham. (*Ibid.*, No. 4).
Also, March 20, 4 Edward VI [1549-50], grant in fee simple by the same to the same (Cante) of the premises comprised in this and the preceding deed; Stokdale so spelt; witnesses, Walter Cawod of Depedale, gent., William Benson of Scardburgh, burgess, William Lokwod of the same, John Hawkyngs, Robert Russell, Nicholas Troughton of Semer; seisin in presence of the same with the addition of [?] Sir William Alottson, James [?] Wales, William Bridkirke, Henry [?] Stowbel, John Bovell, William Alotson, Vincent Allotson, Ralph Thomson. (*Ibid* , No 5)
[4] The grantee is spelt Cauntte.
[5] Parts of this document are in a mouldy condition.

Seamer, esq., and Margaret Thornburgh, daughter and heir of Sir John, of the one part, and Thomas Mompesson of Corton, Wilts., esq., of the other. Whereas Queen Elizabeth on 17 Dec., 3 Elizabeth [1560] by letters patent granted to Sir Henry Gate,[1] knt., deceased, father of Edward Gate, her rectory and parish church of Seamer *alias* Semer and her chapels of Cayton and Ayton,[2] formerly belonging to the monastery of Whittby, with the messuages, houses, buildings, tithe-barns, stables, dovehouses, orchards, gardens, glebelands [*etc.*], tenths and tithes of "garbesheafe," hay, wool and lamb, and all other tithes great and small, situate in Seamer, Pickeringlith, Cayton and Ayton, belonging to the said rectory and chapels, to hold of her manor of East Greenwich, co. Kent, by fealty only in free socage, at a total rent of 34*li*. 9*s*.; and whereas the rectory and chapels descended to Edward Gate as son and heir of Sir Henry, who on 5 April, 35 Elizabeth [1593] demised to Anthony Bennett of East Greenwich the same premises for 1000 years, who on 6 April, same year, demised the same to Edward Gate for 999 years, paying to him (Bennett) 200 marks yearly by quarterly payments in the Chapel of "the Rowles" in Chancery Lane; and whereas on 10 June, 44 Elizabeth [1602], by indenture between Edward Gate of the one part, Sir John Thornburgh, knt., of the second part, and Henry Gate, gent., son and heir apparent of Edward, and Margaret Thornburgh, daughter and heir apparent of Sir John, of the third part, the same premises together with the advowson of the vicarage of Seamer were assigned to Sir John Thornburgh for 99 years. Now, for the sum of 200*li*., Sir John and Edward Gate conveyed the premises to Thomas Mompesson. (*sd*.) Thomas Mompesson.[3]

Dorso : sealed in the presence of Henry Mompesson, Charles Cooke, Thomas . . . . , John Stansall. (*Ibid*., No. 6).

Shelley.

321. July 31, 3 Henry VIII [1511]. Release by John Storr of Walton the elder, kinsman and heir of Joan formerly wife of Robert Storr, deceased, to Robert Storr his son, and the heirs of his body, of all right in the half-manor (*dimedium manerium*) of Shelley, with all lands, tenements, rents and services, meadows, feedings, woods and pastures, with other appurtenances belonging thereto, and also a yearly rent of 7 marks from William Dodworthe, kinsman and heir of Thomas Dodworthe, which rent Thomas Dodworthe and Elizabeth his wife had granted from the manor

[1] A member of the Council in the North, and died in 1589 (*V.C.H., North Riding*, ii, 485).
[2] For this last chapel see above under East Ayton.
[3] Seal : red wax; signet, a bull's head erased.

of Shelley to the said Joan;[1] with remainder to the right heirs of the grantor. Power to distrain in the said manor, if the rent should be in arrear. Witnesses, Edward Ston' of Newbyggyng, John Cheld of Wodthorpe, Roger Lyle of Walton. Walton.[2] (*Lord Allendale, Shelley, No. 1*).

Shepley.

322.   May 25, 36 Henry VIII [1544].   Grant and feoffment by John Jhesope of Shepeley, yeoman, to Joan Jhesope, one of the daughters of Edward Jhesoppe of Cumberworth, of a fourth part of his messuage called Leikhaull[3] and of all his lands and tenements, meadows, woods and pastures, with appurtenances in Shepelay, then in the tenure of the said Edward Jhesope; to hold to her and the heirs lawfully begotten by her and Henry Jhesope his son and heir apparent. Witnesses, John Berdseill of Cumberworth, John Elles of the same, Randill Boterworth of the same, John Bylcliffe. Cumberworth.[4]

Dorso : seisin delivered, same day, in the presence of John Armytteg, Edward Jhesope, Adam Jhesope, and the witnesses to the grant. (*Lord Allendale*, Shepley, No. 4).

323.   Nov. 28, 4 Edward VI [1550].   "A bounder' of all the londes and medowe" of Mr. Thomas Wenteworth of Westbretton, esq., in the tenure of John Jhesup and Henry Jhesup his son and heir apparent, lying within the township of Shepelay and Cumberworthalf, made by them in the presence of Thomas West, gent., Richard Wentworth, gent., Edmund Oxle of Clayton, yeoman, Thomas Firthe, clothier, Edward Firth and John Armyttage.

"In primis oone parcell of medowe lying in a medow of the seid John Jhesupe and Henrye Jhesupe on the sowth parte of their capitall mesuage called Leykehall in the townschipe of Shepelay conteynynge by estymacon two acres abuttyng on a close of the seid Mr. Wentworth called Boswallclyf on the sowth parte and on certeyn meere stones of the east north and west parte. Item oone close called Boswellclif conteynyng by estymacon fyve acres and a half abuttyng of the Byrke royd of the west parte and on the Smythe roid of the east parte and of Nabbe acre on the north parte and of a close of Thomas Burdett and the commen of the sowthe parte." (*Ibid.*, No. 1).

---

[1] This appears to be the meaning; but the document was drawn up with considerable disregard of grammar.   For the grant of the yearly rent of 7 marks in 1449 see vol. iii, No. 340; and for the interest of the Dodworth family in the manor see Morehouse, *Kirkburton*, p. 86

[2] Fragment of seal of red wax.

[3] Leake Hall in Cumberworth Half, Shepley township, Kirkburton parish.

[4] Seal. red wax, small; letters I A.

324. Feb. 12, 6 Edward VI [1551-2]. Grant and feoffment by John Jhesup of Leykehall, co. York, yeoman, and Henry Jhesup his son and heir, in fulfilment of indentures made between them and Charles Turton of Ouerdembye, dated Feb. 8 same year, to Henry Burdett of Dembye, gent., William Turton, William Wodcocke and Thomas Horne, of the messuage and all other lands and tenements, meadows, feedings, woods, underwoods and pastures with appurtenances, lying in the township of Sheplay and Cumberworthalf, then or late in the tenure of Thomas Firth;[1] to the use of the said Henry Jhesup and Alice Turton his future wife, for the term of their life and that of the survivor, and the heirs of their bodies; with remainder to the use of the said Charles Turton, his heirs and assigns.[2]

Dorso : seisin delivered, 15 May same year, in the presence of Thomas Robuck, John Bylclif, John Berdsell. (*Ibid.*, No. 2).

325. Dec. 6, 6 Edward VI [1552]. Award[3] by Godfrey Bossevile of Gonnildthwayth, esq., Ralph Jenkynson of Ouer Denby, yeoman, John Myckelthwayth of Yngburcheworth, yeoman, and Edmund Battley of Huttersfelde, husbandman, in disputes between Charles Turton of Ouer Denby and Henry Jesope, son and heir of John Jesope of Leekhall in Cumberworth, yeoman, with regard to the title of two leases, one made by John and Henry Jesope to Turton, dated Feb. 8, 6 Edward VI [1551-2], in consideration of 20*li*. 3*s*. 4*d*. paid by Turton to Thomas Wentworth, esq., for redeeming all the lands, messuages [*etc.*] then or lately in the tenure of Thomas Fyrthe, as by a deed of sale to Wentworth by Henry Jesope, and the other made by John Jesope to Turton, dated April 15, same year, and also concerning all sums of money promised and given in marriage with Alice daughter of Turton, to Henry Jesope, and also for not well ordering "and dandellyng of the said Alis" by the said Henry, and all other quarrels [*etc.*] between the said parties. The said Ralph, John, and Edmund had been appointed arbitrators "with the umpage" of the said Godfrey. They awarded, first, Turton to enjoy both the said leases and deliver to Henry Jesope "one cowe at noyte"[4] such as should be thought good and [?] "properisfectable" by the arbitrators, in satisfaction of 6*li*. 30*s*. 4*d*. of his wife's portion which Turton and Christopher Barnaby ought to have paid; also if further dissensions arose between Henry and Alice which could not be

[1] On Feb. 5, 5 Edward VI [1550-1] Thomas Wentworth of Westbretton, esq., had appointed John Armyttage and Robert Gledill as joint attorneys to receive from John Jhesupe of Leykehall, yeoman, and Henry Jhesupe his son and heir apparent, seisin of the same premises; Westbretton; seal on a tongue, red wax, small, letters TW. (*Ibid.*, No. 3).
[2] Tags for two seals; only one fragment remains.
[3] Indenture, in English.
[4] A cow in condition of giving milk after calving (*O.E.D.*, s.v. Note).

settled quietly or by the good counsel of Turton, they to keep the arbitrators' award; all debts and quarrels arising before the date of the award to be forgiven; Turton to pay within a year to Henry's creditors the sum of 10*li*. 13s. 4d., on the receipt of which Henry should make a lease for thirteen years to Turton, to begin at the termination of the lease before-mentioned, dated Feb. 8, 6 Edward VI, at a yearly rent of 4d.; also a deed of feoffment made by John Jesope and Henry to Henry Burdett and others, dated Feb. 12, same year, to stand good. (*Ibid.*, No. 6).

326.   June 13, 6 Elizabeth, 1564.   Grant by Henry Jesoppe of Leake Hall in the parish of Burton, yeoman, in consideration of 20*li*. paid by Charles Turton of Belton in the isle of Axholme, co. Lincoln, yeoman, to the latter, his heirs and assigns, of all his messuages or tenements built on, lying in the parish of Burton, called Leake Hall and all other arable lands, meadows, feedings, pastures, woods, underwoods, rents, reversions and services, with appurtenances belonging thereto, then or late in the tenure of John Firthe, Thomas Bilclyffe and the grantor.[1]

Dorso:[2] seisin given, June 20, in the presence of Thomas Bylclyfe, John Fyrthe, Thomas Blakeburne, Thomas Mo[?]rhous, William Turton. (*Ibid.*, No. 5).

Retber Sbitlington.

327.   . . . . . .[3] 14 Edward II [1320-21].   Release by Alice daughter of . . . . son [or daughter] of Sir John de Horbiry[4] to John de Amyas of Thornhill and Peter Hunkell of Thornhill, of all right in all the lands and tenements which had belonged to the said Sir John, her grandfather, in Nether Shitlington and Holynhirst.   Warranty to John and Peter, and the heirs and assigns of John.   Witnesses, John de Denom, William de Bingham, Robert Russell, John Ithon, ... Woderoue, Hugh de Aberford.   Westminster. (*Lord Allendale*, Shitlington, No. 26).[5]

328.   Nov. 4, 4 Henry V [1416].   Demise by John Amyas, esq., to John de Gayrgraue of his manors of Shitlyngton and Holynherste, with all lands, meadows and pastures belonging thereto, which were then in the grantor's own cultivation (*manura et propria cultura*); to hold from the following Martinmas for

---

[1] Seal : red wax, round, ⅝ in.; initials IB.
[2] In English.
[3] Much torn.
[4] He was probably the Sir John brother of Sir Ralph de Horbury, and father of a son named Robert who had an interest in Shitlington (*Y.A.J.*, xxvi, 343).   For a quitclaim by Denise daughter of Sir John de Horbury of her right in apparently the same property see vol. vi, No. 432.
[5] Nos. 1-25 of this series were printed in vol. vi.

the grantor's life, rendering yearly 8*li.* at Whitsuntide and Martinmas in equal portions, beginning at the following Whitsuntide; power to distrain if the rent should be forty days in arrear, and to re-enter if it should be three months in arrear. The demisee to maintain the manors with straw and . . . . . .[1] and other roofing. Mutual seals to either part of the indenture. Witnesses, Thomas Sayuill, Thomas Methelay, Richard Thornhill. Shitlyngton. And if the demisor should take into his hand the wood or any parcel of meadow the demisee should be allotted a corresponding amount in his farm. (*Ibid.*, No. 27).

329. Jan. 24, 9 Henry VII [1493-4]. Grant by Percival Amyas, esq., to William Mirfeld, Thomas Wentworth, Gerard Lacy, Ralph Normavile, Ralph Reresby, Henry Eueryngham, Alexander Drax, and Roger Wombewell the younger, esqs., of all his manors, messuages, lands, tenements, meadows, woods, pastures, reversions, rents and services, with appurtenances in Nethir Shittlyngton, Ossett, Wakefeld, Pontfrett, Marre, Barne-thorpe, Cadeby, Billyngley,[2] Barneburgh, and Stodfold, co. York, and also a yearly rent of 6*s.* and half a pound of pepper of service rent from certain lands and tenements of William Byngley in Nethir Shittlyngton and the service of the said William, his heirs and assigns, for the same,[3] 10*s.* 3*d.* from John Helwys, 20*d.* from William Jacson, 2*s.* from (lately) William Bedford and Ralph Kirkeby, 8*d.* from John Shepard, 10*d.* from John Kyng, all in Nethir Shittlyngton, 3*s.* 1*d.* from John Paslewe, 22*d.* from William Burton, 13½*d.* from Thomas Cokson, 12*d.* from John Audesley, 6*d.* from John Richardson, 6½*d.* from John Grene, 3½*d.* from (lately) Walter Haukesworth, all in Ossett, 6*s.* 8*d.* from William Sproxton in Wakefeld, and 2*s.* from John Barneby in Marre. Appointment of John Amyas son of Roger Amyas and William Morewodde as joint attorneys to enter and deliver seisin. Seal to this tripartite indenture.[4] (*Ibid.*, No. 28).

Skellow.

330. June 6, 13 Edward IV [1473]. Grant by John Bolle of Carcroft to John FitzWilliam of Atewik, esq., Edward Passelwe of Barneby on Don, Robert Haytefeld and Robert Steell of Owston, gents., of a cottage with garden adjacent in Skelhall, another garden in Carcroft, six acres of arable land in the fields of Skelhall, Carcroft and Owston, and three roods of meadow lying in the meadow of Skelhall, with appurtenances. Witnesses, William

[1] Torn.
[2] These two places are inserted above the line.
[3] These phrases are repeated in all the subsequent cases, here abbreviated.
[4] Seal . red wax, small signet; a rose-shaped device.

Gyllyott, chaplain, John Wylson of Athewike, Peter Moyne of the same, Robert Hawmond of Carcroft, Ellis Hussecroft of Skelhall. Carcroft.[1] (*Duke of Leeds*, Hornby Castle Muniments, Skellow, No. 1).

Skelton (Cleveland).

331. Restoration (*reddidisse et quietum clamasse*) by Alice daughter of William Mareschal to her lord P[eter] de Brus[2] and his heirs of any hereditary right in the toft and croft of her father in Scelton, namely 1⅛ acres lying next the toft of the wife of Richard le Wayte towards the north. She had sworn on the gospels in the presence of the parishioners of the church of Scelton never to claim any right therein.[3] Witnesses, Simon de Brus, John de Thocotes, Robert Buscel, William Pick[ewas]tel,[4] Hugh Haubeg', Goce Costard, Adam Scotus, Reginald de Burgate, Ralph le Brazur, Robert de Uplium. (*Duke of Norfolk*, Misc. II, i, No. 9).

332. Grant by Richard Bretun of Scelton to Guy de Roucestria, for his homage and service, of three and a half acres of land in the field of Scelton in Karlecroft, all the land which he had had at Buttes extending on Brakinhoued, three acres of land at Buttes of Salemancros next the half acre of land which William de Witeby had held of the grantor, one acre in Lag . . . es,[5] half an acre in Wanlaus, a rood in Vuerholm, and all the liberty which he had had in the mills of his lord Peter de Brus, namely to grind his corn growing on his own land to the sixteenth measure, and corn, which he purchased, to the twentieth, and immediately after the corn in the granary (*quod est in tramallo*) when his own corn came to the mill; to hold to him and his heirs and assigns of the grantor and his heirs, with all easements within the vill and without; rendering yearly 1*d.* at Christmas for all things. Witnesses, Alan the clerk, John de Thocotes, William de Layrton, William Pickewastel, Alexander Costard, William de Wyteby, Goce Costard, Robert de Wplium, Clement de Beuerlaco, Richard Cornard. (*Ibid.*, II, i, No. 17).

[1] Seal : red wax; broken and blurred.
[2] This document and the next belong to the period earlier than 1272, when by the death of Peter de Brus III, Skelton and Marske in Cleveland fell to the share of his sister and coheir Agnes, wife of Sir Walter de Fauconberge of Rise (*Complete Peerage*, new ed , v, 268) Cf a Skelton deed pd. in *Y.A.J.*, xiii, 52.
[3] Et insuper tactis sacrosanctis ewangeliis iuraui coram parochianis ecclesie de Scelton' quod numquam aliquod ius uel clamium in predicta terra uendicabo.
[4] A small tear in the parchment. See the next deed.
[5] Torn.

333. Grant by Godfrey . . .[1] of Skelton in Clyueland to Richard son of William de Foxholes . . .,[2] his heirs or assigns, of a bovate of land with meadow adjacent and all appurtenances in the vill, field and territory of Skelton in Clyueland; which bovate with the meadow contained fifteen acres of land, of which one and a half acres lay on *le Clyf* between the land of Odenellus de Manfeld on the east and that of Peter son of Ellis on the west, one rood at Stachou, half an acre at Berchillyth, one acre at Westgrenwal, one acre at Estgrenwal, one rood at Biglandes, half a rood at Grenwalendes, one rood at Claphouholm, three roods at Foghou, one and a half acres at Langelandes in two places, one rood at Thorpdale, half an acre at Halholm, one and a half roods at Ouerholm, half an acre at Laulandes, half an acre at Spedmanwra, half a rood at Wandaltes, one acre at Langacres, one and a half roods at Fulfen, one rood at Littellayrlandes, one rood at the end of the vill on the east of the house of Hugh Pickewastel, one rood on the north below the croft of William de Kendal, one and a half roods at Bymanroshathe, half an acre at Thyrnoue below the meadow of the said vill on the north, one rood at Wanlaus, half an acre at *le Brotis*, half an acre at Graueeng on the east, half an acre of meadow between the meadow of the said Odenellus on the east and that of the said Peter on the west, one rood of meadow in the same meadow between the meadow of the said Odenellus and Peter;[3] to hold of the grantor and his heirs, with all appurtenances and common easements, in moors, meadows, feedings and pastures, belonging to the said bovate with meadow adjacent, far and near; rendering yearly to the grantor and his heirs a pair of gloves at Christmas for all secular services. Witnesses, Sir Laurence, parish chaplain of Skelton, Matthew de Glaphou, R[?alph] del Auneye, Michael de Tokotes, Nicholas le hauberger, Hugh Pickewastel, John the smith, William the baker, William Tr . . r, John Play.[4] (*Ibid.*, II, i, No. 21).

334. Thursday, the eve of St. James the Apostle [July 24], 1337. Demise by Sir John de Faucomberg, lord of Skelton, knt., to William son of Thomas de Restona for life of a toft built on with appurtenances in the vill of Skelton, lying between the toft of Sir John on one side and *le Westbek* on the other; to hold of Sir John and his heirs,[5] with all easements within the vill of Skelton and without, far and near; rendering yearly 2s. sterling in equal portions at Martinmas and Whitsuntide, and doing suit of court at Skelton

---

[1] The document is stained in places. Combined with the evidence of the seal the name is probably Piper.

[2] Possibly *clerico* or *clerici*.

[3] The details seem to be 2½ roods short of the 15 acres.

[4] Seal: red wax, pointed oval; broken; the legend . . . [GO]DFRIDI PI . ER shows that it was the grantor's seal.

[5] 'de predicto domino Johanne et heredibus suis' written above the line.

twice yearly, namely, at the next courts after Michaelmas and
Easter. Mutual seals to either part of the indenture.[1] Witnesses,
Richard de Wyresdale, John de Biltona, William del Hay, Peter
Gaunt, Cuthbert Stot. Skelton. (*Ibid.*, II, ii, No. 24).

335.   Eve of Whitsunday [May 15], 1350.   Indenture by
which Walter de Fauconberge, lord of Skelton, demised to Peter
the weaver of Skelton all the close with buildings thereon in
Skelton called Cadicroft, with appurtenances; to hold for life of
the grantor and his heirs, rendering yearly 3s. of silver at Whitsuntide and Martinmas in equal portions, doing two suits of court
yearly at his courts of Skelton after Michaelmas and Easter,
grinding his corn at the grantor's mill, and maintaining all the
houses at his own cost, the grantor finding timber.   Skelton.[2]
(*Ibid.*, II, iii, No. 4).

336.   Wednesday, St. Andrew the Apostle, 30 Edward III
[Nov. 30, 1356].   Indenture witnessing that whereas Sir Walter
son of John de Faucomberge, knt., lord of Skelton in Clyueland,
by his charter[3] had granted to Henry le Goldbetere and Alice his
wife for their lives a messuage and three acres of meadow with
appurtenances in the vill and territory of Skelton, and common of
pasture for twelve cows with their young (*sequela*) three years old,
and forty sheep or ewes, in all the lands and tenements of Sir
Walter in the said vill, common of pasture for four oxen or cows
in his park called Westpark, common of pasture for a mare with
her young three years old in his park called Maugrepark and in a
place called *la Haye*, common of turbary in all his moors and
marshes in Skelton, digging and [?] carrying (*sutandi*) every year
twelve cartloads of turves, and also *housbote* and *haybote* in his
woods in the vill of Skelton, namely by cutting every year twelve
cartloads of wood, and also a yearly rent of a quarter of salt to be
taken yearly at Michaelmas from his manor of Skelton, and licence
to cut and carry forty bundles of heath in all his moors in the said
vill, and a yearly rent of two cartloads of straw to be taken yearly
at Michaelmas from his manor of Skelton, and licence to grind their
corn at all his mills within his lordship of Skelton at the thirtieth
vessel after the first corn found in the granary (*tramall'*) of the
mills, and carriage at his cost for all the said turves, wood, hay,
salt and straw as far as the messuage which they were holding of
him for life in the vill of Skelton; and although Sir Walter had
lately granted to them for their lives a yearly rent of 20*li*. from
his manors in Mersk in Clyueland and Wyththornewyk in Holdernesse in equal portions at Easter and Michaelmas; now Henry and

---

[1] Seal to this part: red wax, hexagonal; a star.
[2] Seal: brown wax, round, ¾ in.; a hawk preying over a nest; legend, a
motto, not deciphered; the last word may be DICAMVS.
[3] per cartam suam cirographatam.

Alice granted that if they held and enjoyed the messuage, three acres [etc.] as aforesaid, and a rent of 10li., the payment of the remaining 10li. mentioned in Sir Walter's charter should cease; and Sir Walter granted that if they did not hold and enjoy the same the payment of the 10li. should hold good. Mutual seals. Skelton.[1] (Ibid., II, iii, No. 8).

337.   May 16, 36 Edward III [1362]. Quitclaim by Walter son and heir of Sir John de Faucombergh of Skelton in Cliuel[and] to John de Whetteley of Thorneton in Crauen, the elder, dwelling in Skelton, his heirs and assigns, of all right in a yearly rent of 15s. 4d. in the vill of Skelton in Clyueland, which Beatrice de Laysingby, sister and heir of John brother and heir of Adam de Skelton, had released in her widowhood to the said Sir John de Faucombergh, his heirs and assigns; and which William de Kyllom, chaplain, had for life of the grant of Adam de Skelton and of the said John his brother. Witnesses, Sirs John de Derlyngton, prior of Giseburn, Thomas son of Sir Marmaduke de Thweng, James de Thoucotes, Thomas son of Sir Walter de Faucombergh of Bylton, Walter de Meryngton of Skelton. Skelton.[2] (Ibid., II, iii, No. 10).

338.   June 20, 1396. Grant by Robert de Grenekeld to John Faucomeberge, his heirs and assigns, of a burgage with croft near Poterowe and four acres of land on les Wandelles in the vill and territory of Skelton, lying on the north of the lands of Adam Milner in the same place, in exchange for a tenement with croft in Estgate formerly belonging to Cuthbert de Langwath. Witnesses, Robert de Neuland, chaplain, Richard de Merske, chaplain, Adam Milnere, Hugh Walker, John de Thorpe.[3] (Ibid., II, iii, No. 17).

339.   Jan. 30, 25 Henry VI [1446-7]. Quitclaim by Katherine widow of Robert Playce to Sir William Neuyll, lord de Faucomberge,[4] of all right in a messuage with appurtenances and four bovates of land with appurtenances in Skelton which had belonged to the said Robert Playce, by reason of any dower falling to her or by any other right.[5] (Ibid., II, iv, No. 8).

340.   April 12, 35 Henry VI [1457]. Grant by Christopher Conyers of Hornby, esq., and John Pygott of Ripon to William Nevyll, lord Fawkonberge, his heirs and assigns, of all their lands

---

[1] Two seals, red wax: (1) round, ⅞ in.; within a geometrical border a shield of arms, a chevron charged with several objects, possibly bezants; legend blurred; (2) round, ⅞ in.; blurred.
[2] Seal: red wax; same as to No. 243 above.
[3] Seal: red wax, round; rubbed, no clear impression.
[4] He had acquired Skelton before 28 April 1422 by marriage with Joan dau. and heir of Sir Thomas Fauconberge (Complete Peerage, new ed., v, 281).
[5] Seal: red wax, small; broken.

and tenements with appurtenances in Skelton in Clevelande which had formerly belonged to John Pygott, father of the said John. Warranty by John and his heirs. Witnesses, Laurence Berwyk, James Towcotes, esqs., Robert Wilkynson, Robert del Hill.[1] (*Ibid.*, II, iv, No. 10).

341. Aug. 20, 12 Edward IV [1472]. Receipt by John Berwyk, esq., from James Strangways, knt., for 10*li.* sterling in addition to 30*li.* already paid, in part payment of 50*li.* due at Martinmas last past for the farm of the castle, manor and lordship of Skelton and all the lands and tenements, rents and services lately belonging to Joan his wife by hereditary right or otherwise, and demised by him to James for the life of the said Joan during his own lifetime.[2] (*Ibid.*, II, iv, No. 11).

1Rortb Skirlaugb.

342. Grant[3] and quitclaim by Robert Bealsieu to Walter de Faucumberge, formerly son of Sir Peter de Faucumberge, his heirs or assigns, of all his land in Norhscyrelaye which he had formerly held of Walter in fee, namely, a croft of five selions lying between the croft of Peter le Huuer on one side and that of Robert styled brother of the lay-brother[4] on the other; and eight selions outside the close lying between the land of Robert styled brother of the lay-brother and the close which Augustin formerly held of Philip de Scyrelaye, extending in length with the length of the said croft from the common road of Scyrelaye as far as the watercourse of Rutona; to hold as his fee with all appurtenances within the vill and without of the grantor and his heirs. Witnesses, Sir Simon de Wytike, Sir Anselm de Harphaym, kts., John de Surdvale, Walter de Appeltona, Roger de Dole, Matthew de Rutona, Robert styled brother of the lay-brother of Scyrelaye, Nicholas Sicling of the same.[5] (*Duke of Norfolk*, Misc., II, i, No. 8).

343. Tuesday after St. Augustine [June 1], 1283. Grant by Robert le Frerbroyer of Northskirlaw and Margaret his wife to Walter son of Sir Walter de Fauconberge, his heirs or assigns, of 2*s.* rent in Northskirlaw, for which Alice daughter of Nicholas Sicling and Maud and Agnes her sisters were bound to them for a toft and croft which they (Alice and the others) were holding of them in Northskirlaw, lying between the toft of Roger the miller on the north and *le Uttegangland* on the south; and all their right

---

[1] Two seals of red wax: signets, (1) a helmet; (2) a bird.
[2] Seal on a tongue of the parchment: red wax; fragments; broken.
[3] For the date see No. 309 above; and the last witness suggests that the date is earlier than No. 343.
[4] Roberti dicti fratris conuersi; 'fratre conuersi' in the witness clause.
[5] Endorsed in a medieval hand: Holdernesse. Northskirlowe.

in the said toft and croft; to hold of the grantors, their heirs or assigns; rendering yearly a rose on St. John the Baptist's day for all secular service. Warranty against all men, Jews and Christians. Witnesses, Sirs Walter de Fauconberg', John de Carleton, William de Fauconberge, John Pasmer, knts., Robert de Hildyard, William de Wytick, Walter de Apelton, Walter Northyby of Ryse. Ryse.[1] (*Ibid.*, II, ii, No. 2).

ᛒortb ᛒtainley.

344. Grant by Simon son of Gospatric de Stainlei to Robert de Seurebi and his heirs, for homage and service, of a toft and six acres of land with appurtenances in Steinlei; to hold of the grantor and his heirs, rendering 8*d*. for all services, 4*d*. at Whitsuntide and 4*d*. at Martinmas. The grantee could constitute anyone he wished as heir of the said lands; and he gave 40s. as a fine. Witnesses [named].[2] (*W. M. Staveley, esq.*, North Stainley, No. 1).

345. Grant by Simon son of Gospatric de Stanlei to Fountains abbey, in pure and perpetual alms, of seven acres of land in the territory of Stanlei; and confirmation of six acres of land which had belonged to Robert de Seuerbi, and quitclaim of the service which the latter had been wont to render to him; and confirmation of three acres of land which had belonged to Aldus de Scipton' with a toft in the vill of Stanlei and the toft of Robert de Seuerbi there, with a similar quitclaim; also grant of common within the vill of Stanlei, as much as belonged to a bovate of land there; to hold of the grantor and his heirs, free from all services. Also confirmation of whatever the abbey had of his fee in Stanlei in accordance with the charters relating thereto. Witnesses [named].[3] (*Ibid.*, No. 2).

346. Saturday before Simon and Jude the Apostles [Oct. 26], 1359. Release by Alice formerly daughter and heir of Adam le Warenner of Bondegat by Rypon and William Lytester of Rypon her nephew, to William Masone[4] of Northstaynlay and Eleanor his wife, their heirs and assigns, of all right in a messuage and fifteen acres of unfree land (*terre bond'*) in the vill and fields of Northstaynlay, with appurtenances. Rypon.[5] (*Ibid.*, No. 3).

347. Record of Court roll. Court of the chapter of Rypon held at Rypon, Saturday before All Saints, 33 Edward III [Oct. 26, 1359]. Alice Warner came and surrendered to the chapter all

---

[1] Two tags for seals; a fragment of one remains, green wax.
[2] For a full transcript and notes see Appendix I.
[3] For a full transcript and notes see *ibid.*
[4] He was dead by 1366; see No. 240 above
[5] Two seals: white wax; one a fragment; the other chipped and blurred.

her right to the use of William Mazon and Eleanor his wife, their heirs or assigns, in a messuage and fifteen acres of land with appurtenances in Northestaynlaye. They came and took the same, and gave to the chapter 6*d.* for fine by the pledge of Richard de Howgraue. And William Littester of Rypon, kinsman of Alice, quitclaimed to William and Eleanor his right therein. Seal of John de Cloutherem, steward of the chapter.[1] (*Ibid.*, No. 4).

348. Copy of Court roll. Court of the chapter of Rypon, Saturday after the Epiphany, 35 Edward [III] [Jan. 8, 1361-2]. John de Wynterburne and Ellen his wife came and surrendered into the hand of the lord a messuage with garden adjacent and nine acres of land with appurtenances in Northstaynelay to the use of William Mazon' and Eleanor his wife, saving however that John Euerwag and Agnes his wife previously made a fine to the lord for the said messuage and half an acre of land containing *del Ouerend* from the meadow called Meker as far as the highway (*altam semitam*) of Staynelay, to hold to John and Agnes and Agnes's heirs from Martinmas 35 Edward III for a term of fifteen years; William and Eleanor would do all services to the chief lord for the messuage and lands during the said term, and they took the same to hold to them and their heirs according to the custom of the manor of the chapter, and made fine to the lord, namely to Sir Richard atte Lane then prebendary of the prebend of Nunwyk, and gave 2*s.* for entry. (*Ibid.*, No. 5).

349. Monday before the Purification of the B.V.M., 2 Henry VI [Jan. 31, 1423-4]. Grant by John Lounde of Masham and Joan his wife to Robert Peyke of Thorp Malsert, his heirs and assigns, of two parts[2] of a messuage with appurtenances in North Staynlay lying between the messuage of the hospital of St. John the Baptist of Rypon on one side and that of John Hollegraue on the other, together with two parts of twelve acres of land and meadow with appurtenances in the territories of North Staynlay, of which two parts of three acres of land lay on Sleteberght between the land lately belonging to Thomas Ingelby on one side and the land of John att Stile, chaplain, on the other, two parts of one and a half acres lay on Sleteberght between the land of the said hospital on one side and that of John Broune on the other, two parts of three roods of land lay in the territory of Cunden abutting on [?] the sloping (*pendentem*) half acre of William att Stile between the land of John Broune on one side and that of the said hospital on the other, two parts of one rood of land lay on the culture of

---

[1] Seal on a tongue of the parchment: green wax, round, ⅞ in.; within a cusped border a shield of arms, quarterly, 1 and 4, a chaplet; 2 and 3, rubbed; * S' IOHANNIS DE CLOTHERVM.   For the arms of Clotherham see *Glover's Visitation*, ed. Foster, p. 234; where the second and third quarters are given as three pheons.

[2] *i.e.*, thirds.

St. Helen there between the land of the hospital on one side and that of John Broune on the other, two parts of one rood of land lay on the said culture abutting on the land of the hospital between the land of John Hollegraue on one side and that of John att Stile, chaplain, on the other, two parts of three roods of land lay there by the land of Emma de Keld on the east. two parts of three roods of land lay there at Cundengapp between the land of John de Hollegraue on one side and that of John Broune on the other, two parts of three roods of land lay in the territories of West Cundene between the land of the abbot of Fountains on one side and that lately belonging to Thomas Ingelby on the other, two parts of one and a half acres of land lay on Lamecroft between the land of the abbot of Fountains on one side and that lately belonging to Ellen de Keld on the other, two parts of one acre of land lay there between the land of the said hospital on one side and that of Emma de Keld on the other, two parts of one and a half acres of land lay in the territory of Lamecroft between the land of the hospital on one side and that of the said abbot on the other, and two parts of three roods of land lay at Gatecotegap in the territory of Counden between the land of the hospital on one side and that of John Hollegraue on the other. Witnesses, William Tempest, knt., William Fencotes, John Pygot, John de Hollegraue, William de Style, John de Peyke, Thomas Fauconberge, John Richmond. North Staynlay.[1] (*Ibid.*, No. 6).

350. Thursday after the Purification of the B.V.M., 2 Henry VI [Feb. 3, 1423-4]. Release by Roger son of John Lounde of Masham and Joan his wife to Robert Peyke of Thorp Malsert, his heirs and assigns, of all right in two parts of a messuage with appurtenances in the vill of North Staynlay and in two parts of twelve acres of land and meadow with appurtenances in the territories of North Staynlay, together with two parts of a messuage and croft with appurtenances in the vill of Thorp Malsert, and two parts of fifteen acres of land and meadow with appurtenances in the territories of Thorpp Malsert, which the said Robert had of the feoffment of John de Lounde his father and Joan his mother. Witnesses, William Tempest, knt., William Fencotes, John Pygott, John Wenslawe, Thomas de Faconberge. Thorp Malsert. (*Ibid.*, No. 7).

351. Record of Court roll. Court of the chapter of Rypon held there, Tuesday the morrow of Simon and Jude the Apostles, 5 Henry VI [Oct. 29, 1426]. John Hollegraue the elder of Staynlay who had held of the lord a messuage and two bovates of land with appurtenances in the vill and territory of North Staynlay, together with half a bovate of land there of the prebend of Nunwyk, died

[1] Two seals of red wax: (1) small signet; (2) round, ⅜ in.; letter W beneath an antique crown.

before that court [was held]; and John Hollegraue his son and heir came and made fine with the lord for these premises, to hold to him, his heirs and assigns, according to the custom of that prebend; he gave 33s. 4d. as fine, did fealty, and was admitted. Seal of William Fencotes, steward;[1] same day. (*Ibid.*, No. 8).

352. July 5, 1429. Grant[2] by John Verty son and heir of Roger Verty of Slenyngforth to Richard Wynpeny of Staynley, his heirs and assigns, of a messuage with meadow adjacent and all appurtenances in the vill and territory of Staynley, lying between the messuage of Ranulf Pygot of Cloterome on one side and the tenement of William de Ingylby of Ripley on the other. Witnesses, Robert Snayth, John Broun, Roger Waryn, chaplain, John Hougraue, William de Stele, Adam Turnoc, Thomas Fauconbergh. Staynley.[3] (*Ibid.*, No. 9).

353. Dec. 30, 30 Henry VI [1451]. Appointment by Richard Taliyour of Wathe of John Percyvale of Ripon as his attorney to deliver to John Hougrave of Westtanfeld seisin of one and a half acres of land in the territory of Northstanlay in accordance with his charter. (*Ibid.*, No. 11).

354. Nov. 8, 13 Edward IV [1473]. Release by Thomas Peke, late of Northstaynley to John Pygot of Ripon, *gentilman*, his heirs and assigns, of all right in a messuage with eight acres of land and a small close (*clausulo*) lately acquired from the lord's waste, with appurtenances lying in the vill and territory of Northstaynley, which he lately had of the grant of Robert Peke his father. Witnesses, John Norton, knt., Christopher Wandisfurth, esq., John Brown the elder, John Symson, Robert Brown. Northstaynley.[4] (*Ibid.*, No. 12).

355. Copy of Court roll. Court of the chapter [of Ripon], Tuesday before the Purification of the B.V.M., 13 Edward IV [Feb. 1, 1473-4]. John Holgraue came and surrendered the reversion of a messuage with thirty acres of land lying in the vill and territory of Northstainlay to the use of William Day, his heirs and assigns; William came and took from the lord, the prebendary of the prebend of Nunwyk in the church of Ripon, the said premises in reversion after the death of the said John; fine, 30s.; pledge, John Broune. (*Ibid.*, No. 13).

[1] Originally on a tongue of the parchment, but missing.
[2] Also, July 6, appointment by John Verty of Topclyf of Robert Snayth and John Broun as his joint attorneys to deliver seisin of the same premises to Richard Wynpeny; the vill described as Northstaynlay; at Topclyf; fragment of seal of red wax. (*Ibid.*, No. 10).
[3] Seal: fragment of red wax; no impression.
[4] Seal: red wax, round, ¾ in ; the lamb and flag; ECCE AGNVS DEI.

356.   March 10, 14 Edward IV [1473-4]. Release[1] by Ralph
Nevile, earl of Westmerland, to John Holgrave of Tanfeld, his
heirs and assigns, of all right in all the lands and tenements, rents
and services, with appurtenances in the vills and territories of
Staynlay, Skelton, Markyngton, and Sutton Holgrave, which he
lately had with William Stele and Robert Thornton, deceased, of
the feoffment of the said John. Witnesses, Nicholas Ward, esq.,
John Brown the elder, John Symson.   Brauncepath.   (*Ibid.*,
No. 14).

357.   May 4, 14 Edward IV [1474]. Grant by John Howgraue
of Westtanfeld to John Symson, William Day and John Day, and
the heirs and assigns of John Day, of a tenement with garden
adjacent and seven acres of land in the vill and territory of Northstaynley, with three acres of land in Sutton and Suttonhowgraue
with appurtenances.   Witnesses, John Broune the elder, John
Broune the younger, John Bell the elder, John Bell the younger,
Robert Wynpeny. North Staynley.[2] (*Ibid.*, No. 15).

358.   May 25, 14 Edward IV [1474]. Release by John Day
to John Symson of all right in a tenement with garden adjacent
and seven and a half acres of land with appurtenances in the
vill and territory of Northstainley, and in three acres of land
lying in Sutton and Suttonhowgr[a]ue which he lately had of the
grant of John Howgraue of Westtanfeld.   Witnesses, Richard
Redhede, John Gybson, Robert Byndlowse, John Clerk. Northstaynley.[3] (*Ibid.*, No. 16).

359.   Sept. 27, 15 Edward IV [1475]. Grant[4] by John Day
of Bisshopside, William Day of Westanfeld, and John Symson of
Sharowe to John Pigot of Ripon, gent., his heirs and assigns, of a
tenement with garden adjacent, and seven and a half acres of land
with appurtenances in the vill and territory of Northstanley, and
three acres of land lying in Sutton and Suttonhowgraue, which
had lately belonged to John Howgraue of Westanfeld; and release
of all their right therein.   Witnesses, Richard Redhede, John
Gybson, Robert Byndlowse, John Clerk, John Brown. Northstanley.[5] (*Ibid.*, No. 17).

[1] Draft or copy; not executed. At the foot: This deide his seilid and
in the kypyng of William Day of Northstanley or his hereis.
[2] Seal: red wax, round, ½ in.; a hare; * PRIVE . . SV.
[3] Seal: red wax; signet; a bird with wings extended; motto not deciphered.
[4] Also, May 10, 16 Edward IV [1476], release by William Day to John
Symson of all right in the same premises, which he had of the grant of
John Howgraue of Westtanfeld, witnesses, John Browne of Staynlay, Robert
Carlell, Robert Wynpeny; at Tanfeld; seal, dark red wax, round; a bird,
probably a hawk, holding a smaller bird in its beak. (*Ibid.*, No. 18).
[5] Three tags for seals, of which the third remains: red wax, round,
7/16 in.; a tree.

360. Sept. 2, 17 Edward IV [1477]. Grant by John Symson, son and heir of John Symson of Sharow, to Richard Pygot, king's serjeant at law, and John Pygot his brother, their heirs and assigns, of all his messuages, lands and tenements with appurtenances in Northstayneley; and appointment of William Pyper, chaplain, and Henry Kagill as joint attorneys to deliver seisin.[1] (*Ibid.*, No. 19).

361. March 26, 1479. This endenture maid the xxvjth day of Marche the yere of the reigne of kynge Edward the iiijth after the conquest of Yngland xixth betwyx Joh' Maners of Rothwell in the counte of Yorke & Johannet his wiff doghter & heire of Henre Dalle lat of Laburne [and] Will'm Knyght sone & heire of the seid Johannet on that oone partie & Joh' Ward one that othere partie wittenessith & recordis at the seid Joh' Johannet his wiff & Will'm has iontely yewyne[2] & enefefyd the seid Joh' Ward a meis ix acres of erable lond with al there appurtenans lygynge in the feld callid Lymkylne in Northstanley os by a deid of feffement vnto the seid Joh' Ward by the seidis Joh' & Johannet his wiff more pleynly is comprehendid & fore the more suyrte the seidis Joh' & Johannet his wiff sal bynd theyme be obligacone in the somme of xxli. vnto the seid Joh' Ward at what tyme the seid Will'm be of compleit age of xxj yere then the seid Will'm to make a sufficient feffement or reles vnto the seid Joh' Ward his heires & his assignes fore euer moyre or elis a fore a justis at the eleccone of the seid Joh' Ward & yff hit happyne the seid Will'm to dy ore he be of the age of xxj yere or elis haue maid none estat at then his nest brothere & heire ore elis any othere that is heire vnto the seid Will'm after the deces of the seid Johannet sall make a sufficient feffement ore reles os hit is a fore rehersid. In witnes whare of thes fore seidis Joh' & Johannet his wiff & the seid Will'm to the partie of this endenture has set to theire sealis in the presens of Joh' Radcliff gentilman Thomas Fisshere Joh' Barbour Joh' Broune Will'm Daa Joh' Daa & othere yewyne the day & yere a fore seid.[3] (*Ibid.*, No. 20).

362. March 27, 19 Edward IV [1479]. Grant[4] by John Maners of Rothwell, co. York, and Joan his wife, daughter and heir of Henry Dalle, late of Laburn, to John Ward of Northstanley, his heirs and assigns, of their messuages and nine acres of arable land lying in the territory and field of Northstanley called Lymkylne, with appurtenances. Witnesses, William Radcliff, gentleman, Thomas Fisshere, John Browne, William Daa, John Daa. Northstanley. (*Ibid.*, No. 21).

[1] Seal: red wax; signet; letter W beneath an antique crown.
[2] Given.
[3] Fragment of seal of red wax on a tongue of the parchment.
[4] Also, same day, appointment of John Smyth as attorney to deliver seisin of the premises; messuage in the singular. (*Ibid.*, No. 22).

363. June 5, 21 Edward IV [1481]. Grant by John Warde of Northstaynley to dame Elizabeth Malorye, widow, and Christopher Clerk, and the heirs and assigns of dame Elizabeth, of a messuage and nine acres of land and meadow lying in the vill and territory of Northstaynley called Lymkylne, with all appurtenances; and release of all right therein. Witnesses, John Brown, William Day, Robert Wynpeny, John Bell, Robert Thomson of Northstaynley. Northstaynley. (*Ibid.*, No. 23).

364. Feb. 10, 22 Edward IV [1482-3]. Release by Richard Wynpeny of Northstaynley to John Wynpeny of the same, his heirs and assigns, of all right in a messuage with meadow adjacent and all appurtenances in the vill and territory of Northstaynley, as in his charter more fully appeared. Witnesses, William Da, Robert Tuke, Richard Fodirgill, John Thekiston, Robert Thomson of Northstaynley. Northstaynley. (*Ibid.*, No. 24).

365. Copy of Court roll.[1] Court of the chapter of Ripon, Oct. 22, 9 Henry VII [1493]. William Day of Northstanlay came and surrendered the reversion after his death of two messuages and thirty acres of land containing three bovates with appurtenances, held of the prebendary of the prebend of Nunwyk, to the use of John Day his younger son, his heirs and assigns; John Day came and took from the lord the premises, and was admitted tenant and did fealty; fine 10s. (*Ibid.*, No. 25).

366. Copy of Court roll. Court of the chapter of Ripon, April 10, 13 Henry VII [1498]. It was found that John Broune of Northestanlay was dead, and had surrendered the reversion of two messuages and three bovates of land held of the prebendary of the prebend of Nunwyk, lying in the vill and territory of Northestanlay, to the use of Ralph Broune his younger son, his heirs and assigns. John Broune, son of the said Ralph, being under age and in the custody of Margaret his mother, took from the said prebendary the said messuages and land, putting his mother in his place, and was admitted tenant and did fealty; fine [*blank*]. (*Ibid.*, No. 27).

[1] Also, on paper in a later hand, copies in English of Court rolls relating to the same premises: (*a*) Dec. 20, 1 Henry VII [1485], admission of John Browne, son and heir of John Browne; (*b*) same entry as above, except that the date is Oct. 21, and fine 13s. 4d.; (*c*) May 10, 6 Henry VII [1491], William Day took the premises which had been seized into the hands of the lord for his default of his account of his office of his graveship; (*d*) undated, similar entry relating to John Browne; fine 13s. 4d.; except in the case of (*b*) the premises are described as being in Northstayneley. (*Ibid.*, No. 26).

367.   Dec. 8, 22 Henry VII [1506].   Grant[1] by John Wynpeny of Ripon to Miles Staveley, gent., and John Staveley, his son and heir apparent, and their heirs, of a messuage built on and a close of meadow adjacent with appurtenances in Northstaneley, then in the tenure of John Wright.   Witnesses, William Dey, Richard Fodergill, Robert Coke, William Raner, John Bakhous.   (*Ibid.*, No. 28).

368.   Feb. 12, 22 Henry VII [1506-7].   Grant by Thomas Pygot, esq., for 3*li*. 5*s*. paid beforehand by Miles Staveley, to him and John Staveley, his son and heir apparent, and their assigns, of a tenement in Northstaneley, then in the tenure of Robert Dogeson; to hold from Martinmas last past for a term of thirteen years.   Mutual seals to either part of the indenture.[2]   (*sd.*) Thomas Pygott.   (*Ibid.*, No. 30).

369.   Oct. 17, 23 Henry VII [1507].   Grant[3] by Robert Wyvell, esq., to Miles Staveley, gent., and John Staveley, his son and heir apparent, their heirs and assigns, of all his messuages, tofts, cottages, lands and tenements, rents and services in North Staneley which had descended to him by hereditary right after the death of John Pygot his uncle.   Witnesses, Robert Midilton, Thomas Mankyn, Thomas Kendall, John Bakhous, John Lofthous. (*sd.*) Rob't Wyvill.[4]   (*Ibid.*, No. 31).

370.   Same day.   Grant[5] by Robert Wyuell, esq., to Miles Staveley, gent., and John Staveley, his son and heir apparent, their heirs and assigns, of the reversion of all the messuages [*etc. as in the preceding deed*], lately belonging to John Pigott, esq., the grantor's uncle, when they should revert after the death of Katherine Pygott, widow, late wife of the said John; which

---

[1] Also, Dec. 26, same year, bond by John Wynpenny of Ripon, *yoman*, to Miles and John Staveley in 100*s*. to ensure their peaceful tenure of the premises without disturbance by John Wynpenny, Isabel his wife or John's heirs; seal on a tongue of the parchment, no impression. (*Ibid.*, No. 29).

[2] Two tags for seals, missing.

[3] Also a release of all right in the same, Oct. 25; witnessed by the last three witnesses in different order; same signature. (*Ibid*, No. 32).

[4] Seal: red wax, signet; not heraldic.

[5] Also, same day, bond by Wyvell to Miles and John Staveley in 40*li* to ensure the payment to them of 33*s*. 4*d*. yearly at Martinmas and Whitsuntide in equal portions during the life of Katherine Pygot, and their peaceful tenure of the premises after her death; (*sd.*) Rob't Wyvill; same seal. (*Ibid*, No 34).

Also, 20 Oct., attornment by Katherine Pigott to Miles and John Staveley by the payment of 1*d*., becoming their tenant; witnesses, John Walle the dean, Thomas Percyvell, chaplain, Thomas Mankyn. (*Ibid.*, No. 35).

Also, 25 Oct., appointment by Katherine Pygott of Thomas Parcivall and William Stabyll, clerks, as joint attorneys to deliver seisin of the premises to Miles and John Staveley; seal, a merchant's mark on a tongue of the parchment. (*Ibid.*, No. 36).

messuages [*etc.*] Katherine was holding for the term of her life; also all his messuages [*etc.*] in Northstaneley. Witnesses, Robert Middilton, and others.[1] (*sd.*) Rob't Wyvill.[2] (*Ibid.*, No. 33).

371. Copy of Court roll. Court of the chapter of Ripon, Monday Oct. 30, 5 Henry VIII [1513]. Joan Broune,[3] sister and heir of John Broune, outside the court surrendered into the hands of Richard Nevell, knt., lord of Latemer, chief steward there, and John Pullayn, ...[4] there, two messuages and three bovates of land with appurtenances in Northestanlay; held of the prebendary of the prebend of Nunwyk, to the use of Miles Stavelay, gent., and John Stavelay, his son and heir, their heirs and assigns, to whom the lord by his steward granted seisin, to hold of the said prebendary and his successors by the services according to the custom of the manor; they give to the lord a fine as appears above, were admitted and did fealty. John Broune, son and heir of John Broune the elder, came in person and for 3*li.* 10*s.* 4*d.* surrendered to Miles and John all his right therein. Miles and John give to the lord a fine for the enrolment of this release as appears above. (*Ibid.*, No. 37).

372. Copy of Court roll.[5] Court of the chapter of Rypon, Feb. 28, 22 Henry VIII [1530-1]. Christopher Hesyllepp by Arcules Loncaster his attorney and Joan his wife, examined by the steward, surrendered into the hands of the steward a third part of a messuage and a third part of four bovates of land with appurtenances in Northstaneley to the use of Miles Stavelay and John Staveley, gents., their heirs and assigns; they came and sought admittance to the premises, which were granted to them; they give to the lord a fine, namely to the prebendary of the prebend of Nunwyk.

To the same court came Margery Day, one of the daughters and coheirs of John Day, who surrendered into the hands of the steward a third part of the same premises to the use of Miles and John [*etc. as before*]. (*Ibid.*, No. 39).

373. April 27, 26 Henry VIII [1534]. Grant by Miles Staueley and John Staueley, his son and heir apparent, to John Browneflete and William Thomlynson, chaplains, of an acre and a rood of land and meadow in Thorpe by Rypon, and four acres

---

[1] Not named.
[2] Seal: red wax, signet; not heraldic.
[3] On Oct. 12, same year, Richard Fletham, bailiff of Wotton, co. Bedford, yeoman, and Joan Broune of the same, spinster, issued a receipt for 11*li.* 10*s.* from Miles Stavelay, gent., for her use, for the same premises. (*Ibid* , No. 38)
[4] Words which seem to be *stu[h] erudit.'*
[5] Also another copy of the second part; Margaret Day so described. (*Ibid.*, No. 39A).

and a rood of land lying in the fields of Rypon, which the grantors lately had of the grant and feoffment of Thomas Darby of York, merchant; with appurtenances; in exchange for a messuage with appurtenances in Northstaynley, eight acres of land there in a place called Lymekylne, and an acre of land there in a place called Sletbargh; with this condition that if the premises in North-staynley were recovered from them by judgment in the king's court, or were burdened by the grant of any annuity, it should be lawful for them to re-enter the premises in Thorpe and Rypon. Also grant by Brownflete and Thomlynson of the premises in Northstaynley, which they lately had of the grant and feoffment of Thomas Bakehous, clerk; with a similar condition.[1]

Dorso: memorandum[2] that Sir John Brownefleyt, chantry priest of the chantry of St. Wilfrid within the collegiate church of Rypon, founded by dame Elizabeth Malory, and Sir John Necoll, priest, delivered possession of the premises in Northstaynley to Miles and John Staveley, gents., on May 9, same year. Witnesses, Sir William Malory, knt., Thomas Blakburne, priest, John Batty, Nicholas Jakson, Ralph Jakson, Ralph Kyrkeby, Roger Turrett, Thomas Turnere, John Coytts. (*Ibid.*, No. 40).

374. Memorandum.[3] Co. York. Parcels of the tenements and possessions lately belonging to the monastery of Fountance in the archdeaconry of Richmond :

Free farm of John Staveley, esq., for certain lands and tenements lately belonging to Margaret Pigott, widow, and afterwards to Miles Staveley in Northstainley, paying yearly at Martinmas   ..   .. 16*d*.

Free farm of the heir of Miles Man for a moiety of a messuage with appurtenances lately belonging to William Smith, also a fourth part of a messuage lately belonging to John Gainesforth in Northstainley, paying yearly as above ..   ..   .. 8*d*.

Free farm of the heir of John Browne for a fourth part of the said messuage with appurtenances there, paying yearly as above
4*d*.

Charged by Mr. Tho. Brinley, auditor. (*Ibid.*, No. 41).

375. Copy of Court roll. Court of the canons and chapter of the church [of Ripon], Feb. 13, 2 Edward VI [1547-8]. John Staveley, esq., who had held of the prebendary of Nunwyke according to the custom of the manor two messuages and three bovates of land and meadow with appurtenances in the vill and fields of Staneley, lately the land of John Broune, two thirds

---

[1] Two seals to this part of the indenture; one in fragments; the other, red wax, signet, a bird
[2] In English.
[3] On paper; in Latin except the last line.

(*partes*) of a messuage and of three bovates of land and meadow divided into three parts lying there, lately the land of John Day, and a messuage, two closes and two bovates of land and meadow with appurtenances in Copthewyke, lately the land of Thomas Coundall, had died, after whose death Ninian Staveley, gent., as son and next heir, came and took from the prebendary the said premises, to hold to him, his heirs and assigns, by a yearly rent, fealty and suit of court; fine in the name of relief as appears above; fealty and admittance.[1] (*Ibid.*, No. 42).

376. Copy of Court roll. Court of the king's exchequer held at Ripon, Monday Nov. 28, 6 Edward VI [1552]. Ninian Staveley, gent., came and took from the king a parcel of waste land in Northstaineley lying on the east *del pulleynkeld*, containing sixty-six ells in length and sixty-three ells in breadth; this was granted by the king's steward to him and his heirs, rendering yearly 12*d.*; fine for entry as above; fealty and admittance.[2] (*Ibid.*, No. 43).

377. Oct. 28, 1 Mary[3] [1553]. Sale by Christopher Staveley of the city of London, *marchaunte*, to Ninian Staveley of Ripon parke, esq., his brother, for a sum of money paid beforehand, of a messuage, buildings, orchards and gardens and all his cottages, tofts, crofts, lands, tenements, meadows, feedings, pastures, commons, woods, underwoods, rents, reversions and services, with appurtenances in Northstaneley, then or lately in the tenure of Christopher Raynner; which messuage [*etc.*] the vendor had for life of the gift of John Stave[le]y his late father, as in his testament and last will more fully appeared. Also appointment of Simon Helmesley and Christopher Strikeland as joint attorneys to enter and deliver seisin. (*sd.*) per me Christopher Staveley grocer.

Dorso: sealed and delivered in the presence of John Hogeson, Christopher Raynerd, Christopher Strikland, Robert Hawe, Robert Mabley, John Strikland, Ninian Graunge; seisin delivered in the presence of the same. (*Ibid.*, No. 44).

Swinton (Wath=upon=Dearne).

378. St. John of Beverley [May 7], 1280. Quitclaim by Emma daughter of Jordan son of Henry de Swinton, in her widow-hood, to dame Alice de Bella aqua, her heirs or assigns, of all right in all the lands and tenements which the latter was holding in the

[1] Below is the name Strikeland
[2] Below is the name Newton.
[3] anno regni domine Marie prime Dei gracia Anglie, Frauncie et Hibernie regine, fidei defensoris et in terra ecclesie Anglicane et Hibernice supremi capitis primo.

vill of Swinton.[1] Witnesses, Robert de Criche, Ranulf de Sonirton, Hugh de Birne, Richard de Hoterington, William son of William de Swinton, John the tailor of the same, William de Waht of the same, Henry the clerk. Kirtelington.[2] (*Duke of Leeds*, Hornby Castle Muniments, Swinton, No. 1).

Thirkleby (Kirby Grindalythe).

379. Sept. 30, 32 Henry VIII [1540]. Appointment by John Staveley of Ripon parke, esq., of Ninian Staveley, his son and heir apparent, and Robert Mease as his joint attorneys to receive seisin of all the lands and tenements with appurtenances in Thurkelby, Duggilby, Caitwike and Bewholme in Holdernes, in accordance with a charter of feoffment of bargain and sale made to him, his heirs and assigns, by John Staveley of Lynby, co. Nottingham, esq., and Constance his wife. (*sd.*) per me Johannem Staveley. (*W. M. Staveley, esq.*, Thirkleby, No. 1).

Thorner.

380. May 8, 6 Henry VI [1428]. Grant by William Rodes, citizen and dyer (*littester*) of York, to Thomas Sclater and Edmund Sclater of Thornour, *yomen*, their heirs and assigns, of a tenement in the vill of Thornour, situate by the cross, and nine acres of land in the fields of the said vill, late in the tenure of William Walker of the same; which premises he lately had of the feoffment of John Tymble of Ledes. Witnesses, Thomas Meteham, Robert Maweleuerer, esqs., Thomas Erle, Thomas Eltoft, Richard Maresshall. Thornour. (*The Rev. P. M. Williams, vicar of Thorner*).

381. Whit Tuesday, 16 Henry VI [June 3, 1438]. Grant by Thomas Sclatter of Thornour to Edmund Sclatter of Thornour and Elizabeth his wife, and Edmund's heirs and assigns, of eight acres of land with appurtenances in Thornour, of which one rood lay in *le Southfelde* in length near *lez Forthgatez*, and abutted on *le pixeldepe* on the north and the land of Thomas Erle on the south; another rood lay in *le Westfelde* between the land of Thomas Meteham, knt., on the west and that of Robert Mirescogh on the east, and abutted on *le Personbrek*; half a rood lay in a place called Carkelowe between the land of the said Thomas Meteham on the west and that of Robert Mirescogh on the east, and abutted

---

[1] Although the place of issue, Kirklington, might suggest Swinton, par. Masham, the Bellew interest (see Hunter, *South Yorkshire*, ii, 76) in Swinton, par. Wath-upon-Dearne, and the witness William de Wath (of Swinton), makes the latter identification reasonably certain.

[2] Seal: green wax, pointed oval, $1\frac{1}{8} \times \frac{3}{4}$ in.; an eight-pointed star;
* S' EMME SWINTVN.

on the land of the said Thomas Meteham towards the north; another half rood lay on Bakstonegraftes between the land of Thomas Herryson on the west and that of Robert Mirescogh on the east, and abutted on the land of the said Thomas Meteham towards the north and south; half an acre lay in *le Westfelde* between the land of Robert Mirescogh on the east, and abutted on Eltoftgate towards the north and on Wynhynges towards the south; another rood lay in *le Westfelde* between the land of Robert Mirescogh on the east and that of Thomas Eltoft on the west, and abutted on Maynynge towards the south and on Eltoftgate towards the north; one piece (*pars*) of land called *a ferthyng* lay in *le Westfelde* between the land of Robert Mirescogh on the east and *le Wynynge* on the west, and abutted on *le Maynynge*; half a rood lay in Thwatesfeld in *le bothom* between the land of the said Thomas Meteham on the north and that of Robert Mirescogh on the south, and abutted on the land of Thomas Meteham towards the west and that of the duchy of Lancaster towards the east; another half acre lay in *lez Thwaytez* between the land of Thomas Meteham on the north and that of Robert Mirescogh on the south, and abutted on Eltoft-bank towards the west; another rood lay in *le Milnefelde* between the land of Robert Mirescogh on the east and that of the rector of Thornour on the west, and abutted on the windmill there towards the south; another half rood lay in *le Milnefelde* between the land of John Aleyn on the west and that of Robert Myrescogh on the east, and abutted on Yorkeslane towards the south; another acre lay in *le Milnefelde* between the land of Thomas Eltoft on the west and that of Thomas Meteham on the east, and abutted on the land of the same Thomas towards the north; another acre lay in *le Kirkfelde* between the land of William Symson on the north and that of Robert Mirescogh on the south, and abutted on *le Espgapp'* towards the east and the church there on the west; another acre lay in the said furlong (*stadio*) between the land of Robert Mirescogh on the north and that of Thomas Meteham on the south, and abutted on *le Espgapp'* towards the east and the said church towards the west; another half rood lay in Kirkfelde by Kelthwayteyate between the land of Robert Mirescogh on the east and that of the said Thomas Meteham on the west, and abutted on the land of the same Thomas towards the south; another half rood lay on the furlong (*stadium*) of Grenegate between the land of the said Thomas Meteham on either side, and abutted on *le Grenegate* leading to Litelmore towards the west; another half acre lay in Kelthwayt between the land of Thomas Meteham on the west and that of Robert Mirescogh on the east, and abutted on the road leading from Kelthwaytyate to *le Estmore*; three roods lay in Kelthwayt in the place called Highrawes between the land of Thomas Eltoft on the east and that of Thomas Erley on the west; another half acre lay in *le Stokynge* between the land of John Hull on the north and that of the said Edmund on the

south, and abutted on the land of the said Thomas Meteham;
another rood lay in *lez crounedforlonges* between the land of
Thomas Eltoft on the east and that of the said Thomas Meteham
on the west, and abutted on the land of the same Thomas towards
the north; another half rood lay in Kelthwayt between the land of
Thomas Eltoft on the east and that of the said Thomas Meteham
on the west, and abutted on Kelthwaytwell towards the south.[1]
Witnesses, Robert Mauleuerer, Aluered Manston, Thomas Swalowe,
rector of Thornour, Thomas Eltoftes, Robert Mede. Thornour.[2]

382. Sept. 1, 22 Henry VI [1443]. Grant by Edmund
Sclatter and Elizabeth his wife to William Symson and Joan his
wife, their daughter, of the reversion after their death and the
death of the survivor, of a messuage and two acres of land with
appurtenances in Thornour; which messuage was situate by the
cross between the tenement of Thomas Metham, knt., on the west
and that of John Patryk on the east, and of the two acres half an
acre, namely four *londez*, abutted on Eltoftgate on the west,
another half acre lay in a headland by *le longbalk*, another half
acre at *le Esshenhede*, and another half acre in *le Stokynge* on the
south; to hold to them and the heirs of Joan's body, rendering 8*d.*
to the chief lords of the fee at the usual terms. Should Joan have
female issue and not male the elder sister should have the premises,
to her and the heirs of her body. With remainder in default of
Joan's issue to Alice their daughter, Joan's sister, and the heirs
of her body; and successive remainders in tail to John son of
William Sclatter, late of Houden, and to Thomas Sclatter their
brother, and remainder to Richard Marsshall, parker of Roundhawe,
and William his son, their heirs and assigns. Witnesses, William
Gascoigne, knt., John Gascoigne, esq., Thomas Elys, Thomas
Erle, William Patryk. Thornour.

Thorp Arch, Etc.

383. Tuesday, feast of St. William, 4 Edward II [June 8,
1311]. Indenture[3] witnessing that Nicholas de Stapelton, one of
the heirs of Laderina de Brus,[4] and Alan de Folyfayt, attorney of

---

[1] The lands specified add up to 8 acres, the 'farthing' being taken as
half a rood.

[2] Seal· red wax; small; gothic letter T.   [3] In French

[4] Laderina, one of the four sisters and heirs of Peter de Brus, who died
in 1272, married John de Bellew, who died in 1301; her heirs were Nicholas
de Stapelton her grandson and Joan her younger dau., wife of Aucher
FitzHenry (see *Complete Peerage*, new ed., ii, 101). For Laderina's share of
the Brus inheritance see the inq. after the death of John de Bellew in 1301,
when she was dead and her heirs were as above (*Cal. Inq. p. m.*, iv, No. 45).
It seems that dame Isabel widow of Sir John de Bellew, mentioned in the
present document, was his second wife; and the evidence of the seal suggests
that she may have been a Ros. But no second wife is given in *Complete
Peerage, loc. cit.*

Sir Aucher son of Henry and Joan his (Aucher's) wife, had received from dame Isabel, widow of Sir John de Belewe, forty-three[1] charters relating to the Brus inheritance, which dame Isabel had in custody: (1)[2] indenture between Peter de Brus the third and the prior of the Park[3]—20 acres and one rood of land in Thorp; (2) quitclaim of William de Percy—2 marks' rent from the mill of Thorp; (3) charter of Stephen son of Roger de Barneby—1½ acres in Camelsford; (4) quitclaim of Rabot son of Walter de Bouyngton—2 bovates of land in Tibthorp; (5) writing of the prior of St. Oswald—chantry of Scokirk; (6) quitclaim of Joan widow of Richard de Wilesthorp—10 marks' rent in Wilesthorp; (7) writing of Roger de Smytheton—Little Cathal; (8) writing of William de Hedon—2 bovates of land in Walton; (9) quitclaim of Wymer widow of William le mouner of Thorp; (10) quitclaim of Robert le Vauasour to Juetta (*Jowete*) de Arche; (11) writing of William Fairfax to Sir Peter de Brus—land in Walton; (12) writing of Richard de Wymondthorp to Sir John de Belewe—tenements in Estbronne; (13) writing of Peter de Fountaygnes to Hugh de Collum—40s. rent in Carlton and Camelsford; (14) charter of Robert *a la filie* to Peter son of Peter de Brus—a bovate of land in Tibthorp; (15) indenture of Walter de Faucomberge—services in Appelton; (16) quitclaim of Peter de Fountaygnes to Peter de Brus—40s. rent; (17) charter of Berard de Camelsford—a toft in Camelsford; (18) charter of Giles brother of Berard de Fontaignes—an acre of land in Camelsford; (19) quitclaim of Thomas de Beleby to Sir Peter de Brus—20s. rent in Camelsford; (20) writing of Richard de Langthuayt to Sir Peter de Brus—land in Camelsford; (21) indenture between Sir Peter de Brus and John de Cliueland—tenements in Carlton; (22) quitclaim of Rabot son of Walter de Bouyngton to Peter de Brus—a bovate of land in Tibthorp; (23) a letter patent of Peter de Brus to Henry de Leyrton; (24) writing indented between the abbot of Selby and Sir Peter de Brus—an acre of land in Carlton; (25) charter of Gregory de Skelton to Thomas de Heiton—tenements in Camelsford; (26) charter of William de Aton to Thomas de Heiton—a villein and half a bovate of land in Camelsford; (27) writing indented between Robert brother of Richard de Wilesthorp and master Richard de Arnale—manor of Wylesthorp and other tenements; (28) another writing indented between the same—same manor; (29) indenture between Sir Peter de Brus and the prior of Holy Trinity, York and others—manor of Wylesthorp; (30) quitclaim of Alan de Arches to Adam de Brus—3 carucates of land in Walton; (31) writing indented of Peter de Brus; (32) writing indented between Sir John de Bellewe and Laurence son of Thomas de Lancastre—manor of Eston;

---

[1] Apparently only forty-two are specified.
[2] These numbers are not in the original and are only inserted here for convenience.
[3] Healaugh Park.

(33) indenture between Peter de Brus and Richard de Colthorp—a bovate of land and a toft in Thorp; (34) confirmation of Sir Peter de Brus to William de Lairton—100s. rent; (35) charter of Robert de Tolby to William de Hedon—2 bovates of land in Walton; (36) quitclaim of Thomas de . . . .[1] to Sir Thomas de Brus—tenements in Camelsford; (37) writing of Henry son of William son of Thomas to Sir Peter de Brus—2½ acres of land in Thorp; (38) charter of William de Sausey to Sir Peter de Brus—12 bovates of land in Thorp; (39) quitclaim of Terry de Ribrok to Sir Peter de Brus—73 acres of land and 2 tofts in Thorp de Arches; (40) indenture between Sir Peter de Brus and the prior of St. Oswald—chantry at Scokirk; (41) charter of the king—warren of Carlton; (42) indenture between Sir John de Bellewe and William son of Alexander de Walton. Mutual seals of Isabel and of Nicholas and Alan to either part of the indenture.[2] Witnesses, Sir Robert de Plumpton, Sir John de Walkingham, Sir Randolf de Blawmusters, Walter de Osgotby, Ralph de Scotton.   York.   (*Duke of Norfolk*, Misc., II, ii, No. 6).

Thorpe Salvin.

384.   Saturday after St. Mary Magdalene, 13 Edward III [July 24, 1339].   Inspection and confirmation by John son of John de Upsale of the charter of John his father to Hugh de Kyueton, his heirs and assigns, of a plot of land called Andreuflat and a culture called Milneflat with appurtenances in Thorprikenyld. Witnesses, Adam Bernard, Stephen de Wighton, William Frebois, John Giles, chaplain, William de Shirokes.   Thorprikenild.[3] (*Duke of Leeds*, Hornby Castle Muniments, Box V, No. 23).[4]

385.   Sunday after Easter [April 14], 1341.   Grant by Robert de Calington of Thorp Rykenyld to Sir Anketin Saluayn, knt., his heirs and assigns, of a yearly rent of 5s. from all his lands and tenements which he then had of the grant and feoffment of Godard de Brampton and Alice his wife in Thorp Rykenild, into whosesoever hands they might come, to be taken at the usual terms by equal portions; with power to distrain therein if the rent should be in arrear.   Witnesses, John de Uppesal the elder, John de Uppesal the younger, William Freboys, John Giles, chaplain, William del Beche.   Thorp Rykenild.[5]   (*Ibid.*, No. 24).

[1] Name erased.

[2] Seal to this part: red wax, round, outer rim missing, shield of arms remains; fretty, impaling three water-bougets (dimidiated). 'Fretty' suggests the arms of Bellew; and, if this seal was used by dame Isabel, having been John de Bellew's, it may be that the arms on the impalement (? the arms of Ros) were hers.   [3] Seal: white wax, small; blurred.

[4] Nos. 1 to 18 of this series were printed in vol. vii.

[5] Seal: dark red wax, round, ¾ in.; a stag's head cabossed, a cross above and a crescent and star below; * TIME TE DEVM.

386. Aug. 23, 1341, 15 Edward III. Grant[1] by Antony son of Ellis son of William de Thorp Rykenild, dwelling in Spillesby, to Sir Anketin Saluayn, knt., his heirs and assigns, of all the lands with appurtenances, which had formerly belonged to Ellis his father, namely, those which the grantor had of the grant and feoffment of William Freboys in Thorp Rykenild, namely, one and a half acres at Mikelthwayt between the land of William Freboys on either side abutting towards *Suth* and *North* on the land of Sir Anketin, three acres at Hegh Stubbyng between the land of John de Uppesal and William Freboys, abutting towards *Suth* on the pasture *del Suthwod* and towards *North* on the land formerly belonging to Emma Durraunt, half an acre in the same between the land of William Freboys and Margery Gilli, abutting *Suth* on the land of John de Barleburgh and *North* on the land formerly belonging to the said Emma, one acre at Honysik on the *south* side between the land of John de Uppesal and William Freboys, abutting *Suth* on the land of Thomas Chaumbrelayn and *North* on the land of John de Uppesal, three roods at Haraldcroft between the land of William Freboys and Thomas Chapman, abutting *Est* on the land of John Uppesal and *West* on the land of Sir Anketin, one rood at Lytlehowe between the land of William Freboys on either side, abutting *Est* on Turnestubbyng and *West* on the road leading to Whitewell, one acre beyond the same road between the land of John de Uppesal and that formerly belonging to Emma Durraunt, abutting *Est* on *le Rugh* and *West* on Hertehilstret, half an acre at Loskehowe between the land of William de Shirokes on either side, abutting *Est* on the land of John Giles, chaplain, and *West* on Hertehilstret, one rood on the *West* side of the orchard (*orchardi*) of John de Uppesal between the land of William Freboys and Margery Gilli, abutting *Est* on the said orchard and *West* on the land of Sir Anketin, one rood of land at the same between the land of Sir Anketin and William Freboys, abutting *Est* on *le Wolfepitt* and *West* on the land of the said John Giles, one rood beyond the road leading to Hertehill between the land of John de Uppesal and William de Shirokes, abutting *South* on the land of Sir Anketin and *North* on Personcroft, one rood at Goldehil between the land of John de Uppesal and William de Shirokes, abutting *Est* on the land of John de Uppesal and William Freboys and *West* on Hertehilstret, one rood at Layrepittes between the land of John de Uppesal and William de Shirokes, abutting *South* on Hertehilgat and *North* on Layrepittes, half an acre at the same between the land of Sir Anketin and William de Shirok', abutting *Est* on the land of John de Uppesal and *West* on Her-

---

[1] Also, attached, Sunday before St. Margaret, same year, appointment by the grantor of Thomas Knyght of Luda, clerk, as attorney to receive seisin in his name; and another appointment, same day and some of the same witnesses as to the grant, to deliver seisin; both have the same seal as to the grant.

tehilstret, three roods at Langewhitecres between the lands of
William Freboys and Thomas Chapman, abutting *South* on the
land of Robert de Calyngton and *North* on that of John de Uppesal,
one and a half acres on the *Est* side of Wylliamdal between the
land of Sir Anketin on one side and that of John de Uppesal and
William Freboys on the other, abutting *South* on the land of John
de Uppesal and *North* on Stakkedalhill, and two roods beyond
the road leading to Anstan in scattered lots (*diuisim*) between
the land of John de Uppesal and William Freboys, abutting *Est*
on the land of Sir Anketin and *West* on the land formerly belonging
to John Gilli; with easements. Witnesses, John de Uppesal the
elder, John de Uppesal the younger, William Freboys, William de
Beche, Robert de Calyngton, Roger the chaplain, John Giles, chaplain, Robert Wybbe, Thomas Smyth, William de Rypon. Thorp
Rykenild.[1] (*Ibid.*, No. 25).

387.   Invention of the Cross [May 3], 1344. Demise[2] by
Thomas Chaumbrelayn of Rolleton, the elder, to Sir Anketin
Saluayn, knt., lord of Thorp Rykenyld, of a plot of land called
. . . .[3] lying in Thorp Rykenyld next between the toft of Sir
John de Kyueton on the west[4] side and that of William de . . . .[3]
on the east, abutting towards the north on the common road and
towards the south on the land of the said Sir John; to hold with
all easements for a term of six years of the demisor and his heirs,
rendering yearly a rose at the feast of the Nativity of St. John the
Baptist for all services. Mutual seals to either part of the indenture.
Witnesses, John de Uppesal the younger, William de Shyrokes,
William de Bech, Sir John Giles, chaplain, Richard de Brampton.
Thorp Rykenyld.[5] (*Ibid.*, No. 19).

388.   July 27, 1347, 21 Edward III.   Grant by Thomas
Chapman of Thorp Rikenyld to Nicholas Saluayn, lord of Thorp
Rikenyld, his heirs and assigns, for the grantor's life, of all his
arable land and wood lying in different places in the territory of
Thorp Rikenyld, with appurtenances and easements; doing on the
grantor's behalf to the chief lords of the fee the services due.
Witnesses, Hugh de Totehill, Richard de Kyueton, John Cayli,
William de Beche, William de Shirokes, Thomas Smyth. Thorp
Rykenild.[6] (*Ibid.*, No. 26).

[1] Seal: yellow-brown wax, round, ¾ in ; a hare riding a dog; the legend
may be ALLONE I RIDE.
[2] An erasure after *concessisse*.
[3] Erased.
[4] *ex West parte*, and in the other cases the English words *est, north,* and
south are used
[5] Seal: dark red wax; oval, 1⅙ × 1⅙ in.; St. Margaret standing on a
dragon, holding a cross in her left hand, a palm branch beside her on her
right; * SAVN . CA MARG . . . A.
[6] Seal· red wax, round, *c.* ¾ in ; the sacred monogram beneath a three-
pointed object; legend blurred.

389. Monday before the Conversion of St. Paul, 22 Edward III [Jan. 19, 1348-9]. Agreement[1] between Nicholas Saluayn, lord of Thorp Rykenild, on one part, and John Coke of Malteby, William Dedenstowe and John Brian del Ker, on the other part, witnessing that the former had sold and delivered to the latter all manner of wood ripe for sale from a piece (*place*) of his wood of Thorp Rykenild, namely, from the piece called Asenergap as far as the water called Haghwell, and from the road going to the meadow as far as the end of the wood towards the east, and from . . . .[2] of Cayliwod as far as the highroad marching between [the land of] the said Nicholas and Branteclyf, except a border of ten feet, namely, from Caylywod as far as Assylcroft and from there as far as the highroad going out of the wood and then as far as the said meadow. The purchasers would begin to cut the wood any day they pleased after the agreement, and would clear the said piece before the following Michaelmas; and as soon as it was cleared it would be immediately taken into the vendor's hand. Nicholas granted to them, their men and all others buying the said wood free entry and exit to carry it within his wood and outside on his demesne throughout his lordship anywhere that was necessary, except land that was sown, during the said term; and if they did damage they should do satisfaction according to the amount of the damage. He also granted them a place for a forge in his wood and outside at their will, and also pasture in the same place for their beasts carrying the wood. Thorp Rykenild.[3] (*Ibid.*, No. 21).

390. Wednesday before St. Gregory the Pope, 23 Edward III [March 11, 1348-9]. Grant by William de Amyas of Notingham to John de Morleye, his kinsman, his heirs and assigns, of two bovates of land in Thorpe Salueyn, which he had of the grant and feoffment of Thomas Chaumberleyn of Thorpe Rikenyld, and which had formerly belonged to Agnes Salueyn; rendering yearly 13s. 4d. sterling at the feast of the Invention of the Cross and Martinmas in equal portions; with power to distrain or enter if the rent should be in arrear. Witnesses, John de Amyas, Richard de Brampton, Robert del Hull of Thorpe. Thorpe Rikenyld.[4] (*Ibid.*, No. 27).

391. Sunday before the Nativity of Our Lady, 24 Edward III [Sept. 5, 1350]. Covenants[5] between William de Schirokis and John Wyrth of Hoggisthorpe by which the latter would find for

---

[1] In French.
[2] 'e de laoure de Cayliwod.' The meaning of this appears to be obscure; but it may mean 'from the outskirts of Cayliwod.'
[3] Three tags for seals; only blurred fragments of yellow wax remain.
[4] Seal: dark red wax, round, ¾ in.; a bird; * CROV [?]ME DAT; placed upside-down on the tag.
[5] In French.

the former reasonable sustenance for the term of the former's life, namely, bread and ale (*seruose*) and a mess from the kitchen (*cosyn*) daily, and clothing and lodging, namely, before Christmas one cloak of new cloth, and at Christmas one year a suitable robe[1] and yearly a coat with a hat, the year in which he took his robe being that in which he would not take the coat; and would give him yearly for stockings and shoes 2s. yearly at Whitsuntide and Martinmas, and find him linen sheets and bedding; and also in every third year a robe. Should John fail in any part of this corrody William could enter all the lands and tenements in Thorperikenild formerly in his possession.   Thorpe Rikenild.[2]   (*Ibid.*, No. 20).

392.   Thursday, St. Barnabas the Apostle [June 11], 1355. Grant by Nicholas Saluayn, lord of Thorp Rykenild to Robert Wybbe of Thorp Rykenild and Joan his wife, of the toft which they inhabited, and his (the grantor's) common oven (*furnum*) and also eighteen acres of arable land lying throughout different places of the fields, which they had earlier held of him; to hold with appurtenances for the term of their lives and that of the survivor of the grantor and his heirs, rendering yearly 16s. of silver at the terms of Martinmas and Whitsuntide in equal portions, and doing on his behalf the service belonging to the castle of Tykhil. Mutual seals to either part of the indenture.[3] Witnesses, John de Uppesal, William son of Gregory, William Turnur, Roger Wybbe, Richard Gilly. Thorp Rykenild. (*Ibid.*, No. 28).

393.   Saturday, St. Peter ad vincula [Aug. 1], 1355, 29 Edward III. Demise by Nicholas Saluayn, lord of Thorp Rykenild, to John de Uppesal of the same, his tenant, of his manor of Thorp Rykenild with demesne lands and meadows belonging thereto; to hold for John's life of Nicholas and his heirs, rendering yearly for the following three years 50s. sterling at Martinmas and Whitsuntide in equal portions, and thereafter 20*li.* of silver yearly at the same terms; with power to enter and hold the same with all goods and chattels found therein, if the rent should be in arrear for fifteen days. John would acquit Nicholas and his heirs of all the service for the said manor belonging to the castle of Tyckill, saving to John fines and ward fees[4] (*wardefes*) belonging to the said manor. Warranty, saving to Nicholas the chambers over the

---

[1] This word indicates a complete outfit of clothes, which he was apparently to have every third year; but the arrangement is not very clearly expressed.

[2] Seal (detached): red wax, round, ⅞ in.; apparently an animal rampant; blurred.

[3] Seal: white wax, round, ⅞ in.; within a curved border with three points a shield, bearing a label and two objects resembling fish between three stars; legend chipped and indecipherable.

[4] Compositions for castle guard.

great gate.[1] John to maintain all houses and walls of the manor, and to leave it in as good state or better. Mutual seals to either part of the indenture.[2] Witnesses, Sir John de Kyueton, master William de Anstan, William son of Alexander, Sir Richard Gilli, chaplain, John Giles of Thorp Rykenild. Thorp Rykenild. (*Ibid.*, No. 29).

394. April 10, 32 Edward III [1358]. Grant[3] by Nicholas son of Anketin Saluayn, knt., to William de Sandford, clerk, his heirs and assigns, of the manor of Thorpe Saluayn with appurtenances, rents, services of freemen and other things belonging thereto, and also the rent of 19s. which Robert Wybbe rendered to him yearly for certain lands which he was holding of him for life in the same vill. Also the reversion of all the tenements and the common bakehouse (*pistrina*) which the said Robert was holding of the grantor for life in the same vill, the reversion of which after Robert's death belonged to the grantor and his heirs. Witnesses, Peter. de Nuttle, sheriff of Yorkshire, John de Langeton, mayor of York, Ralph de Lascels, knt., Roger de Lascels, knt., John de Neuton, Richard de Rouclif. York.[4] (*Ibid.*, No. 30).

395. April 11, 32 Edward III [1358]. Indenture[5] between Sir Nicholas son of Anketyn Saluayn, knt., on one part, and William de Sandford the elder and Thomas Dannay son of John Dannay of Crosbygerard, on the other, witnessing that whereas William and Thomas were bound to Sir Nicholas in 400*li.* sterling by a statute merchant to be paid at the feast of the Trinity next ensuing, Sir Nicholas granted that if they or one of them should pay to John de Langeton, mayor of York, at York at the same feast or before 200*li.* in gold or silver the said statute merchant should be annulled. Mutual seals.[6] York. (*Ibid.*, No. 30B).

396. May 24, 32 Edward III [1358]. Grant[7] by Thomas Lelegrane of Tyuerington to William de Sandford, clerk, his heirs and assigns, of a messuage, six acres of land, and a wood called Wodewardhill, with appurtenances in the vill of Thorpe Saluayn.

[1] saluis michi cameris annexis super magnas portas.
[2] Seal: white wax, oval, small; apparently an animal resembling a rabbit along the major axis; rubbed and legend blurred.
[3] Also, same day and place, appointment of Thomas Dannay as attorney to deliver seisin; in French; same seal on a tongue. (*Ibid.*, No. 30A).
[4] Seal: red wax, round, ⅞ in.; a cusped panel, the ground sown with fleurs-de-lis, on which is a helmet surmounted by the crest of a boar's head and neck, and below a shield of arms, couché, a chevron between three charges which are probably boars' heads couped; S' : NICOLAI SALWNNE . This is doubtless the same seal as that described in vol. i, p. 123n.
[5] In French.
[6] Same seal as to the preceding deed.
[7] Also, on the following day, appointment by the same (Lelegrayne) of Thomas Donnay to deliver seisin; same seal. (*Ibid.*, No. 31A).

Witnesses, John de Langeton, mayor of York, Ralph de Lascels, knt., Roger de Lascels, knt., John de Neuton. York.[1] (*Ibid.*, No. 31).

397. Saturday after St. Peter in cathedra, 35 Edward III [Feb. 27, 1360-1]. Grant[2] by William de Shirehokes to William de Sandford, clerk, his heirs and assigns, of all the lands and tenements, rents and services, which he had in the vill of Thorpe Saluayn, with appurtenances. Witnesses, William Gregson, John de Styrapp, Richard Gilly, chaplain, John Giles, Thomas le Maszoun of Thorpe, William de Dukmanton, Alan Nasse, Robert Wibbe del Holme. Thorpe Saluayn.[3] (*Ibid.*, No. 32).

398. Monday before the Nativity of the B.V.M., 36 Edward III [Sept. 5, 1362]. Surrender by Richard Gilly, chaplain, to William de Sandford of one and a half roods of land with appurtenances in Thorpe Salueyn, lying on Haraldcroft, which he had formerly held of Nicholas son of Anketin Salueyn, knt., by military service. Thorpe Salueyn.[4] (*Ibid.*, No. 34).

399. Tuesday before the Annunciation of the B.V.M., 37 Edward III [March 21, 1362-3]. Release by William de Dokmanton son of William de Dokmanton the elder to William de Sandford, of all right in four and a half acres of land with appurtenances in Thorpe Saluayn, which the latter had of the grant and feoffment of William de Dokmanton his father. Witnesses, John de Keton, William Gregson, Richard Gilly, chaplain, William Tournour, John Gyles, John Beche. Thorpe Saluayn.[5] (*Ibid.*, No. 35).

400. Invention of the Cross, 41 Edward III [May 3, 1367]. Grant by Richard de Ekynton to Richard Gylly of Thorpsalueyn, chaplain, his heirs and assigns, of all the lands and tenements which he had in the vill of Thorpsalueyn and its fields, with appurtenances. Witnesses, John Gyles of Thorpsalueyn, Thomas Masun, John de Leker, Robert Ibotsun, all of the same. Thorpsalueyn.[6] (*Ibid.*, No. 37).

401. Friday after St. John the Baptist, 41 Edward III [June 25, 1367]. Release by John Upsal to John de Kyueton of a

[1] Seal: red wax; same as to No. 392 above.
[2] Also, attached, another example of the same grant. Also, on the following day, release by John de Hoggesthorpe to the grantee of all right in all the lands and tenements in the same vill which the grantee lately had of the grant and feoffment of William de Shirehokes; same witnesses; seal, red wax, round, ⅞ in.; the sacred monogram beneath two sprigs; * PRIVE SVM VOD[?]T. (*Ibid.*, No. 33).
[3] Seal: red wax, oval, 1¼ × ¾ in.; not deciphered; not heraldic.
[4] Seal: brown wax, round, ¾ in.; a four-leafed flower.
[5] Slit for tag; but apparently no tag was inserted.
[6] Fragment of seal of yellow wax.

messuage and nine acres of land with appurtenances in Thorpe Riknild, which Thomas Wallar was holding for the term of his life. Kyueton.[1] (*Ibid.*, No. 36).

402. Saturday, the morrow of St. Matthew the Apostle, 43 Edward III [Sept. 22, 1369]. Release by Isabel widow of Nicholas Saluayn, knt., in her widowhood, to William de Sandford, lord of Thorpe Saluayn, of all actions of seeking any dower against him of the endowment of the said Nicholas in respect of any lands or tenements which had belonged to the latter. Witnesses, John Marreys, Thomas Louell of Skelton, Roger Dautre, John Lascels, Thomas Dannay. In the abbey of St. Mary, York.[2] (*Ibid.*, No. 38)

403. Tuesday, the eve of St. Peter ad vincula, 49 Edward III [July 31, 1375]. Release by Thomas de Sandford, brother and heir of William de Sandford the elder, clerk (*clerici*), to Thomas Dannay, William de Sandford the younger, clerk, and William de Hornby, of all right in the manors of Thorpe Saluayn and Herthil with appurtenances, into which manors they had entered immediately after the death of William his brother. Thorpe Saluayn.[3] (*Ibid.*, No. 39).[4]

404. Whit Monday [May 11], 1383. Grant by William son of John de Dukmanton, dwelling in Cloune, to Walter son of William de Dukmanton, his heirs or assigns, of all the lands and tenements with appurtenances which he had in the vill and territories of Thorpe Saluayn of the grant of Alice daughter of John Gilly of Rykenildthorpe. Witnesses, William Turnor, Thomas Waller, Ellis Milner, John Wybbe, Robert son of Isabel de Thorpe Saluayn. Thorpe Saluayn.[5] (*Ibid.*, No. 41).

405. The Ascension, 4 Henry IV [May 24, 1403]. Indenture between Edmund Sandford son of Edmund Sandford, knt., (*militis*) and William Louet of Hertyll, witnessing that the former demised at farm to the latter [and] Agnes his wife, their heirs and assigns, related by blood (*consanguineis*), a toft in Hertyll between the messuage of Richard Wade on the north and the toft of Alice Bernerd on the south, with the garden and one bovate of land and meadow belonging thereto, and appurtenances, which formerly

---

[1] Fragment of seal of red wax; a bird or animal
[2] Seal: red wax, same as to No 392 above.
[3] Seal: dark brown wax, round, $\frac{7}{8}$ in ; within a cusped panel a shield of arms, ermine, on a chief two boars' heads couped; ★ SIGILLVM THOME DE [?]SANDFORD.
[4] No. 40 is a copy of the indenture dated Monday after St. Barnabas, 3 Richard II [June 18, 1380], founding a chantry in the chapel of St. Mary on the north side of Thorpe Saluayn [church], and of the letters patent dated 12 Nov. 3 Richard II [1379]; of these there are full abstracts in *Cal. Pat Rolls*, 1377-81, pp 402, 519
[5] Seal: greenish-brown wax, round; blurred.

belonged to Stephen Jurdan, chaplain; to hold of Edmund, his heirs
and assigns, rendering yearly to them 6s. sterling in equal portions
at the following Martinmas and Whitsuntide, and so from year to
year, and also the payment of the forinsec rent as accustomed, and
doing two suits (*aduentus*) yearly at Edmund's court at Hertyll
without greater service. William to maintain the toft at his own
cost and leave it in good state. Edmund would deliver sufficient
timber for the toft and a new building if William and Agnes should
wish to build one, together with underwood for fencing the garden
when necessary. Power to distrain for the rent of 6s. if it should
be a month in arrear. Should William wish to plant trees in the
garden he could reasonably cut (*amputare*) them for mending his
ploughs and carts without Edmund's leave.   Mutual seals.[1]
Witnesses, William Mody of Hertyll, William Belgh of the same,
John Ferrour of the same. Thorpe Salueyn. (*Ibid.*, No. 42).

406.   Feb. 21, 6 Henry IV [1404-5].   Indenture between
Thomas de Hornby and Edmund de Sandford, witnessing that
whereas Edmund was bound to Thomas in 60*li.* sterling, of which
Edmund had received 45*li.* by the hand of Thomas, Thomas
granted that if Edmund should find for John, Peter, and James,
sons of John the brother of the said Thomas, food, clothing, and
school fees (*stipendium scole*) and other necessaries suitable to their
estate while they enjoyed[2] the schools in Thorpsalueyn, until each
of them expended 15*li.*, if it happened that each of them dwelt
(*morari*) so long with Edmund, and if any one of them should
depart from Edmund's company (*comitina*) and the said schools
before spending 15*li.* and Edmund should deliver to him the
residue of the 15*li.* on his departure, and also if any one of them
should die before spending or having 15*li.* and Edmund should
deliver the residue to those who survived, and lastly if each of them
died before spending or having 15*li.* and Edmund should grant
and distribute the residue of all their portions, neither spent nor
delivered, to chaplains and the sick and bedridden poor to pray
in masses and prayers for the souls of William de Sandford, clerk,
Edmund de Hornby and Margaret his wife, John, William, and
Thomas, their sons, and all their benefactors and the faithful
departed, then the said bond should be annulled. Edmund swore
on the gospels to fulfil the terms of the indenture. Mutual seals.[3]
(*Ibid.*, No. 43).

407.   Jan. 6, 1411[-2].   Notification by John Mordon, donzel,
(*domicellus*) and Robert de Laghton, clerk, notary public, that

[1] Seal: red wax; small signet, a shield of arms, apparently two fishes in
pale.
[2] A literal translation of 'fruuntur.'
[3] Fragment of seal: an oblong-shaped signet with lettering which may
be [H]ornby.

ten, eleven or twelve years ago a certain Nicholas Kueton, then summoned to a certain cross called Lady Crosse by the vill of Thorpe Saluayne, obeyed Sir Edmund de Sandeford, knt., then esq., as his lord, recognized him as his lord, and did homage for the lands and tenements which he had held and claimed to hold of him, in their presence and in the presence of John Checton, John Turnour and many others. Because their seals were unknown they had procured the seals of the archdeacon of York[1] and the dean of the deanery of Doncastr' to be affixed to these presents. Thorpe. (*Ibid.*, No. 43A).

408. March 4, 9 Henry VI [1430-1]. Grant by John Rokley, chaplain, to Nicholas Blakburn, citizen and merchant of York, William Daud, and William Swaynby, chaplain, of a messuage and thirty acres of land with appurtenances lying in the vill and territory of Thorp Saluayn, which he lately had of the grant and feoffment of Nicholas Keton. Witnesses, John Melton, knt., John Warenes, John Serleby, Edmund Daynyll, William Gylby. Thorp Saluayn.[2] (*Ibid.*, No. 44).

409. Eve of the Apostles Peter and Paul, 11 Henry VI [June 28, 1433]. Grant by Richard son of John Gylly of Thorp Rikenild to Brian de Sandford, esq., his heirs and assigns, of all his lands and tenements with appurtenances which he had in the vill and fields of Thorp Rikenild after the death of John his father. Witnesses, John Wastnays, Hugh Crescy, Edmund Deenyll, William de Kyueton, Edmund Proktour, Thomas Gibb. Thorpe Rikenild.[3] (*Ibid.*, No. 45).

410. Feb. 27, 16 Henry VI [1437-8]. Grant by Thomas Drake, *wallere* of Beghton, and Elizabeth his wife to Edmund Fitzwilliam, esq., Robert Donham, Thomas Folby, clerk, [and] Edmund Tayliour of Blida, of a messuage with appurtenances in the vill and fields of Thorpsalvayn which they lately had of the grant and feoffment of Nicholas Gaushyll, esq. Witnesses, John Melton, knt., Nicholas Gaushyll, esq., Hugh Cresy, esq., Thomas Melton, John Turnour. Thorpesalvayn.[4] (*Ibid.*, No. 46).

411. March 9, 1450[-1]. Indenture witnessing that John Marchall, clerk, canon of the cathedral church of York, chosen as arbitrator between the venerable and religious man Charles Flemmyng, prior of Wirksop, diocese of York, patron, as he

---

[1] There is a blurred word after *Ebor'* which may be *Offic'*, and the official of the archdeaconry may be intended; unfortunately the seals which may have been on a tongue of the parchment have disappeared.

[2] Seal: red wax, small signet; letters IR beneath an antique crown.

[3] Seal: red wax, small; not heraldic.

[4] Two seals, red wax: (1) letter T beneath an antique crown; (2) no impression.

asserted, of the perpetual chantry in the chapel of B.M. of Thorpe Salvan, parish of Laghton, diocese of York, and Sir Thomas Folby, chaplain of the said chantry and lately possessor of the same, touching certain questions and debates lately moved between them, and especially the right and title to the said chantry and the amoval of the said Sir Thomas from the same, having heard the answers of either side, gave his judgment after deliberation to the following effect· that the said Sir Thomas be restored to the possession of the said chantry and possess it again with his goods left there, notwithstanding the said amoval by prior Charles, because he was not the ordinary of the said Sir Thomas. Also, after inspecting the ordination of the said chantry and perceiving its tenor and moved by other things bearing on the matter, he gave his judgment that Sir Thomas Folby, having previously had possession of the chantry and a yearly pension of six marks given to him by the prior, if he should be freely and canonically provided with another competent benefice, either in a perpetual chantry or a parish church or a vicarage of the yearly value of 8*li*., as compensation for such a yearly pension or benefice, he should immediately resign the chantry in the chapel of Thorpe Salvan absolutely and leave it vacant at the will of the prior or other patron for disposal in accordance with the form of the said ordination. York. (*Ibid.*, No. 47).

412.   Dec. 8, 6 Edward IV [1466].   Grant[1] by Henry Sandford and Margaret his wife to John Stotusbury and Agnes his wife, their heirs and assigns, of a messuage built on with a garden adjacent, with all lands and other appurtenances within the vill of Thorpe Salvayn and its territory, which they had of the grant of Peter Frechewell of Staley, esq.   Witnesses, Sir John Lilly, abbot of Rufford, Robert Bateley, chaplain, John Bosvyle, William Clogh, William Upsall.   Thorpe Salvayn.[2]   (*Ibid.*, No. 48).

413.   March 26, 20 Edward IV [1480].   To all true peple of Crist unto whome this present writyng schall come to be sene ore herde we Willelmus Bliton of Knesall esquiere Sir Ric' Craven vicare of Knesall Robertus Perkere yoman Balyffe of the same toune Nich' Bakeley Will' Banast' Will' Pyche John Chapman Thomas Goldsmyth John Travman Ricardus Burnell John Hyrst and Ric' Mason of the same toun send gretyng in oure lorde gode euerlastyng and foreasmuch as hit ys meritorie & medefull forto bere wyttnez of trouth in al dowtefull materys beyng in wariance

---

[1] On June 8, 7 Edward IV [1467] the grantees appointed Bartholomew Halley and William Upsall as joint attorneys to deliver seisin of the same premises to John Daud and Clemence his wife, in accordance with their charter; witnesses, Edmund Sandford, esq., Thomas Folby, chaplain, James Mansell; same place; two broken seals on a tongue of the parchment. (*Ibid.*, No 49)

[2] Two tags for seals: red wax; letters.

and trawas therefore we are steryed and movyd by the waye of charite forto bere wittnez and recorde of trouth that where Will' Uppesall now decessyd late beyng oure neghbure atte Knesall hade a kynswoman dwelyng with hym in Knesall callyd Johanna Anwyk the whych Johanna he sayde unto us suld be hys ryght here after hys decesse and oppon that ofte and mony tymez offerd hyre to marie unto dyuerys persons of oure neghburs the whych Johanna we recorde to be ryght here and eneritabull to all the lyffelod of the sade Will' Uppesall lying within the toun and in the lordschype of Thoroph Rekynyll and this we wil proue as the lawe will qwhen we be lawfully required that hyt ys truthe whyt oute forgyng fenyng ore falsehede. In wittnez and recorde [?]here of we all a fore sade and ilkon of us be oure selfe to thys present hath sett oure seallez. Gevyn att Knesall . . . .[1] (*Ibid.*, No. 50).

414. March 10, 22 Edward IV [1481-2]. Grant by Walter Rotheley and Reginald Marbury to Henry Sandford, his heirs and assigns, of a messuage with appurtenances in Thorpe Saluyn which they lately had of Henry's grant and feoffment, and which Henry had of the grant of Brian Sandford, knt., his father; with all lands, meadows, feedings, pastures, woods, underwoods and all appurtenances in the vill and fields of Thorpe aforesaid. Witnesses, William Multon of Ufford, Henry Polard of Marram, William Halman. Peturburgh.[2] (*Ibid.*, No. 51).

415. March 8, 2 Richard III [1484-5]. Indenture[3] by which John Sandforde of Thorppsaluen, esq., and Brian Sandford, his son and heir, demised to Thomas Kame of the same and his heirs a place with a mill belonging thereto, called the Moremilne, with its profits from Whitsunday next following for a term of twenty years, yielding to them 26s. 8d. by equal portions at Martinmas and Whitsuntide. Thomas to do the repairs except timber, stones and all other "irengeyre,"[4] which would be found by John and Brian. The indenture to be void if the rent were forty days in arrear, or if Thomas or his heirs should take "anymans leuerey[5] or clothing during the seid terme bot of the seid John or Bryan or seke any lordship or maistership bot theires." Mutual seals.[6] (*Ibid.*, No. 52).

416. June 23, 5 Henry VII [1490]. Grant by John Tailliour *alias* John Swetnam of Thropen, co. York, to Brian Sandford, esq., and Elizabeth his wife, and Brian's heirs, of his manor of Thropen, with all the lands and tenements, meadows, feedings

---

[1] Twelve seals on five tags: dark red wax; devices, not heraldic.

[2] Two seals: dark red wax; (1) broken and blurred; (2) round, ½ in.; a shield of arms, on a cross engrailed between a charge in each quarter (possibly a fish) an annulet

[3] In English.   [4] Iron gear.   [5] Livery.

[6] Seal: red wax; broken and indistinct.

and pastures, woods, commons, wardships, marriages, escheats, rents, services and reversions with all appurtenances which he had in the vill and fields of Thropen or elsewhere belonging to the said manor. Witnesses, George Ingram of Dynnyngton, Christopher Syms, Thomas Moldson, John Cokson, Ralph Ingram, Robert Langley, all of the same, Robert Burton of Wallyngwellez.[1] (*Ibid.*, No. 52A).

417. Nov. 16, 9 Henry VII [1493]. Indenture[2] by which Brian Sandford of Thorpesilvayne, esq., should have of Thomas Turnour of the same, yeoman, by the way of exchange, his close lying within the park of Thorpe aforesaid, whereof the bigger part lay east and west, and the less part lay north and south, the south head lying against the way going to Nether Thorpe, and the north head "buttyng of the bigger parte of the said close"; to hold to Brian and his assigns during the life of Brian and Thomas and of the survivor. Thomas should have of Brian his part of Honysyke-close lying in the south field of Thorpe for the same term, and should have it yearly lying several from Candlemas to Michaelmas or for a longer period while it lay several, paying to Brian 8s. yearly at Martinmas, with power to Brian to distrain if the rent should be fourteen days in arrear. Should Thomas be "intryppid"[3] or troubled by anyone in his occupation thereof he could re-enter the other close. Mutual seals.[4] (*Ibid.*, No. 53).

418. Dec. 28, 12 Henry VII [1496]. Bond by Christopher Wylkynson of Wodesetts, co. York, husbandman, John Whitacres and Thomas Whytacrez, both of the same, husbandmen, to Brian Sandford, esq.,[5] in 20*li.* to be paid at the Purification of the B.V.M. next following. Thorpsiluan.

The condition[6] of the bond was to ensure that they should keep the peace against all the king's people, especially against John Wylkyn of Wodesetts. (*Ibid.*, No. 54).

Thorpe Langton (co. Leicester).

419. Tuesday before St. Margaret, 11 Edward III [July 15, 1337]. Indenture witnessing that whereas Robert Salueyn of Thorpe by Langeton[7] had quitclaimed to Robert son of William

[1] Seal: dark red wax; signet, letters TA.
[2] In English   [3] Interrupted.
[4] Seal: red wax; letters BW; broken.
[5] armigero pro corpore domini. It is doubtful whether this means esquire of the king's body or esquire of Sandford's superior lord.
[6] In English.
[7] There seems little doubt that the place is Thorpe Langton, co. Leicester, as there is a deed in *Cat. Anc. Deeds*, ii, 394, by which Robert Salveyn of Thorp by Langeton made a grant of land in Slawston (*c.* 2½ miles distant) in 1346.

Ayleward of Thorpe all his right in two messuages lying in Thorpe by the messuage formerly belonging to Alexander Salueyn on the east, Robert Salueyn bound himself, his heirs and assigns, to acquit the same with appurtenances against the chief lords and anyone else in respect of rents, suits of court and all other services which could be exacted therefrom; and to secure this he had granted by charter to Robert son of William Ayleward 12d. yearly rent to be taken yearly at Michaelmas from his lands and tenements into whosesoever hands they might fall; now Robert son of William Ayleward granted that this rent was not to be paid as long as Robert Salueyn acquitted the said two messuages; but if he failed to do so Robert son of William Ayleward would have power to distrain for the rent. Mutual seals.[1] Witnesses, John Ayer, John West, Thomas West, Robert Baroun, Henry Pe[?]ldyn. Thorpe. (*Duke of Leeds*, Hornby Castle Muniments, Box V, No. 22).

Treeton.

420. Friday, St. Lucy the Virgin and Martyr, 5 Edward III [Dec. 13, 1331]. Grant by Thomas Furniuall the elder, lord of Hallumshire and of Wyrkesop, to Joan his younger daughter of his two manors in Treton, co. York, with all the lands and tenements which he then had in the vill; with all appurtenances as in messuages, tofts, crofts, arable lands, meadows, feedings, pastures, woods, moors, marshes, turbaries, fisheries, mills, rents and services of free tenants, with their wardships, marriages, reliefs, scutages and escheats, villeins and their holdings, sequels, chattels, services and customs, cottars and their cottages, profits and perquisites of courts and all other commodities belonging; to hold for her life, rendering during the next ensuing six years a rose at the feast of St. John the Baptist for all services, and thereafter 100 marks of silver yearly at Michaelmas; with reversion to the grantor and his heirs after her death. Mutual seals to either part of the indenture.[2] Witnesses, Sir Robert de Pyrpount, Thomas de Longeuilers, knts., John de Bolyngbrok, John de Gayteford, Robert de Burton of Wyrkesop, William de Gayteford. Wyrkesop. (*Duke of Norfolk*, Misc., II, ii, No. 21).

421. Saturday, St. Luke the Evangelist, 12 Henry IV [Oct. 18, 1410]. Grant by Hugh Burgh, Gryffin de Hynton and John Bukenhull, chaplain, to dame Maud, wife of John Talbot, lord de Fournyvall, her heirs and assigns, of their manors and

---

[1] Seal : brown wax, oval, $\frac{7}{8} \times \frac{3}{4}$ in ; within a cusped border an animal passant along the major axis; legend not deciphered.
[2] Seal : red wax, round, $\frac{3}{4}$ in.; two human figures, head and shoulders, facing one another, a spray of flowers between them; legend, probably a motto, not deciphered.

lordships of Treton and Wyston, with the advowsons of those churches and all appurtenances, and all their lands and tenements, rents and services with appurtenances in co. York, which they lately had of the feoffment of the said John Talbot and Maud his wife.[1] (*Ibid.*, II, iv, No. 3).

Upsall (South Kilvington).

422. Tuesday, the morrow of St. Denis, 3 Edward III [Oct. 10, 1329]. Indenture[2] between Sir Geoffrey le Scrope and Sir Geoffrey de Upsale witnessing that, whereas the latter was holding the manor and wood of Upsale for life of the former's inheritance by fine levied in the king's court and the former had brought a writ of waste against the latter by reason of waste made in the said wood, the latter in order to have a release and quittance of the said waste surrendered to the former all the wood of Loftscough, Gildhousdale, Orberghraue with all the wood and coppices beyond the rabbit-warren (*conyngger*) of Upsale on one side and the moor of Baggeby on the other, and the highroad extending from the south of the park of Upsale called Cliuelandgate on one side and the lands of South Kiluyngton and Tresk on the other, to hold to him and his heirs quit of the latter and his heirs for ever, so that it should be lawful for the former and his heirs to fell the said wood and coppices and remove timber at will, saving corn and meadows, and inclose them for purposes of cutting when the wood should be ten years old. In return the former quitclaimed to the latter all action of waste and trespass made by him and his men in the manor and wood. Mutual seals.[3] Sandhall. (*Duke of Norfolk*, Misc., II, ii, No. 19).

Wakefield.

423. March 31, 15 Elizabeth [1573]. Grant by John Batte of Birstall, gent., to Anne Batte, widow, late wife of Henry Batte of Haghe, co. York, deceased, his father,[4] of a yearly rent of 53s. 4d. from a messuage or burgage with appurtenances in Wakefeld, called Cliff, then in the tenure of John Broke and his assigns, and from two messuages or tenements and two crofts adjacent with appurtenances in Drighlyngton, then in the tenures of Christopher Halidaye and John Tynker; to hold for life, payable

---

[1] Seal : red wax; signet; letter [?] P.
[2] In French.
[3] Seal to this part of the indenture : black wax, oval, ⅞ × ⅝ in.; a shield of arms, a cross; ornamental border in place of legend. As this is not the Scrope arms the seal was probably Upsale's
[4] These facts confirm and add to the account of the Batte family of Oakwell given in *Dugdale's Visitation*, ed. J. W. Clay, vol. 1, p. 353.

at Whitsuntide and Martinmas in equal portions; with power to distrain if more than twenty days in arrear. He had placed her in seisin of the rent by the payment of 4*d*. of silver. (*sd*.) per me Johannem Batte.[1]

Dorso : sealed and delivered in the presence of Robert Popeley, Richard Wentworthe, John Popeley, John Dighton, gents., William Grene, John Kitson, William Grayve, with also the delivery of the said 4*d*. (*Lord Allendale*, Wakefield, No. 2).[2]

Wales.

424.   Grant by Richard son of Robert Bouet of Anstan to John Bouet, clerk, his heirs or assigns, of two and a half acres of land and an acre of meadow with appurtenances in the vill and territory of Walys by Hertehull, lying in length and breadth between two bounds by the land of Thomas the reeve of Walys on the east and abutting at the south end on the stream of Hertehull; to hold with all easements of the chief lord of the fee by the service due for all secular services. Witnesses, Hugh de Keuton, John de Keuton, Eustace de Walyswode, William de Tatewyk, William Bouet, Alexander son of William, Robert son of William, Nicholas de Keuton, Simon Litonell.[3]   (*Duke of Norfolk*, Misc., II, i, No. 4).

Wath=upon=Dearne.

425.   Grant by Robert son of Peter the clerk of Wath to Robert son of John de Scelmarthorp, his heirs or assigns, of a rood of land lying in the east field of Wath in length and breadth between the land of Peter the clerk and that of Richard Rudde,[4] and abutting on the road leading towards Swinton and extending towards [?] Theuest'uyc; to hold of the chief lord of the fee, doing the service due. Witnesses, Adam de Brerethwysil, Roger Per, John de le Brom, William Alered, Robert le [?]Carter, clerk. (*Duke of Norfolk*, Misc., II, i, No. 3).

426.   All Saints [Nov. 1], 1323. Quitclaim by Sybil, formerly wife of William Witric, of all right in the land and tenement which she claimed to exact from Robert Gene of Wath in the name of her dower in the said vill of Wath or without. Witnesses, Ralph Bacun, John de Scyris, John Gilberd, John de Brom, John the smith, Roger [?]his] son.[5]   Wath. (*Ibid*., II, ii, No. 15).

[1] Seal : red wax, round, ⅝ in.; an interlaced design.
[2] No. 1 of this series was printed in vol. vi.
[3] Seal : brown wax, round, 11/16 in.; a bird over a nest; legend not deciphered
[4] The word *quondam* follows.   [5] *Rogero filio*, simply.

427. Sunday after St. Gordian and St. Epimachus, 28 Edward III [May 11, 1354]. Release and quitclaim by John de Letwell, tailor, dwelling in Blida, to Hugh son of Roger the cook and Alice daughter of Reiner Yongsmith, his wife, and the heirs of their bodies, of all right in all the tenements, lands and meadows in the vill, field and meadows of Wath which he had of the feoffment of Alice daughter of Reiner Yongsmith of Wath; with reversion, in default of issue, to the heirs of Alice. Wath. (*Ibid.*, II, iii, No. 7).

Wentworth.

428. Eve of St. Laurence the Martyr, 16 Henry VI [Aug. 9, 1438]. Grant by Alice Moslyngdene of Warmesworth, daughter and heir of John Toppynge of Wyntworth, in her widowhood, to Thomas Wodhall of Wyntworth, his heirs and assigns, of all her lands and tenements, rents, services, wood and meadow with all appurtenances, which had descended to her by hereditary right after the death of John Toppynge of Wyntworth, her father, in the vill and territory of Wyntworth. Witnesses, Thomas Wentworth, William Stede, Robert Lee, William Silcok, Robert Anabull. Wermesworth.[1] (*Duke of Norfolk*, Misc., II, iv, No. 6).

Wheatley (Doncaster).

429. St. Benedict the Abbot [March 21], 1294[-5]. Grant by Richard son and heir of Thomas Fraunfre of Donecastre to Robert son of Henry Stirton' of the same, his heirs or assigns, for a sum of money given beforehand, of an acre and a half of land lying in the field of Waytelay called Neuton, namely, between the land formerly belonging to Robert de Lomby on one side and that formerly belonging to William Wride on the other, of which one end abutted on the moor of Waytelay and the other on the highroad; rendering yearly to the chief lord of the fee 4*d.* at the four terms of the year customary in Donecastre, and to the grantor and his heirs a grain of pepper at Christmas for all secular service. Witnesses, John son of Ellen, William Turtays, William de Chilterne, Reginald de Messingham, Nigel de Mar, Ellis le Tauerner, Richard Pluket, clerk.[2] (*Y.A.S.*, DD 20).

Whitby.

430. St. Peter ad vincula [Aug. 1], 1410. Quitclaim by John Suthwyk and Alice his wife to Roger Peche, his heirs and assigns, of all right in a messuage lying in Whiteby in the street

[1] Seal : red wax; signet; a standing female or ecclesiastical figure.
[2] Seal: green wax, round, $\frac{13}{16}$ in.; a star; * S' R[ICARD]I . FRAVNFER.

(*vico*) called Grapt[?]mitlane.[1] Witnesses, William del Hall, William Kilwardby, William Hersand, Ralph Gouere, Thomas Hersand. Whiteby.[2] (*Duke of Norfolk*, Misc., II, iv, No. 2).

Wborlton.

431. Grant by Geoffrey Leuedyman to Sir Nicholas de Meynill and his heirs, of two and a half acres of land in the field of Weruelton towards the south, namely, towards Herehow and Snythum in three cultures called Langelandes, Scalestedis and Depedalle, and one and a half acres and half a rood of land in the field of Weruelton towards the north, namely, in the park; in exchange for two and a half acres of land in the field of Weruelton towards the south, namely, towards Snythum and Herehou in five cultures called Hexildsamflat, Thomasflat, Petrusflat Valays, Roberdbosseflat, and Rayschayth, and for one and a half acres and half a rood of land in the field of Weruelton towards the south, namely, towards Moregate in a culture called Bosseflat; with all easements within the vill and without. Mutual seals to either part of the indenture. Witnesses, John de Meynill, Robert de Meynill of Hilton, John de Meynill of Rungeton, Thomas de Semer, Roger Sturmy of Faiceby, Robert de Pothow, John de Gowton. (*Duke of Norfolk*, Misc., II, i, No. 15).

432. July 8, 8 Henry VII [1493]. Grant, indented, by James Strangwais, knt., Thomas Darell, James Strangwais of Sneton, Richard Aclom and Thomas Seurtes, esqs., Robert Marshall, *gentil*[*man*], Henry Traham, chaplain, and William Hille, *yoman*, to Richard Strangwais, second son of the said James, and his assigns, of a yearly rent of 10*li.* from the manor of Whorlton and from all lands and tenements in Whorlton, in equal portions at Whitsuntide and Martinmas, until he should be promoted to an ecclesiastical benefice, office or lands of the value of 20 marks yearly; to hold for Richard's life in fee simple or fee tail; with power to distrain; the grantors to be exempt from personal liability.[3] (*Ibid.*, II, iv, No. 18).

Wombwell.

433. Assumption of B.V.M. [Aug. 15], 1444. Grant by Henry Hall of Smythlay and Helen his wife to John Taylbott, knt., Thomas Haryngton, knt., John Wombewell, esq., John

---

[1] Four minims before the second 't.' There is a Grape lane in Whitby; the name occurs in 1426 (Atkinson, *Memorials of Old Whitby*, p. 188) and in the 16th cent. (*Whitby Chartulary*, ii, pp. 721, 723).

[2] Two seals on one tag: brown wax; signets; one has a shield, but not apparently armorial.

[3] Slits for eight tags; five with seals remain; all red wax, small; (1) a six-petalled flower; (3) letter I; none armorial.

Bosvile, rector of a moiety of the church of Derfeld, Nicholas Lyghtorese and John Hall, their heirs and assigns, of all their lands and tenements, rents and services with appurtenances in Smythlay[1] in Wombewell; and of all their goods and chattels, movable and immovable, wherever found. Witnesses, Thomas Wombewell, esq., John Roklay, esq., John Munke, John Taylzoure, Robert Wyscardrode. Smythlay in Wombewell. (*Sir Thomas Pilkington*).

434. Jan. 26, 16 Henry [VII] [1500-1]. Letters patent,[2] appointing Humphrey Conyngesby and James Hobart as justices with their associates to take an assize of novel disseisin which Robert Walmersley, clerk, and James Croft, clerk, had brought by writ against Alexander Drax, esq., and others concerning tenements in Wombewell and Broddesworth. Westminster.[3] (*Bradford Public Libraries*, Misc. MSS.).

Woolley.

435. Grant by William son of Adam son of John de Mora to Thomas son of John the [?]mason (*?cimentar'*) of Wlweley, his heirs or assigns, of an assart called Robbe rode as it lay in length and breadth in the territory of Wlweley Morhuses on the west of the croft of Henry de Mora; with all easements within the vill of Wlweley and without; to hold of the chief lords of the fee. Witnesses, Henry de Biry, John de Steynton, Adam de Biry, Robert de Ponte fracto, Richard de Mora, John son of Robert, John de Haukedone, clerk.[4] (*Lord Allendale*, Woolley, No. 1).[5]

436. Grant by Thomas de Mar of Wluelay to Thomas Abot of the same, his heirs or assigns, of half an acre of land with appurtenances in the field of Wluelay, lying by Bernardflat, four selions of land lying in different places on the field of the said vill called Oldfeld, and four selions of land lying on *le Hawe*; to

[1] Smithley, a hamlet in Wombewell.
[2] The names of the justices and their activities in Yorkshire at this time make the date certain; see *Cal. Pat. Rolls*, 1494-1509, particularly pp. 246-7, although these letters patent are not enrolled. Moreover Alexander Drax was dead by 19 March 1501-2 (*ibid.*, p. 271); see the pedigree of that family in *South Yorkshire*, ii, 108, where the date of his death is given as 10 Aug. 1501. The king cannot therefore be Henry VIII.
[3] Fragment of seal of white wax on a tongue of the parchment.
[4] Seal : yellow wax, pointed oval, 1¼ × ⅞ in.; a conventional device; + S' WILL[E]L[M]I FIL ADE.
[5] For Woolley Moorhouse, to which these deeds mainly relate, see Mr. J. W. Walker's paper on Woolley in *Y.A.J.*, xxvii, pp. 249 *et seq.*, where there is a pedigree of the Stainton family, showing the descent to Elizabeth dau. and heir of Laurence Stainton of Woolley Moorhouse, who married Thomas Popeley in 1489. *Cf.* also no. 490 in vol. i of this series (date 1393), and no. 530 in vol. ii (date 1350).

hold of the chief lord of the fee. Witnesses, Henry de Biry, John his son, William son of John de Wluelay, John son of Henry le Marshal, Thomas le Masun.[1] (*Ibid.*, No. 47).

437. Grant by Thomas de Marisco to William de Steinton and his heirs or assigns of 2s. yearly rent from the tenement which Thomas Sand held; to hold of the chief lords of the fee. Witnesses, John de Steynton', Godfrey his brother, William de Notton', Robert de Mora, John the clerk.[2] (*Ibid.*, No. 49).

438. Grant for life by Alice formerly wife of John de Hoppewod, in her widowhood, to Henry son of Henry Achard of Wluelay of all that plot of arable land lying together in the vill and territory of Wluelay in a place called *le Brek*, with all easements; with remainder to Robert the grantor's son. Witnesses, Thomas de Staynton, Robert his brother, William son of John, Henry son of Anabel, Adam Ward.[3] (*Ibid.*, No. 3).

439. Grant by Adam Ward son of John the smith to Thomas de Staynton, his heirs or assigns, of two acres of land with appurtenances in Wuluelay lying in different places, of which one and a half roods lay on *le Hou* between the land of Margaret de Staynton on the south and that of Thomas Abbot on the north, half a rood lay between the land of William de Notton on the south and that of Thomas Abbot on the north, two selions in Oldfeld between the land of William de Notton on the south and that of Thomas Abbot on the north, one selion in the same field between the land of Thomas Abbot on the south and that of Margaret de Staynton on the north, one rood towards Wyndhil between the land of John son of Richard de Mora on the south and that of Henry Achard on the north, and one rood on *Aycolt heued* between the land of the said Thomas de Staynton on the south and that of John de Schepelay on the north; to hold of the chief lords of the fee. Witnesses, Robert de Staynton, William de Notton, Robert de Pontefr[acto], William son of John, Thomas Abbot.[4] (*Ibid.*, No. 2).

440. Sunday after the Assumption of the B.M., 21 Edward [I] [Aug. 16, 1293]. Grant by Adam le Ward of Wolflay and Margaret his wife to John son of Thomas de Staynton and his heirs of a garden inclosed, abutting on the garden of John son of Thomas de Wolflay towards the north and the garden of John de Crigeleston towards the west, with complete entry as far as the highroad towards the west; which garden and entry the said John de Crigeleston had held in the previous year; with all appurtenances in the

[1] Seal : white wax, broken and rubbed.
[2] Endorsed in a medieval hand : Wolfuelay.
[3] Seal : white wax, pointed oval, broken and blurred.
[4] Seal : white wax, small; something within two interlaced squares.

vill of Wolflay; to hold of the chief lords of the fee by a rose yearly at the Nativity of St. John the Baptist for all secular services. Witnesses, William de Notton, John de Dronsfeld, John son of Thomas de Wolflay, John de Wetelay, William de Keueresford. Wolflay.[1] (*Ibid.*, No. 50).

441. St. Gregory the Pope [March 12], 1325[-6]. Grant by Thomas son of William de Wlfwelaymorehous' to Hawise of Coldehindelay of his messuage with buildings, and all his land with meadows and appurtenances, lying in the vill of Wlfwelay at Morehous'; to hold for life with reversion to the grantor or his heirs. Witnesses, Thomas de Staynton, Robert his brother, Robert de Pontefracto, William son of John, Henry de Morehous'. Wlfwelay.[2] (*Ibid.*, No. 22).

442. Sunday before St. Margaret the Virgin [July 15], 1330. Grant by Robert de Pontefracto of Wollaymorehouse and Agnes Lemyng his wife to Adam Sprigonel and Margaret his wife and their heirs, of all their lands and tenements, with meadows and feedings adjacent and appurtenances, within the bounds of Wollay, lying in separate lots outside the separate inclosure of the grantees; which inclosure the grantees had of the grant of the said Robert; to hold for the term of the grantors' lives, with reversion to Robert's right heirs. Witnesses, Thomas de Staynton, Henry de Birthwayt, Richard de la more, Henry son of Amabel, Roger Alcok. Wollaymorehouse.[3] (*Ibid.*, No. 23).

443. SS. Philip and James [May 1], 1331. Grant by Henry son of Anabel de Woluelaymorhouses to John son of Adam son of Maud, the carpenter of Woluelay, his heirs and assigns, of a plot (*placeam*) of arable land and meadow lying in length and breadth in *le Morfeld* between the land of John son of Richard del More on one side and that of John le Wryth on the other, and abutting on the land of Roger del More at one end and that of Thomas son of William at the other; with all easements. Witnesses, Thomas de Staynton, William son of John, Roger del More, Richard son of Robert, John son of Thomas. Woluelay.[4] (*Ibid.*, No. 51).

444. Michaelmas [Sept. 29], 1333, 7 Edward III. Grant by John son of Richard de Mora to Juliana widow of Roger de Woluelaymorhous', her heirs and assigns, of half an acre of land with appurtenances, lying in the croft formerly belonging to Henry de

[1] Two seals, yellow-brown wax : (1) round, ⅝ in.; a squirrel; * I CRAKE NOTIS ; (2) oval, 1 × ¾ in.; apparently a conventional representation of St John the Baptist, holding an Agnus Dei plaque; * ECCE ANGNVS DEI.
[2] Seal : yellow wax, pointed oval, *c.* 1¼ × ¾ in.; possibly a hawk preying over a nest ; blurred.
[3] Seal : broken and blurred.
[4] Seal . yellow wax, round, ⅝ in.; a quatrefoil; . . . . . LEL AMI.

Mora in Woluelay, in exchange for half a selion of land lying on the north side of the vill of Woluelay. Witnesses, Thomas de Staynton, Adam Sprigonell, William son of John de Wolueley, John son of Thomas of the same, Henry son of Anabel of the same. Woluelay.[1] (*Ibid.*, No. 52).

445. Friday after Michaelmas, 11 Edward III [Oct. 3, 1337]. Grant by Henry son of Anabel de Wolueley to Robert son of John the carpenter of the same, and Agnes the grantor's daughter and the heirs of their bodies, of a messuage with appurtenances in Wolueley, lying in length and breadth between the messuage of the said John on one side and a plot of land called Malincroft on the other; to hold by the services of $\frac{1}{2}d$. yearly at Christmas; with reversion to the grantor and his heirs. Witnesses, Thomas de Staynton, William de Notton, John de Pull, Robert Munk of Chevet, Richard de Bretton. Wolueley.[2] (*Ibid.*, No. 37).

446. Sunday before Palm Sunday [April 2], 1340. Quitclaim by Alice daughter of Robert de Pontefracto of Wouelay-moreouse, in her virginity, to Adam Sprigonel and Margaret his wife, of all right in all the lands and tenements, meadows, woods, pastures or other appurtenances, which Adam and Margaret then had within the bounds of Wouelay of the gift of Robert, Alice's father, and of the grant of the said Robert and Agnes de Lemyng. Witnesses, Thomas de Staynton, Adam del More, Richard son of Robert of the same, John son of Thomas of the same, Henry son of Anabel, John de Whetelay, Robert Whiteheued. At the church of Wouelay.[3] (*Ibid.*, No. 34).

447. Sunday after St. Dunstan the Bishop [May 20], 1341. Quitclaim by Richard son of Robert Hubbe of Wluelaymorehuse to John his uncle of the same and Robert his (John's) son, and Robert's heirs and assigns, of all right in a toft containing an acre of land and four and a half acres of land with appurtenances in the territory of Wollaymorhouse. Witnesses, Robert de Staynton, John de Whetelay, Adam del More, Adam Sprigonell, William son of Richard del More. Wollay.[4] (*Ibid.*, No. 36).

448. Monday, St. Martin the Bishop [Nov. 11], 1342. Grant by Henry son of Anabel de Woluelay Morehouse to Robert son of John the carpenter del Morehouses and Agnes his wife and the heirs of their bodies, of eight acres and half a rood of land with appurtenances in Morehouses, of which two and a half acres and

[1] Seal : yellow-brown wax, round, $\frac{5}{8}$ in.; an animal; indistinct.
[2] Seal : yellow wax, round, $\frac{3}{4}$ in., blurred and broken.
[3] Seal : yellow wax, round, $\frac{5}{8}$ in.; a bird, * IE SV VNVTEL.
[4] Seal : yellow-brown wax, round, $\frac{3}{4}$ in.; a round object with two legs; legend not deciphered.

half a rood with the meadow adjacent lay between the land of Thomas de Mora on the south and the common pasture on the north and abutted at one end on the common lane of Morehouses towards the east and at the other end on the moor towards the west, lying in a place called Faldeworthyng; three roods lay together in Faldeworthyng between the land of Thomas de Mora on the south and that of John de Mora on the north, abutting at one end on the common lane of Morehouses towards the east and at the other end on the moor towards the west; two acres with a messuage lay together in a place called Kylneflat in Faldeworthyng, abutting at either end as before and lying between the land of Thomas de Mora on the south and that of John de Mora on the north; half an acre lay on Faldeworthyng between the land of John de Mora and that of Adam [de] Mora by Birkynwell, abutting at one end on the stile (*scalam*) of the said lane and at the other end on the moor towards the west; three roods lay together on Stonyrodes between the land of John de Mora on the north and that of Adam [de] Mora on the south, abutting at one end on Sissecroft towards the east and at the other on *les Bentes*; three roods lay together on Stonyrodes between the land of Adam Ward on the north and that formerly belonging to Henry de Mora on the south, abutting at one end on the lands of John the carpenter and Thomas son of William de Mora on Hallestedes and at the other on *les Bentes*; and three roods lay together on Stonyrodes between the land formerly belonging to Henry de Mora on the north and that of John the carpenter on the south, abutting at one end on Hallestedes towards the east and at the other on *les Bentes* towards the west; with reversion to the said Robert, his heirs and assigns. Witnesses, Thomas de Staynton, Robert his son, John de Whetelay, Adam de Mora, Adam Sprigonell. Woluelay.[1] (*Ibid.*, No. 4).

449.   Sunday after St. Matthew the Apostle, 17 Edward III [Sept. 28, 1343]. Grant by John Abot of Wolflay and Margaret his wife to John Helwis of Westbretton and his heirs, of a toft and croft with adjacent land, containing altogether half an acre as it lay abutting on the land of the church on the south side, and on the north on the highroad, together with the house built thereon and appurtenances in Wolflay; which premises William Pulhore had formerly held of the grantor's father Thomas Abott; rendering yearly 1*d.* at the Nativity of St. John the Baptist. Witnesses, Adam del More, John son of Thomas de Wolflay, John de Wetelay of the same, Robert del Hill of the same, John son of Adam of the same. Wolflay.[2] (*Ibid.*, No. 5).

450.   Sunday after the Conversion of St. Paul, 18 Edward

---

[1] Seal : white wax, heater shaped; blurred.
[2] Two seals : white wax; one bears a bird and the other a fleur-de-lis.

III [Feb. 1, 1343-4]. Grant by Robert son of Alice Achard to John de Staynton and his heirs of a yearly rent of 40*d.* sterling at the Nativity of St. John the Baptist from a plot (*placea*) of land within the bounds of Wolflay called *le Brek*, until Robert should pay John 13*s.* 4*d.* of silver; with power to John to distrain on the plot called *le Brek* if the rent should be in arrear. Witnesses, William de Notton, Adam del More, John son of Thomas, John de Whetelay of Wolflay, Robert de Cotheworth. Wolflay.[1] (*Ibid.*, No. 53).

451. Wednesday, St. Giles the Abbot, 18 Edward III [Sept. 1, 1344]. Grant by Henry son of Anabel de Wollaymorehouses to Agnes his daughter, her heirs and assigns, of an acre of arable land lying within the bounds of Wollay Mourehousis called *le Engeaccre*. Witnesses, Robert de Staynton, John de Whetelay, John son of Thomas de Wollay, Adam son of Thomas de Wollay, William son of Richard del More. Wollay.[2] (*Ibid.*, No. 7).

452. Sunday after St. Edmund the King [Nov. 21], 1344. Grant by Henry son of Anabel de Woulfelaymorhouses to Agnes his daughter and her heirs or assigns, of an acre and a rood of land in the fields of Woulfelaymorhouses, of which three roods lay together between the land formerly belonging to Adam son of Thomas de Staynton on the north and the land of Thomas son of William del More on the south, and half an acre lay in a place called Stonerodes between the land of Thomas son of William on the south and the land of Adam Warde on the north. Witnesses, Thomas de Staynton, John de Whetelay, Adam son of Thomas de Staynton. Woulfelaymorhouses.[3] (*Ibid.*, No. 6).

453. Sunday after St. Tiburtius and St. Valerian, 19 Edward III [April 17, 1345]. Grant by Robert son of Alice Hopwod to John son of Thomas de Staynton and his heirs, of a plot of land called *le Brek* in the territory of Wollay. Witnesses, William de Notton, John de Whetelay, Adam son of Thomas de Staynton de Mora, John son of Thomas de Wollay, Adam le Ward of the same. Wollay.[4] (*Ibid.*, No. 39).

454. Monday after St. John of Beverley, 19 Edward III [May 9, 1345]. Grant by Adam son of Thomas de Staynton and Juliana his wife to John son of Thomas de Wolflay, his heirs or assigns, of an acre of land lying in the field of Wolflay by *le Faregat* on the north, abutting on *le Clyf* on the west, which they had of the feoffment of Adam de Byrthwayt; in exchange for a plot of

[1] Seal · brown wax, round, ⅝ in.; a squirrel; * I CRAKE NOTIS.
[2] Seal . brown wax, round, ⅝ in.; a bird, legend not deciphered.
[3] Seal · dark brown wax, small and blurred.
[4] Seal . same as to No. 447 above.

land called Dobrod with 20s. sterling which he (the grantor) had given John beforehand for the said plot which the grantor and his wife had of John's grant. Witnesses, Thomas de Staynton, William de Notton, Robert de Staynton, John de Whetelay, Robert del Hill. Wolflay.[1] (Ibid., No. 38).

455. Thursday after St. William of York, Archbishop, 19 Edward III [June 9, 1345]. Grant[2] by John Abot of Wolflay and Margaret his wife to John son of Thomas de Staynton and his heirs, of all his land in Holdfeld except Dobrod, namely, beginning on the north side of Holdfeld one selion lying between the land of Scheplayoxgang on the north and that of Sir John Darcy on the south, another selion between the land of Scheplayoxgang on the north and that of John son of Thomas de Wolflay on the south, a third selion between the land of Thomas de Staynton on either side, a fourth between the land of Scheplayoxgang on the north and that of Thomas de Staynton on the south, a fifth between the land of Thomas de Staynton on the north, and on the south one selion lay between the said selion and the land of the church, and a sixth selion between the land of Scheplayoxgang on the north and that of Thomas de Staynton on the south; these six selions lay for[3] two acres of land and abutted towards the east on le Hawe; also five selions in Holdfeld lying together for one and a half acres between the land of Thomas de Staynton on the north and that of Sir John Darcy on the south; together with appurtenances within the bounds of Wolflay; rendering yearly to the chief lords of the fee a rose at the Nativity of St. John the Baptist for all secular services. Witnesses, William de Notton, John de Dronsfeld, John de Whetelay of Wolflay, John son of Thomas of the same, William son of John of the same. Wolflay.[4] (Ibid., No. 8).

456. Sunday, St. Gregory the Pope, 20 Edward III [March 12, 1345-6]. Grant by John Hobbe, carpenter, de Mora, to John son of Thomas de Staynton, his heirs or assigns, of the messuage with buildings, and all his lands and tenements with appurtenances which William Hobbe his father formerly held of the feoffment of Margaret de Staynton in her widowhood in the field of Wolflay-morehouse. Witnesses, William de Notton, John de Dronsfeld, Henry Lascy, Adam son of Thomas de Staynton, John de Whetelay of Wolflay, John son of Thomas of the same. Wolflay.[5] (Ibid., No. 9).

[1] Two seals, brown wax : (1) a bird; . . . IESV; (2) same as to No. 447 above.
[2] Also, same day, a grant by the same to the same of the same land, but without the specifications as to boundaries; the land abutted towards the east on le Haw; same seals. (Ibid., No. 8A)
[3] Meaning 'were computed at.'
[4] Two seals : brown-yellow wax, round, ⅝ in ; (1) a fleur-de-lis; (2) same as to No. 447 above.
[5] Seal : brown wax, small; blurred.

457. Sunday after St. Wilfrid, Archbishop of York, 20 Edward III [Oct. 8, 1346]. Grant by John de Mora to the same, of all his lands and tenements called Mokocland within the bounds of Wolflay. Witnesses, William de Notton, John de Turribus, John de Dronfeld, John son of Thomas de Wolflay, John de Wetelay. Wolflay.[1] (*Ibid.*, No. 40).

458. Friday after St. Luke the Evangelist, 20 Edward III [Oct. 20, 1346]. Grant by John the carpenter de Mora to the same, of all his lands and tenements in Wolflaymorhouses which he had of the grant and feoffment of Adam Achard of Grimesthorpp. Witnesses, William de Notton, John Toures, John de Dronsfeld, John de Wetelay, John son of Thomas de Wolflay. Wolflay. (*Ibid.*, No. 41).

459. Friday after All Saints, 20 Edward III [Nov. 3, 1346]. Grant by John de Mora to the same, of a piece of land called Symcroft with appurtenances in Wolflaymorhouses, abutting at one end towards the east on the croft of Adam Sprigonell. Witnesses, William de Notton, John de Turribus, John de Dronsfeld, John de Wetelay of Wolflay, John son of Thomas of the same. Wolflay.[2] (*Ibid.*, No. 24).

460. Sunday after Martinmas, 20 Edward III [Nov. 12, 1346]. Grant by Agnes widow of Robert the carpenter de Mora to the same, of a toft with adjacent croft and appurtenances in Wolflaymorhouses, lying between the messuage of the said John (the grantee) on one side and a plot of land called Thorncroft on the other. Witnesses, William de Notton, John de Turribus, John de Dronfeld, John de Wetelay of Wolflay, John son of Thomas of the same. Wolflaymorhouse.[3] (*Ibid.*, No. 42).

461. Conversion of St. Paul, 21 Edward III [Jan. 25, 1346-7].[4] Grant and quitclaim by Agnes widow of Robert the carpenter de Mora, and Elizabeth her sister, and John son of Robert Jouet of Westbretton and Alice his wife to John de Staynton, his heirs and assigns, of all the lands and tenements which John had of the grant of Henry Anabell within the bounds of Wolflaymorhouses; with appurtenances. Witnesses, William de Notton, John de Turribus, John de Dronsfeld, John de Wettelay, John son of Thomas de Wolflay. Wolflay.[5] (*Ibid.*, No. 54).

[1] Seal : brown wax, small, an animal.
[2] Seal : brown wax, round, ⅝ in.; a squirrel; * I CRAKE NOTIS.
[3] Seal . yellow-brown wax, small, a knot; PRIVE SV.
[4] *Cf.* No. 467 below.
[5] The same four seals as to No. 467, though arranged in a different order.

462.   Thursday before St. George the Martyr [April 19], 1347.   Whereas[1] John de Birthwayt and Diota his wife had granted to Adam de Birthwayt, his heirs and assigns, a plot of land with appurtenances in the field *del More* in the vill and territory of Wlfley called Cristcroft, Adam granted that if he held the plot longer than twelve years he and his heirs would render yearly to John and Diota and their heirs 12*d*., half at Martinmas and half at Whitsuntide.   Witnesses, William de Ketilbarthorp, Robert de Cotheworth, Thomas de Heton, Robert Addy of Kesseburgh, Robert son of Peter of the same. Bergh.[2] (*Ibid.*, No. 31).

463.   Sunday after the Ascension, 21 Edward III [May 13, 1347].   Grant by John de Mora, carpenter, to John son of Thomas de Staynton, his heirs and assigns, of all his lands and tenements within the bounds of Wolflay and Wolflaymorhouses. Witnesses, William de Notton, John de Turribus, John de Drons-feld, John de Wetelay of Wolflay, William de Keuersford. Wolflay-morhouses.[3] (*Ibid.*, No. 11).

464.   Sunday after St. Laurence, 21 Edward III [Aug. 12, 1347].   Grant by John Abot of Wolflay and Margaret his wife to John son of Thomas de Staynton, his heirs and assigns, of half an acre of land with appurtenances in the vill of Wolflay,[4] abutting at one end on the east side of Schepelayhenge. Witnesses, John de Dronsfeld, John son of Thomas de Wolflay, John de Wettelay, William de Keueresford, Robert del Hill. Wolflay.[5] (*Ibid.*, No. 12).

465.   Martinmas, 21 Edward III [Nov. 11, 1347].   Grant[6] by John de Mora to John de Staynton, his heirs and assigns, of a messuage with appurtenances in Wolflaymorhouses, lying by the messuage of Adam de Mora on the east, in exchange for an acre of land in the vill of Wolflay, namely, half an acre lying in *le Schorthefolrawes* which the grantee had of the gift of William son of Richard son of Christiana de Wolflay, and the other half acre abutting on Schepelayheng which the grantee had of the gift of John Abot.   Witnesses, William de Notton, John de Turribus, John de Dronsfeld, Thomas le Bosevill, Thomas de Dodworth. Wolflay.[7] (*Ibid.*, No. 43).

[1] Indenture.

[2] Seal : yellow-brown wax, oval; blurred.

[3] Seal : yellow-brown wax, oval, 1 × ⅞ in.; a shield of arms within a geometrical border; blurred.

[4] Also spelt Wollay.

[5] Two tags; one has a broken seal of yellow wax; a small animal, probably a squirrel.

[6] Indented.

[7] Seal : brown wax, small, an animal.

466.   St. Thomas the Apostle, 21 Edward III [Dec. 21, 1347]. Grant[1] by Adam de Mora and Juliana his wife to John de Staynton, his heirs and assigns, of a garden with appurtenances in Wolflay-morhouses, lying by *le Walkeryerd* on the north as far as the new ditch, in exchange for a garden which the grantee had of the gift of John de Mora, lying by the grantors' messuage on the east, in Wollaymorhouses.   Witnesses, William de Notton, John de Turribus, John de Dronsfeld, John de Wetelay, John son of Thomas de Wolflay.   Wolflay.[2]   (*Ibid.*, No. 44).

467.   St. Hilary, 21 Edward III [Jan. 13, 1347-8].   Grant and quitclaim by Agnes, widow of Robert the carpenter de Mora, Elizabeth daughter of Henry Amabel de Mora, and John son of Robert Jouet of Westbretton and Alice his (John's) wife, to John de Staynton, his heirs and assigns, of all the lands and tenements which the latter had of the grant of Henry Amabel in Wolflay-morhouses and which the said Henry had held of the said John de Staynton.   Witnesses, William de Keuerisford, Thomas de Dod-worth, John de Wettelay, Adam de Mora, John son of Thomas de Wolflay, Edmund de Wettelay.   Wolflay.[3]   (*Ibid.*, No. 10).

468.   Sunday after the Annunciation of the B.M. [March 30], 1348, 22 Edward III.   Grant by Adam Warde of Wolfylei and Margaret his wife to Adam son of Thomas de Staynton, his heirs or assigns, of two acres of arable land lying separately (*par-ticulariter*) in the fields of Wolfiley, of which one acre lay in the west field of the vill of Wolfyley between the land of John son of Thomas on the north side and that which Agnes daughter of William de Notton was holding of the gift of Sir John de Arci on the south, abutting at the east end on *le hadeland* of Smethefeld and at the west end on Wolfyleyclyf; half an acre lay in the same *furlang* between the land which John son of Thomas was holding on the north and that of John del Morre on the south, abutting at the east end on *le hadeland* of Smethefeld and at the west end on Wolfyleyclyf; and half an acre lay in the same *furlang* between the land which William de Notton was holding on the south and that of John son of Thomas on the north; with all appurtenances and easements.   Witnesses, John de Staynton, Thomas his brother, John de Byry, John son of Thomas, Robert del Hull of Wolfiley. Wolfyley.[4]   (*Ibid.*, No. 55).

[1] Indented.

[2] Two seals : (1) same as the second seal to No. 440 above, (2) small, an animal.

[3] Four seals, brown wax : (1) round, $\frac{5}{8}$ in.; a bull's head cabossed; * [?] PRIVE SV; (ii) oval, 1 × $\frac{3}{4}$ in.; a shield of arms within a geometrical border, bearing three stars or crosses within a bordure; legend, a motto, not deciphered; (iii) same as to No 440 above; (iv) round, $\frac{5}{8}$ in.; a squirrel; * I CRAKE NOTIS.

[4] Two seals, yellow-brown wax: (1) oval, blurred; (2) round, $\frac{3}{4}$ in.; the Lamb and flag; legend not deciphered.

469.   May 3, 22 Edward III [1348]. Grant by Henry Amable of Wolflaymorhouses to John son of Thomas de Staynton, his heirs and assigns, of all his lands and tenements with appurtenances within the bounds of Wolflaymorhouses, together with the reversion of all the tenements which Adam de Mora was holding of his demise within the said bounds.   Witnesses, William de Notton, John de Turribus. John de Dronsfeld, John de Bretton, John son of Thomas de Wolflay.   Wolflay.[1]   (*Ibid.*, No. 45).

470.   St. Luke the Evangelist, 22 Edward III [Oct. 18, 1348].   Grant by Thomas de Staynton to John de Staynton, his son, his heirs and assigns, of all the land called Malsard with the adjacent meadow with appurtenances within the bounds of Wolflaymorhouses, rendering yearly to the chief lords of the fee a rose at the Nativity of St. John the Baptist for all secular services. Witnesses, William de Notton, John de Turribus, John de Dronsfeld, John de Wettelay of Wolflay, John son of Thomas of the same.   Wolflay.[2]   (*Ibid.*, No. 13).

471.   St. Thomas the Apostle, 22 Edward III [Dec. 21, 1348].   Grant[3] by John de Whetelay of Woluelay to John son of Thomas de Staynton of the same, his heirs and assigns, of a yearly rent of 8*d*. with the lordships, services and other appurtenances, to be taken at Martinmas from thirty acres of land in Woluelaymorehouses, which Ralph de Wyngerworth had held, and from all Wyppowerod lying between Wyngerwrode and the dike (*foueam*) in Woluelaycliff; of which lands and tenements John Tyrell son of Ralph de Bursecliff had enfeoffed Alexander de Merkschagh, and from which the said John Tyrell had made a yearly payment of 8*d*. at Martinmas to the fee of Biry[4] in Woluelay, and of 4*d*. to the fee of Dighton in the same.   Witnesses, John Tours, John de Dronsfeld, Hugh de Brerelay, Thomas Bosseuile, Thomas de Doddeworth, Walter Page of Kesseburgh.   Woluelay.[5]   (*Ibid.*, No. 56).

472.   The Epiphany, 22 Edward III [Jan. 6, 1348-9]. Release[6] by John de Wettelay of Wolflay to John son of Thomas

---

[1] Seal : brown wax, oval, 1 × ¾ in.; a shield of arms within a geometrical border, bearing three stars or crosses within a bordure; legend, a motto, not deciphered.

[2] Seal : yellow wax, round, ⅞ in.; a conventional tree with two birds in the branches; legend, a motto, not deciphered

[3] Also another deed, precisely the same, except for variations in spelling, *e.g.*, Wetelay, Wlfelay, Wingerwrthe, Wippourode, Tirel, Merschaghe; same seal.   (*Ibid.*, No. 56A)

[4] For the Bury and Deighton fees in Woolley see Mr. Walker's paper in *Y A J.*, xxvii, *loc. cit.*

[5] Seal: red wax, same as to No. 440 above.

[6] Also another release to the same effect, with slightly different wording; same witnesses and seal   (*Ibid.*, No. 57A).

de Staynton of the yearly rent of 8*d.* which Henry de Biry and his ancestors were wont to take from the lands and tenements which Henry Amable and his ancestors had held within the bounds of Wolflaymorhouses. Witnesses, William de Notton, John de Turribus, John de Dro[n]sfeld, John de Gundelthwayt, William de Keuersford. Wolflay.[1] (*Ibid.*, No. 57).

473. 10 Kal. April, 23 Edward III [March 23, 1348-9]. Grant by William son of Adam le Ward of Wolflay to John son of Thomas de Staynton, his heirs and assigns, of all his land in the croft by *le Wetrod* on the north side in Wolflaymorhouses, except the acre of land in the said croft on the north side of *le Wetrod* on which his house was situate and which he was holding of St. Mary; and of all his land in Goderker in Wolflaymorhouses. Witnesses, William de Notton, John de Turribus, John de Dronsfeld, Adam Spregonell, John de Wettelay. Wolflay.[2] (*Ibid.*, No. 58).

474. May 10, 23 Edward III [1349]. Grant and surrender by Adam le Ward of Wolflay to John son of Thomas de Staynton, his heirs and assigns, of all his meadow in Goderker within the bounds of Wolflaymorhouses which he (Adam) had held by courtesy (*per legem Anglie*) of the inheritance of William his son, and of all the lands and tenements which John had at that date within the said bounds of the grant of the said William. Witnesses, William de Notton, John de Turribus, John de Dronsfeld, John de Wettelay of Wolflay, John son of Thomas of the same. Wolflay.[3] (*Ibid.*, No. 59).

475. Sunday before St. Margaret the Virgin [July 19], 1349, 23 Edward III. Grant by John Wright son of Adam Molleson of Wollay to Adam son of Thomas de Staynton dwelling in Wollaymorehouse and Juliana his wife, and the survivor, and Adam's heirs and assigns, of a plot of land and meadow as it lay in length and breadth in a field there called *le Morefeld* between the land of John de Staynton on either side, and abutting on the land of William Waree towards the east and on the meadow of John de Staynton towards the west, for a certain sum of money given beforehand; the grantor had the premises of the grant and feoffment of Henry son of Anabel de Wollaymorehouse. Witnesses, Robert de Staynton, John de Staynton, William de Staynton, John de Wheitlay, John son of Thomas de Wollay, William de Gyldosom, Thomas de Lepton, clerk. Wollaymorehouse.[4] (*Ibid.*, No. 14).

[1] Seal : brown wax, round, ⅝ in., a bull's head cabossed; * [PRIV]E SV.
[2] Seal : brown wax, round, ⅝ in.; a squirrel; [* I CRAKE NOTIS].
[3] Seal : brown wax, pointed oval, 1⅜ × ¾ in ; a bird, ✠ SIGILLVM

. . . . .
[4] Seal : yellow wax, round, ⅜ in.; the Agnus Dei; legend not deciphered.

476. St. Giles the Abbot, 23 Edward III [Sept. 1, 1349]. Quitclaim by John del Haghe to John son of Thomas de Staynton of a yearly rent of 2s. which John had of his demise for life in the vill of Wolflay. Witnesses, William de Notton, John de Turribus, John de Dronsfeld, [? Richard] Addy, John de Bretton. Le Haghe on Dirne by Byrthwayt.[1] (*Ibid.*, No. 60).

477. Saturday after the Decollation of St. John the Baptist, 23 Edward III [Sept. 5, 1349]. Grant by Adam son of Thomas de Staynton and Juliana his wife, to William son of the said Thomas, his heirs or assigns, of all the lands and tenements which they had of the gift and feoffment of Thomas son of William de Woluelaymorehouse and Hawise his wife, with two acres of arable land which they had of the gift and feoffment of Adam del Ward and Margaret his wife, a plot of land and meadow *en le Morefeld* (gift of John son of Adam Molson of Woluelay), a plot of arable land called Dobrode (gift of John son of Thomas de Woluelay), an acre of land lying in Woluelaymorehouse (gift of John del Rodes of Gunnelthwayt Rodes), half an acre of land (gift of Adam Sprigonell and Margaret his wife), a yearly rent of 1d. (gift of Henry son of Anabel de Woluelaymorehouse), and a garden (gift of John de Staynton). Witnesses, Robert de Staynton, John Tourse, John de Dronsefeld, John de Whetelay, John son of Thomas de Woluelay. Woluelay.[2] (*Ibid.*, No. 27).

478. Sunday after St. Giles, 23 Edward III [Sept. 6, 1349]. Grant by Adam son of Thomas de Staynton and Juliana his wife, to the same, of an acre of land with meadow adjacent in *le Morefeld* in the vill of Woluelay called Eyngeaker, which he had of the gift and feoffment of Agnes wife of Robert le Whyryght. Witnesses, William de Notton, Robert de Staynton, John de Tourse, John de Dronsefeld, John de Whetelay. Woluelay.[3] (*Ibid.*, No. 15).

479. Wednesday after Michaelmas, 23 Edward III [Sept. 30, 1349]. Grant by William de Staynton son of Thomas de Staynton to Adam son of the said Thomas, and Juliana his wife, of all the lands and tenements which he had of their grant in the vill of Wolvelay; to hold for their lives, with reversion to the grantor. Witnesses, William de Notton, Robert de Staynton, John Tourse, John de Dronsefeld, John de Whetlay. Woluelay. (*Ibid.*, No. 25).

480. Martinmas, 23 Edward III [Nov. 11, 1349]. Grant by Thomas son of Thomas de Staynton to John his brother, his

---

[1] Seal : brown wax, round, ⅜ in.; a squirrel; * I CRAKE NOTIS.
[2] Two seals : yellow wax; (1) round, ¾ in.; an animal, possibly a hare; (2) round, 1⅛ in.; an animal resembling a stag on a branch; legends blurred.
[3] Two tags; one has a seal of white wax with a floral device, much blurred.

heirs and assigns, of a piece of land and meadow within the bounds of Wolflaymorhouses, called *le Kelnecroft*. Witnesses, William de Notton, John de Turribus, John de Dronsfeld, John de Bretton, John de Wettelay of Wolflay. Wolflay.[1] (*Ibid.*, No. 26).

481. Aug. 21, 24 Edward III [1350]. Quitclaim by Alice, daughter of Adam Sprigonell and Margaret his wife, to John son of Thomas de Staynton of all right in the tenement called *le Kylncroft* within the bounds of Wuluelay Morehouse. Witnesses, William de Notton, John de Tours, William de Mirfeld, Laurence de Dronsfeld, John de Bretton. Wuluelay.[2] (*Ibid.*, No. 33).

482. Monday, St. John of Beverley,[3] 25 Edward III [? May 7, 1351]. Grant by John de Mora of Wollay to Adam son of Thomas de Staynton, his heirs and assigns, of one and a half acres of land lying in Bernardflattes, which he had of the gift of John de Staynton within the bounds of Wolflay, and abutted on the west side on *le Clif*. Witnesses, John Dronsfeld, John de Staynton, Thomas his brother, John de Whetlay, John son of Thomas de Wollay. Wollay.[4] (*Ibid.*, No. 61).

483. Sunday after St. Thomas the Apostle [Dec. 23], 1352. Grant by John de Crygelston of Woluelay to John son of Thomas de Staynton, his heirs or assigns, of all his lands and tenements which he held in Woluelay by curtesy (*per legem Anglie*) after the death of Alice his wife, Witnesses, William de Notton, Robert de Staynton, John de Dronsfeld, John de Gunnylthwayt, Adam del more of Woluelay. Woluelay.[5] (*Ibid.*, No. 28).

484. Sunday after the Epiphany [Jan. 13], 1352[-3]. Grant by John son of Thomas de Woluelay to John son of Thomas de Staynton, his heirs or assigns, of an acre of land lying by *le Fargate* on the north side in the field of Woluelay, and one and a half roods of meadow in the field of Woluelaymorhouses, abutting towards the east on two selions of William Warde. Witnesses, William de Notton, Robert de Staynton, Adam del More, William de Gildoshome, John de Whetelay. Woluelay.[6] (*Ibid.*, No. 16).

[1] Seal : red wax, round, ¾ in.; a hawk preying over a nest; the legend may be * SVM DELICATVS.
[2] Seal : red wax, small, a bird.
[3] The feast of St. John of Beverley, May 7, fell on a Saturday in 25 Edward III (1351); and the feast of his translation, Oct. 25, fell on a Tuesday. Neither of these corresponds. But May 7 fell on a Monday in 1352.
[4] Seal : brown wax, round, ¾ in ; a lion rampant; * SVM LEO FORTIS.
[5] Seal : brown wax, round, ¾ in.; a quatrefoil; legend, a motto, not deciphered.
[6] Seal : brown wax, round, ¾ in.; a lion rampant; * SVM LEO FORTIS.

485.   April 3, 1360. Quitclaim by John son of Robert the carpenter of Woluelaymorhouses to John son of Thomas de Staynton of Woluelay, of all right in all the lands and tenements with appurtenances, which the said John de Staynton had in Woluelaymorhouses of the gift of Agnes, the quitclaimor's mother, of John the carpenter, his ancestor, and of his own or any of his ancestors. Witnesses, Thomas de Bessevile,[1] John de Dronsfeld, John Thours, John de Whetelay, William de Gildoshome. Woluelay morhouses.[2] (*Ibid.*, No. 35).

486.   Wednesday, June 5, 38 Edward III [1364]. Release by Adam de Staynton of Woluelaymorehouses to John de Staynton of Woluelaymorhouses of all personal actions by reason of any trespass. Woluelaymorhouses.[3] (*Ibid.*, No. 62).

487.   Sunday after the Epiphany [Jan. 12], 1364[-5]. Grant by Thomas de Staynton of Woluelay to Adam de Staynton and Juliana his wife of Woluelaymorehouses, for their lives and that of the survivor, of all the lands and tenements with meadows, woods, and appurtenances, which he had of the gift and feoffment of the said Adam within the bounds of Woluelay and Woluelaymorehouses; rendering yearly 5s. at Whitsuntide and Martinmas in equal portions. Witnesses, John de Whetelay, William de Gildoshome, Walter Page, John Walker, Henry del Hagh. Woluelaymorhouses.[4] (*Ibid.*, No. 48).

488.   Wednesday after St. Peter in cathedra [Feb. 26], 1364[-5]. Quitclaim[5] by John de Staynton and Joan his wife to John son of Thomas de Woluelay, of all right which they had in the messuages, lands and tenements in Woluelay by reason of a certain feoffment made to them by the said John son of Thomas, which were then in the latter's hand, namely those which he had in Woluelay by hereditary right after the death of Thomas his father. Witnesses, Sirs Robert de Staynton, Henry de Sotehill, knts., Thomas de Staynton, John de Bretton, John de Whetelay of Woluelay. Woluelay.[6] (*Ibid.*, No. 32).

489.   Friday after St. Katherine the Virgin, 40 Edward III [Nov. 27, 1366]. Grant by John del More of Wollay to John son of Thomas de Steynton, his heirs and assigns, of all his lands and tenements with appurtenances in Wollay, abutting on Wollayclyf

---

[1] Probably an error for Bossevile.
[2] Seal : same as to No. 440 above.
[3] Seal on a tongue of the parchment : brown wax, round, ¾ in.; indistinct, perhaps a hawk preying over a nest.
[4] Seal : yellow wax, round, ¾ in.; an animal; legend indecipherable.
[5] Indenture.
[6] Two seals, yellow wax : (1) round, 9/16 in.; a shield of arms, blurred; (2) round. ¾ in.; a hawk preying over a hare; * ALAS IE SVPRIS.

towards *les Morehous* towards the west, which he lately had of
Sir John Darcy, knt., in exchange for an assart called Alaynrode[1]
in Wollay. Witnesses, Thomas de Steynton, John son of Thomas
de Wollay, John de Whetelay, John de Dronsfeld, John de Bretton.
Wollay.[2] (*Ibid.*, No. 18).

490.   Thursday after the Conception of the B.M. [Dec. 10],
1366. Grant by John son of Richard de Mora of Woluelay to John
son of Thomas de Staynton of Woluelay, his heirs or assigns, of
three arable acres of land lying in the fields of Woluelay in different
places, namely one and a half acres in one parcel (*perticularit'*)
between *le Morecrosse* and Oldefeld, and one and a half acres in
another parcel between *le Morecrosse* and *le Wyndmilnestigh*,
abutting on *le Westecliff* towards *le Morehouses*, which he had
had by hereditary right after the death of his father. Witnesses,
John de Dronsfeld, John Tours, John de Whetelay, John son of
Thomas de Woluelay, William de Gildoshome. Woluelay.[3] (*Ibid.*,
No. 17).

491.   Saturday after St. Peter ad vincula [Aug. 5], 1385.
Grant by John son of Thomas Helwys of Wollay to John son of
Thomas de Staynton, his heirs or assigns, of a toft with croft
adjacent with appurtenances, containing half an acre, in the
same [Wollay], as it lay between the land of the church on the
south side and the high road towards the north on the other,
which had lately belonged to William Pulhore. Witnesses, John
Woderouf, John de Dronfeld, Thomas de Staynton, William de
Doddeworth, Henry del Hagh, Richard de Keresford. Wollay.[4]
(*Ibid.*, No. 19).

492.   Sunday, Michaelmas, 11 Richard II [Sept. 29, 1387].
Grant[5] by John son of Thomas de Staynton, dwelling (*manens*)
in *le Morehous*, to William his son and Elizabeth, the latter's wife,
daughter of John Dronsfeld, and to their heirs lawfully begotten,
of all the messuages, lands and tenements, meadows, woods and
pastures, with appurtenances in the vill of Wollay and in Wollay
Morehous, together with the rents and services of all his tenants
there; to hold by the service of a rose yearly at the Nativity of
St. John the Baptist if demanded, and doing on his behalf the
services due to the lords of the fees; with reversion, in default
of issue, to the grantor and his heirs. Witnesses, Thomas Boseuill

---

[1] A footnote on the fold of the parchment in a contemporary hand,
saying (in Latin) that sometimes they called it Alaynrode, sometimes
Hicdunrode, and now they call it Breryrode.
   [2] Seal : yellow wax, round, *c* ¾ in.; possibly a bird, legend not deciphered.
   [3] Seal . yellow wax; same as to No. 440 above.
   [4] Seal : yellow wax, round, ¾ in.; a hawk preying over a hare; * ALAS
IE SVPRIS.
   [5] Indented.

of Erdeslay, Richard Woderoue, Nicholas Burdet, John Wyntworth of Elmesale, Richard de Rymyngton, Thomas de Whetelay,
John Swalewell, William de Dodworth. Wollay.[1] (*Ibid.*, No. 30).

493. Same day. Whereas John Stanton had enfeoffed
William Stanton and Elizabeth his wife in all his tenements in
Wolfeley and Wolfeley Morhous, the latter granted to the former
that he could live in their houses at Morehouse, where he was
wont to dwell, until the following Easter, and meanwhile have all
necessary easements without waste, remove all his goods and
chattels and dispose of them at will, and feed all his cattle couchant
therein in the common pasture and uncultivated lands until Lady
Day following and in the fallow lands until they should be sown.
Wolfeley Morhouse.[2] (*Ibid.*, No. 20).

494. Eve of the Conversion of St. Paul, 11 Richard II
[Jan. 24, 1387-8]. Quitclaim by Frances widow of John de Staynton of Wlley to Thomas de Staynton of Wlueley and Robert son of
the said John of all right in all the movable goods and chattels
which had belonged to the said John whether bequeathed to her
or not. Witnesses, Sir Robert Charethero, Sir John de Snydale,
chaplains, Thomas de Wheteley of Wlueley. Les Morehous in
Wlueley. (*Ibid.*, No. 63).

495. Aug. 9, 3 Henry IV [1402]. Quitclaim by Robert de
Staynton, son of Thomas son of Thomas de Staynton of Wollay,
to William Dronsfeld, knt., of all right in an assart in Wollaymorehouses containing twenty acres of land called *le Northrode*,
lying between Nobilrode on the east and *le Stubbyng* on the
west, formerly belonging to Thomas his father.[3] (*Ibid.*, No. 46).

496. St. Dunstan, 8 Henry VI [May 19, 1430]. Grant by
John Stanton of Woluelay to Richard Oxspryng, William Oxspryng, William Dyghton, [and] John Dyghton, chaplain, of all
his lands, tenements, meadows, woods, pastures, rents and services,
with appurtenances in the vill and territories of Woluelay. Witnesses, William Haghe, Robert Haghe, Thomas Ward, Richard
Dyghton, John Birton. Woluelay.[4] (*Ibid.*, No. 29).

497. June 9, 20 Edward IV [1480]. Grant by Laurence
Steynton to Thomas Popeley and his assigns for the term of his
life of a yearly rent of 13s. 4d. from all his lands, meadows and

---

[1] Seal : brown wax, round, *c.* ⅞ in.; a shield of arms, rubbed, possibly
semé with crosses; S' : IOH'IS : DE : [?]STAYNTON.
[2] Fragment of seal of red wax on a tongue of the parchment
[3] Seal : brown wax, round, ⅞ in.; within a triangular cusped frame a
shield of arms, three crosses patée; S' ROBERTI STAYNTON in black
letter; fine impression.
[4] Fragment of seal on a tongue of the parchment.

pastures with appurtenances in Wolley and Wolley Morehous, at two terms of the year, namely Martinmas and Whitsuntide, in equal portions; with power to distrain if the rent should be in arrear for forty days.[1] (*Ibid.*, No. 64).

498. Oct. 5, 5 Henry VII [1489]. Grant by Robert Rilston, son and heir of Edmund Rilston, late of Woluelay, to Thomas Popelay of Woluelay, of a yearly rent of 3*s.* 4*d.* from a messuage and certain lands and meadows with appurtenances in Wollay Morhous within the bounds of Wollay, lately belonging to Thomas Warde, to be paid at Martinmas, also another yearly rent of 21*d.* from another messuage [*etc.*] in Wollay, lately belonging to Thomas Warde, together with all the service of the heir of Thomas Warde, and wardships, reliefs, escheats, marriages, and other services of the heirs and assigns of the said Thomas Warde. Witnesses, Richard Woderoue, Matthew Wyntworth, esqs., Richard Whetlay, William Hynchclyff, William Dyghton. (*Ibid.*, No. 21).

499. Wednesday after the Assumption of the B.M., 11 Edward [II][2] [Aug. 17, 1317]. Grant by Adam de Prestewyche and Alice his wife to Sir John de Arcy, lord of Notton, and Emmeline his wife, and John's heirs and assigns, of all their lands and tenements, rents and services, with appurtenances in the vill and territory of Wlueley, with all buildings erected thereon, all corn growing therein, and all goods and chattels thereon; and all easements; to hold of the chief lords of the fee by the accustomed services. Witnesses, Nicholas de Worteley, John de Turribus, William de Migeley, Godfrey de Steynton, John de Burton, Henry de Byrthwayt, Richard de Ryhale. Wlueley. (*Duke of Norfolk*, Misc., II, ii, No. 3).

500. Martinmas [Nov. 11], 1318. Agreement between John de Darcy and Henry Achard of Wluelay, by which the former demised to the latter the messuage and all the land with appurtenances which the latter formerly held in the vill and territory of Woluelay of the demise of John de Felton; to hold for a term of fourteen years, rendering yearly to John and his heirs 8*s.* 6*d.* in equal portions at Whitsuntide and Martinmas, and 2*d.* for wapentake fine, and 15*d.* [?] for the farm of the castle of Pontefract, and doing the king's forinsec service belonging to the tenement, for all secular service; at the end of the term the premises

[1] Seal : red wax, round, ¼ in.; a shield of arms, a fess between three crosses patée.
[2] anno regni regis Edwardi undecimo. Both the handwriting and the tenendum clause suggest that the date is not 11 Edward I. The grantee was Sir John Darcy who was under age in 1292 and married Emmeline Heron (through whom he obtained Notton); she was aged 7½ in May 1297; and as he married a second wife in 1329 the date of this deed must certainly be 11 Edward II; see *Complete Peerage*, new ed., iv. 58.

to revert to John and his heirs in as good state or better. Mutual
seals to either part of the indenture. Witnesses, Godfrey de
Staynton, William de Notton, Robert de Staynton, William son
of John de Woluelay, Thomas Abot of the same. (*Ibid.*, II, ii,
No. 10).

501. St. Barnabas the Apostle, 12 Edward II[1] [June 11,
1319]. Grant by Henry Achard of Wolueley to Sir John de Arcy
and Emmeline his wife, their heirs or assigns, of a certain assart
called Cokerode lying on the south side of Thurstonhagh. Witnesses, William de Miggeley, Godfrey de Staynton, Thomas his
brother, Robert de Barneby, William son of John de Wolueley.
Notton.[2] (*Ibid.*, II, ii, No. 11).

502. St. Margaret, 14 Edward III [July 20, 1340]. Grant by
William son of Henry de Fincheden to Sir John Darcy, son of Sir
John Darcy *le Cosyn*, knt., his heirs and assigns, of a rent of 10*s*.
from his tenement in Wllay Wodehouse which he had of the
gift and feoffment of John de A . . .,[3] and in whosesoever hands
it might fall; to be paid in equal portions at Martinmas and Whitsuntide; with power to distrain if the rent should be a month in
arrear. Witnesses, Sir Henry de Sothill, knt., John his son, Thomas
de Staynton, Robert his son, Thomas Cresacre. Wllay Wodehouse.[4]
(*Ibid.*, II, iii, No. 1).

Wyten (? Whitton, co. Lincoln).

503. Saturday after St. Dionisius [Oct. 12], 1308. Demise
by [? Walter de] Faucumberge, knt., to Peter le Marays of . . .[5]
and Beatrice his wife, for their lives or that of the survivor or their
assigns, of a toft in the vill of Wyten[6] with all buildings thereon
and with all the length and breadth as it lay between the toft of
Maud Coti and that of Sir Simon the chaplain, and extended in

[1] E. fil.' r[egis] E.
[2] Acta et data apud Notton.
[3] Torn.
[4] Seal : red wax, oval, 1 × ¾ in.; beneath a canopy a kneeling figure
before the Virgin and Child; below a shield of arms, rubbed; AVE MARIA
GRA' PLE[N]A.
[5] The document is badly torn, with a large hole in the centre.
[6] No place in Yorkshire seems to fit. There was no Fauconberg interest
in Wyton, par. Swine. The most likely suggestion seems to be Whitton, co.
Lincoln, on the Humber, *c.* 2 miles n.w. of Winteringham; and West Halton
(*cf.* one of the witnesses) is about the same distance to the south A Marsh
farm (*cf.* the name of the grantee) is close by In 1303 William de Faucunberge held 1¼ fees in Whitene [Whitton] which Peter de Faucunberge formerly
held (*Feudal Aids*, iii, 166). The Fauconberg interest arose through the
marriage of Walter de Fauconberg of Rise (father of Peter) to Agnes, lady of
Whitton, dau. and coh. of Simon FitzSimon (*Complete Peerage*, new ed.,
v, 268*n*)

length from the common road of the vill as far as the toft of John *ad aulam* and Simon Bue; to hold of the grantor and his heirs, with free entry and exit within the vill of Wyten and without and all easements in ways, paths, waters, meadows, feedings and pastures; rendering yearly 5*s.* namely, 15*d.* at [Christmas], 15*d.* at Easter, [15*d.*] at St. John the Baptist's day, and [15*d.*] at Michaelmas, for all services except one suit [of court] at . . . . Mutual seals to either part of the indenture. Witnesses, Simon Bigot, Thomas de Kinton, John Marais, Adam de Aytyebi, dwelling in Wyten, Robert Frauntenant of Halton, Ralph Amelin. Wyten. (*Duke of Norfolk*, Misc., II, ii, No. 4).

Wedingham.

504.   Thursday after St. Luke the Evangelist, —[1] Richard II. Release by Joan widow of Thomas de Potthow to Sir Philip Darcy, lord de Menyll, of all right in all the lands and tenements which she had of the feoffment of Sir Nicholas de Menyll, lord of Wherlton, in the vills of Yedyngham and West Haslarton.[2] (*Duke of Norfolk*, Misc., II, iii, No. 18).

505.   St. Peter ad vincula, 22 Richard II [Aug. 1, 1398]. Grant by Philip, lord Darcy and de Menyll, to John Darcy his son for life, of all his lands and tenements, rents and services, with appurtenances in the vills of Heslerton and Yedyngham, paying to the chief lords of the fee the services due. Witnesses, Richard Darcy, John Gunthorpe, Hugh de Mitforth, Walter Toppcliff, Geoffrey de Walton.[3] (*Ibid.*, II, iii, No. 19).

Work.

506.   Grant and quitclaim by Ralph de Esingwald and Rose (*Rosya*) his wife to Roger de Karleton, citizen of York, his heirs or assigns, of a yearly rent of 4*s.* which they were wont to take in the city of York in a shop (*selda*) in the street (*vico*) of Fossegate, of the fee of the master and brethren of the house of Eskedale of the order of Grandmont; which rent they had purchased of John son of Simon de Rypon, whose charter they had delivered to Roger. Witnesses, Walter de Stokes, mayor of York,[4] Henry de Holteby,

[1] Stained.
[2] Seal : red wax, shield shaped; a bird passant and something above; not apparently armorial.
[3] Seal : red wax, small, octagonal; above a helmet a crest, on a chapeau a bull statant guardant.
[4] According to the list in Drake, *Eboracum*, p. 359, he was mayor in 1271, 1278 and 1279; and as the next two witnesses are not described as bailiffs the most likely year is 1279.

John the spicer (*speciar'*), Paulinus the goldsmith, Stephen de Morton, Robert de Routhecliue, German de Barneby, Robert de Setrington, Nicholas del [?]Ouing, baker, Roger de Hoby, William de Grymeston.[1] (*Duke of Leeds*, Hornby Castle Muniments, York, No. 1).

507. St. Edmund the Archbishop [Nov. 16], 1301. Grant by Nicholas son of Ralph de Esingwald to Walter de Cotingwyth, girdler (*zonar'*) of York, and Tiffany widow of William de Brandesby, his wife, of the grantor's messuage in Marketeschire in York, lying in breadth between the land of William de Burton on one side and that formerly belonging to Peter le Cuper on the other, and extending in length from the highstreet in front as far as the land of John Ossemod behind; with all buildings and appurtenances; to hold for their lives and the life of the survivor, rendering yearly 24s. sterling, half at Whitsuntide and half at Martinmas. If any of Walter's heirs or assigns after the death of Walter and Tiffany should wish to hold the messuage they should render yearly 40s. sterling, or else deliver it up in as good a state as ever in their lifetime. Walter and Tiffany to repair and maintain the messuage at their own cost, and no buildings to be pulled down or alienated. Mutual seals to either part of the indenture.[2] Witnesses, John le Spicer, mayor of York, William de Osenay, William Spry and Michael the usher (*ostiar'*), bailiffs, John de Bromholme, Thomas de Wyteby, Nicholas de Seterington, John Ossomod, Ranulf the tailor, William Durant, Walter Fraunceys, John de Walkingham, Robert the clerk. Power to enter and distrain if the rent should be in arrear. York. (*Ibid.*, No. 2).

508. Sunday before St. Thomas the Apostle [Dec. 19], 1322, 16 Edward II. Grant by Thomas son of William le Agguiller of York to Thomas Duraunt, citizen and merchant of York, and Ellen his wife, and the heirs and assigns of Thomas, of all his land with buildings and appurtenances in Fossegate, York, lying in breadth between the land of the grantees on one side and that of the brethren of Mount Carmel of York on the other, and in length from the highstreet of Fossegate in front as far as the land of the said brethren behind; which land he formerly had of the feoffment of Nicholas son of Ralph de Esyngwald. Witnesses, Nicholas de Langton, mayor of York, Nicholas Fouke, Robert del Wald, Robert de Molseby, bailiffs, Roger Basy, William de Redenesse, Robert de Ponteburgo, Thomas de Alwarthorp, Richard de Duffeld, Nicholas de Sexdecim vallibus, John de Walmesford, William de Horneby, John de Selby, apothecary, Robert de

---

[1] Two seals of white wax : (1) fragmentary; (2) pointed oval, *c.* 1 × ⅝ in.; head and shoulders of a man to the dexter; legend blurred and top part chipped away.
[2] Missing from this part.

Appelby, William de Snayth, John de Selby le hoser, William de Langwath, Giles le hoser, William de Esyngwald, Roger le Wild, Adam de Fymmer, William de Appelby, clerk. York.[1] (*Ibid.*, No. 3).

509. Saturday after St. Nicholas, 17 Edward II [Dec. 10, 1323]. Whereas John son of Nicholas son of Ralph de Esingwald had granted to Thomas Durant, citizen of York, a yearly rent of 22s. 3d. from the messuage in Marketschire in York, which Walter de Cotynwith had held for life, and the said John for greater security had bound himself to Thomas in the form of the statute of Acton Burnel in three sacks of good wool of the market price of 20li. to be paid at Easter, 1327, Thomas now granted that if he enjoyed the rent for fifteen years and if John did not alienate the tenement after Walter's death within the said term except to Thomas, at a sum as much as John could obtain from anyone else, the feoffment of the rent and also the bond should be of no effect. Should Thomas be impleaded or molested in respect of the rent during the said term so as to incur costs (*misas vel custus*) beyond the sum of 40s., John granted that Thomas, his heirs or assigns, should retain the rent until such costs were settled. Thomas granted that he would pay to John immediately after the end of the term 40s. if he had enjoyed the rent for the said term. Mutual seals to either part of the indenture.[2] York. (*Ibid.*, No. 4).

510. Saturday after St. Nicholas, 17 Edward II [Dec. 10, 1323]. Whereas Walter de Cotyngwith, girdler (*zonar'*) of York, had granted to Thomas Duraunt, citizen of York, all the messuage with appurtenances which he had of the grant of Nicholas son of Ralph de Esingwald for his (Walter's) life, lying in *le Marketschire* in York, in length from the high street in front as far as the land formerly belonging to John Ossemund behind, Thomas now granted it to Adam de Fymmer, his heirs and assigns, to hold for Walter's life, rendering yearly to Thomas and his heirs 27s. of silver at Whitsuntide and Martinmas in equal portions; Adam to maintain it in roofing only at his own cost. Mutual seals to either part of the indenture.[3] Witnesses, Nicholas de Langeton, mayor of York, Nigel de Menyngthorp, John de Collum, Richard de Balne, bailiffs, Robert de Ponteburgi, John de Seleby, apothecary, John Cleruous, William de Snayth, Nicholas Brade. York. (*Ibid.*, No. 5).

511. Monday, St. Gregory the Pope [March 12], 1323[-4], 17 Edward II. Grant by William son of Richard le Spicer of

[1] Seal : brown wax, small; a bird looking back; legend blurred.
[2] Seal to this part : brown wax, round, ⅞ in.; an eight-pointed star;
* S' IOHIS FIL' NICH'I D'ESINGWALD.
[3] Fragment of seal of brown wax to this part.

York and Maud his wife to Thomas Duraunt, citizen of York, his heirs and assigns, of a messuage with appurtenances in Market-skire, York, lying in breadth between the tenement formerly belonging to Nicholas son of Ralph de Esingwald, which the grantee had of the grant of Walter de Cotyngwith for the latter's life, on one side and the tenement formerly belonging to Robert son of John de Seleby on the other, and extending in length from the highstreet (*via regia*) in front as far as the tenement formerly belonging to John Ossemond behind.   Witnesses, Nicholas de Langeton, mayor of York, John de Collum, Nigel de Menyngthorp, Richard de Balne, bailiffs, Robert de Ponte Burgi, William de Horneby, John de Seleby, *spicer*. John de Seleby, *hosier*, Robert de Tweng, William de Esingwald, William de Snayth, William de Ponte Burgi, William Cokerel, *spicer*.   York.[1]   (*Ibid.*, No. 6).

512.   April 16, 1332, 6 Edward III.   Release by Walter de Askeham, son and heir of John de Askeham, formerly citizen of York, deceased, in his full age, to William de Eskryk, cordwainer (*allutario*) of York, of all right in the land with buildings and appurtenances in Fossegat in York, which the latter formerly had of his grant and feoffment, saving only a yearly rent of 2*s.*; which land lay in breadth between that formerly belonging to John Osmode on one side and that of master John de Selby and that formerly belonging to Thomas de Calueton on the other, and in length from the highstreet of Fossegat in front as far as the king's dike (*guteram*) behind, together with a house called *le Turfhous* on the other side of the dike towards the lane called Trichourlane. Witnesses, Richard de Huntyngton, William de Redenesse, William de Ponteburgi, William de Estryngton, Richard de Tichill, William de Langwath, John de Heworth, Thomas de Benyngbourgh, Richard de Shyrburn, John de Walton, William de Appelby of York, clerk, Nicholas Ellerker of York, clerk.   York.[2]   (*Ibid.*, No. 7).

513.   Sunday after St. James the Apostle [July 29], 1341, 15 Edward III.   Grant[3] by Thomas Fairfax, son and heir of the late John Fairfax, to Thomas Duraunt, citizen of York, his heirs and assigns, of a yearly rent of 4*s.* of silver which he was wont to take from a shop of the said Thomas with appurtenances in Ousegate in York, lying in breadth between the land of John de Cleruaux on one side and that of Richard de Leycestre on the other, and in length from the highstreet in front as far as the land

---

[1] Two seals: greenish-brown wax; (1) round, $\frac{11}{16}$ in ; a device; legend blurred; (2) round, $\frac{5}{8}$ in.; a hare; * SO HOV SO HOV.

[2] Seal : green wax, small; a lion rampant holding a sword; legend not deciphered.   There is a medieval endorsement to the effect that this is *secunda relaxacio*.

[3] Also a release by the same to the same of all right in the same, Sunday after St. Peter ad vincula (Aug. 5), same year; same witnesses, Ripon preceding Craik, and same seal. (*Ibid.*, No. 8A).

of the said Richard. Witnesses, Nicholas de Langeton, mayor of York, John de Crayk, John de Ripon, John de Acom, bailiffs, John de Cleruaux, John de Selby, Richard de Leicestre, William de Beuerlaco, John de Cleruaux the younger, Henry de Kelkfeld, Peter de Haxiholm, Robert Calamyn. York.[1] (*Ibid.*, No. 8).

514. Oct. 10, 1353, 27 Edward III. Release by Walter de Kelsterne, citizen of York, to John de Gertheston, citizen of York, of all right in a messuage with buildings and appurtenances in Walmegate in York, lying in breadth between the land of Adam de Escrik on one side and that of Sir Thomas de Tweng, rector of Lithum, on the other, and in length from the highstreet of Walmegate in front as far as the lane called Noutegale behind; which messuage John had of the grant and feoffment of Walter. Witnesses, John de Langton, mayor of York, John de Allerton, William de Beuerlay, Robert de Howme, bailiffs, Roger de Normanuill, John Haunsard, William de Allerton, Robert de Skelton, William de Otryngton, clerk. York.[2] (*Ibid.*, No. 9).

515. April 5, 28 Edward III [1354]. Release by John de Gertheston, citizen of York, to master John de Barton of Naburn of all right in the same messuage [*described as in the previous deed*].[3] Witnesses, John de Langeton, mayor of York, John de Allerton, William Leuedychapman, Robert de Holme, bailiffs, Roger Normanuill, John Haunsard, William de Vlueston, fellow citizens, John de Caue, clerk. Naburn. (*Ibid.*, No. 10).

516. Thursday after the Annunciation of the B.V.M., 34 Edward III [March 26, 1360]. Grant by Thomas del Bothe and Richard de Conyngesthorpe to John de Caue and William le Porter of Knaresburgh, chaplains, their heirs and assigns, of their messuage with appurtenances, lying in Walmegate in York between the land of Nicholas Toller on one side and that of Alan del Brewhous and *le Fishmarket* on the other, and abutting on the highstreet in front and the water of Fosse behind. Witnesses, John de Langton, mayor of York, William Frankysh, Ralph de Horneby, Robert de Ampelford, bailiffs, John Haunsard, Robert de Skelton, William de Vlueston, citizens. York.[4] (*Ibid.*, No. 11).

[1] Seal : greenish-brown wax, round, ⅞ in.; within a cusped and traceried border a lozenge-shaped shield of arms, a lion rampant over a barrulet; legend consisting of letters between each cusp, not deciphered If the grantor was the Thomas son of John Fairfax of Walton (see J. W. Clay, *Ext. and Dorm. Peerages*, p. 63) his arms seem to have been *argent, 3 bars gemelles gules, over all a lion rampant sable.*
[2] Seal red wax, round, ⅞ in , a device within a traceried border, blurred.
[3] Variations in spelling : Escryk, Lythom, Noutegayle.
[4] Two seals, red wax : (1) round, *c.* 1 in ; within a traceried border a shield of arms, probably a chevron engrailed; blurred and much chipped; (2) round, ⅞ in.; within a cusped border a shield of arms, a chevron engrailed between three animals; * S' RIC'I DE . CONINGE[S]THOR[P].

517. April 30, 11 Henry IV [1410]. Release[1] by John Quixlay, citizen of York, to John Laundeuyll and John Watton, chaplains, of all right in all the lands and tenements, with buildings and appurtenances in Fossegate, York, lying together in breadth between the lane called Osmondlane leading to the chief messuage formerly belonging to John de Barden on one side and the tenement of Henry Wyman and John Maltster on the other, and in length from the high street in front as far as the land of the mayor and community of York and that formerly belonging to Adam de Brigg and as far as the royal dike and beyond the said dike as far as the land of Walter de Askham and that of the chief messuage formerly belonging to the said John de Barden behind; which right he had by reason of a certain feoffment previously made to him. Witnesses, John de Bolton, mayor of York, John de Northeby, Robert del Gare, sheriffs, John Brathwayt, Thomas de Santon, Richard de Thoresby. York.[2] (*Ibid.*, No. 12).

518. May 12, 1 Henry VI [1423]. Release by Thomas Gaunt, clerk, and John Seggefeld, chaplain, to Nicholas Blakburn the elder, citizen and merchant of York, of all right in the capital messuage with appurtenances, which had lately belonged to Adam de Bank in Northstrete in York, and in all lands and tenements with appurtenances in Fossegate in York, lying together between a certain lane called Bardenlane on one side and the lands and tenements lately belonging to the said [*sic*] John Barden on the other. Witnesses, Thomas Esyngwald, mayor of York, William Craven, Thomas Kyrkham, sheriffs, William Ormeshed, John Loufthouse, John Aldsta[?]innor, William Brandesby. York.[3] (*Ibid.*, No. 14).

519. Sept. 6, 32 Henry VI [1453]. Demise by William Craven of York, *gentilman*, to Robert Wardrop and John Shirwod of the capital messuage with two tenements annexed and appurtenances in Northstrete in York, which had formerly belonged to Nicholas Blakburn, lately citizen and merchant of York, and which after the death of Margaret Blakburn ought to revert to Christopher her son, in virtue of letters of attorney made to William by Christopher as follows : Nov. 4, 28 Henry VI [1449]; appointment by Christopher Blakburn of York, *gentilman*, of William Craven of York, *gentilman*, as attorney to demise all his lands and tenements in York and the suburb which ought to descend to him by tail

[1] Also, same day, release by Alice widow of John de Barden to the same of all right in the same; Wyman described as citizen and merchant of York; witnesses the same mayor and sheriffs, with John de Brathwayt William Bowes, Peter Bukcy and Thomas Bracebrigg. Seal : red wax, small signet; a device. (*Ibid.*, No. 13).

[2] Seal : red wax, small; a shield of arms, on a cross a cross flory, a roundel on each arm of the main cross.

[3] Two seals: red wax, small; devices.

from Nicholas Blakburn, lately citizen and alderman of York, his father, or Nicholas Blakburn, formerly citizen and alderman of York, his grandfather, and to change tenancies, with power to distrain: to hold from the following Nativity of the B.V.M. to the following Martinmas and thereafter for a term of four years, rendering yearly to Christopher 40s. sterling at Whitsuntide and Martinmas in equal portions, with power to Christopher to distrain. The demisees had entered into bonds for 8*li*. Mutual seals to either part of the indenture.[1] (*Ibid.*, No. 15).

/Disccllanea.

520. 9 Edward IV (146⅝—14⅖⅗). Rental of Richard Wentworth, esq. of all rents and services in Westbretton, Cumberworth, Clayton, Netherbretton, Darton, Sandall, Rodirham, Staynton, Everton, and Elmessall.

WESTBRETTON

From the said lord for certain lands and meadows	13*li*. 15s. 10*d*.
John Syke of Bulclyffe for certain lands and meadows	5*li*.
The water-mill, yearly	4 marks 10s.
Agnes Walker for one messuage with certain lands and meadows	7 marks
Robert Oxele for [ditto]	13s. 4*d*.
John Grene for [ditto]	10s.
Robert Coweherde for one cottage	3s. 4*d*.
Robert Vescy for one messuage, etc.	13s. 4*d*.
William Tutehill for [ditto]	33s. 4*d*.
William Eyrton for [ditto]	16s. 8*d*.
John Erle for one cottage, yearly	2s.
William Walton for one messuage, etc. ..	26s. 8*d*.
John Jacson for [ditto]	20s.
John Sekker for [ditto]	10s.
Richard Cowherde for [ditto]	11s.
Thomas Tasker for [ditto]	3s.
Richard Erle for [ditto]	12s.
William Kynge for [ditto]	6s. 8*d*.
William Erle for [ditto]	14s.
Laurence Lee for [ditto]	11s. 8*d*.
John Genne for [ditto]	7s. 8*d*.
Richard Parkyn for [ditto]	6s. 8*d*.
John Erle, junior, for one cottage, yearly ..	3s.
John Halle for one messuage, etc.	9s.
John Machon for [ditto]	6s.
John Hykke for one cottage, yearly	3s.
William Vessy for rent of assize	1*d*.

[1] Seal to this part : red wax, small; letters.

CUMBERWORTH

John Wodcoke for one messuage, etc...	..	20s.
John Wodderoffe for rent of assize, yearly	..	6s. 8d.
the same for assize, yearly ..	..	2s. 4½d.
Nicholas Turton for rent of assize, yearly	..	12d.
William Jesope for [ditto] ..	..	3s. 4d.
the same for rent at will ..	..	3s. 4d.
Adam Jesop for rent of assize, yearly ..	..	3d.
John Wodcoke for [ditto] ..	..	3d.
Aymer Burdet for [ditto] ..	..	19½d.
Richard Symmes for [ditto] ..	..	¾d.

CLAYTON

John Oxle for one messuage, etc.	..	45s.
Adam Woldale for [ditto] ..	..	7s.

NETHERBRETTON

Thomas Mooke for [ditto] ..	..	10s.
Richard Denton for rent of assize, yearly	..	2s.

DARTON

John Wylcoke for one messuage, etc...	..	20s.
John Haghe for rent of assize, yearly	..	6d.
William Sparke for intercommoning, yearly	..	10s.
John Hagh for [ditto] ..	..	3s. 4d.

SANDALL

John Lokwod for one messuage, etc. ..	..	6s. 8d.

RODERHAM

William Gurry for rent of assize, yearly	..	15d.
Robert Hill for [ditto] ..	..	15d.
John Mersburgh for [ditto] ..	..	3s.
Richard Cutliere for rent at will ..	..	16s.

STAYNTON

[blank] Scotton for one messuage, etc...	..	6s. 8d.

EVERTON

[blank] for two acres of land and meadow	..	6d.

ELMESSALL

John Wodde for one messuage, etc. ..	..	26s. 8d.

(*Lord Allendale*, Bretton, No. 9).

521. July 12, 17 Henry VII [1502]. Grant by Matthew Wentworth, esq.,[1] to dame Margaret Seint George, widow, of an annuity or yearly rent of 7*li*. 6*s*. 8*d*. for the term of her life; to be taken from the issues of his manor or lordship of Everton, co. Nottingham, in equal portions at Martinmas and Whitsuntide, or within forty days; with power to distrain. Seisin granted by the payment of 4*d*. Mutual seals to either part of the indenture.[2] J. Worsopp. (notarial mark).[3] (*Lord Allendale*, Everton, No. 1).

[1] Of West Bretton. His will was dated 10 Nov. 1505 and pr. on the following 10 Jan. (*Test. Ebor.*, iv, 240). Margaret St. George was the widow of his uncle William Wentworth of Gamlingay, co. Nottingham, who made his will and died in 1497 (*ibid.*, p. 240*n*). But in this reference co. Nottingham must be an error for co. Cambridge; for the interest of the St. George family there, and also that of Avenel (mentioned in the will), see *Feudal Aids*, i, 188.

[2] Seal : red wax, small signet; an eagle displayed.

[3] Endorsed in probably a seventeenth-century hand : An annuitie to the Ladie Margerett Saint George once a Wentworth in Henrie the 7th time.

APPENDIX.

ORIGINAL TEXTS.

No. 205.   *Frontispiece.*

Omnibus sancte matris ecclesie filiis has litteras uisuris uel audituris Willelmus de Mala Palude canonicus Ebor' . salutem . in domino. Nouerit uniuersitas uestra quod cum Willelmus filius Herberti breue justiciarii de recto decano et capitulo Ebor' . attulisset conquerendo de me quod dimidiam carrucatam terre ei deforciaui in Grimeston' . quam iure hereditario idem Willelmus filius Herberti de me et canonicis successoribus meis tenere clamauit . questio inter nos in hunc modum sopita est. Scilicet quod ego recognoui prefato Willelmo duas bouatas predicte dimidie carrucate terre . et eum de eis saisiui in presencia decani et capituli Ebor' . per fustum et baculum . et inde coram eis homagium suum cepi . ita quod predictus Willelmus filius Herberti et heredes eius tenebunt in feudo et hereditate predictas duas bouatas terre in Grimeston . cum omnibus liberis pertinenciis suis infra uillam et extra de me et canonicis successoribus meis imperpetuum . libere . honorifice . et quiete . reddendo inde annuatim michi et successoribus meis pro omni seruicio et exactione tres solidos et duos denarios . scilicet decem et nouem denarios ad Pentecosten . et decem et nouem denarios ad festum sancti Martini. Predictus uero Willelmus reddidit in manum meam alias duas bouatas quas petierat . illas scilicet quas Ricardus tenuerat . michi et successoribus meis tenendas. Memoratus etiam Willelmus filius Herberti concessit Beatrici[1] matri mee unam predictarum bouatarum quas ei recognoui tenendam tota uita sua . reddendo inde annuatim predicto Willelmo filio Herberti duos solidos et duos denarios . medietatem ad Pentecosten . et medietatem ad festum sancti Martini . et post decessum predicte . B . matris mee . eadem bouata sine contradictione aliqua reuertetur ad prefatum Willelmum filium Herberti. Ne autem hoc in dubium possit reuocari . illud presentis scripti testimonio et sigilli mei apposicione corroboraui. Hiis testibus . Simone decano . Hamone thesaurario . Adam de Torner . archidiacono . Ebor[acensi] . Willelmo archidiacono . de Nothingh[am] . Hugone Murdac . Willelmo de Stiandebi . magistro Lisia . Willelmo de Caua . canonicis . Arundello . Roberto de sancto Saluatore . Waltero . Hugone . capellanis . Radulfo Nuuel . Johanne Blundo . Radulfo Fin . Johanne filio Stephani . Matheo fratre meo . Waltero clerico . Roberto de Briningeston' . Alano Jordani . Waltero fratre eius . Thoma clerico . Paulino filio Roberti . Hugone filio Gileberti . Thoma filio Herberti . Roberto de Mileford.

---

[1] A small hole in the parchment.

SEAL : green wax, pointed oval, 1⅞ × 1¼ in.; a stag courant along the major axis, with interlacing foliage; ✠ SIGILL' : WILL'MI : DE : MALAPALVDE.

Endorsed in a medieval hand : Grymes[t]on.

This charter was formerly in the Phillipps collection (MS. 27837), and was acquired by the Yorkshire Archæological Society after the sale of a further portion of that collection at Sotheby's on 25 June 1935 (Cat. No. 498).

The grantor was probably the William de Male Palu who rendered an account of 100*li.* in Yorkshire at Michaelmas 1182 for a *donum* to be in the king's custody and protection as his clerk.[1] As William de Malapalude, canon of York, he issued a charter giving to his kinsman, Robert the clerk, 2 bovates of land in Burneston at a yearly rent of a talent, in the period 1184-1203.[2] As a canon of York he witnessed a charter relating to Jolby, of probable date 1201, which was also witnessed by the first four and six other witnesses to the present charter.[3] As Hamo did not become treasurer of York until after the election of his predecessor master Eustace as bishop of Ely on 10 Aug. 1197,[4] and as Adam de Thorner apparently ceased to be archdeacon of York at some time during the year 1201,[5] the extreme limits 1197-1201 can be assigned for the present charter.

There are several Grimstons in Yorkshire, and it is not easy to identify the present one with certainty. In 1284-85, of the 3 carucates in Grimston, par. Dunnington, one carucate belonged to the liberty of St. Peter, of the gift of Ulf;[6] which shows that the benefaction was no recent one. At the same period Grimston, par. Gilling, was held of the same liberty.[7] But on the whole the most likely evidence points to Grimston, par. Kirkby Wharfe; for archbishop William in the period 1153-54 had assigned 20 bovates of land in Barkston and Grimston [par. Kirkby Wharfe] and tithe of the demesne and mill of [North] Milford, to augment the prebend of Habblesthorpe, then held by Thomas [Becket], provost of Beverley, to hold to him and his successors as canons;[8] and perhaps the last witness to the present charter, Robert de Mileford [Milford], points in the same direction. If this identification is correct it may be supposed that William de Mala Palude held the prebend of Habblesthorpe. It will be noticed that the charter shows that his mother was named Beatrice, and that he had a brother named Matthew. The witness Robert de Briningeston' suggests the place Burneston where William gave land to a kinsman, as mentioned above.

No. 344.

Sciant presentes et futuri quod ego Symon filius Gospatricii de Stainlei concessi et dedi et presenti carta . mea confirmaui Roberto de Seurebi et heredibus suis pro homagio et seruitio suo quoddam toftum et sex acras terre cum omnibus pertinentiis in Steinlei . unde Gamell' filius Orm' tenuit toftum et tres acras terre et dimidiam . scilicet . in crofto . unam acram et dimidiam . et unam acram et dimidiam in occidentali parte de Heremitesrane . et

[1] *Pipe Roll* 28 *Hen. II*, p. 45; the sum was finally paid at Mich. 1187 (*ibid.*, 33 *Hen. II*, p. 85).
[2] *E.Y.C.*, v, no. 332, where some notes about him are given.
[3] *Ibid.*, note to no. 253.
[4] See 'The Early Treasurers of York' in *Y.A.J.*, vol. xxxv.
[5] *E.Y.C.*, v, notes to nos. 253, 302.
[6] *Feudal Aids*, vi, 34.
[7] *Ibid.*, pp. 67, 69.
[8] *E.Y.C.*, i, no. 155.

dimidiam acram in Cumbedene . et duas acras iuxta Grengailgate .
et dimidiam acram iuxta fontem sancte Helene . illi et heredibus
suis tenenda de me et de heredibus meis in feodo et hereditate
libere . quiete et honorifice cum omnibus aisiamentis et libertati-
bus . in bosco . et plano . in prato et pastura et pascuis . et in
omnibus locis et rebus ad predictas terras pertinentibus infra
uillam et extra . reddendo mihi et heredibus meis per annum octo
denarios pro omnibus seruitiis . quatuor denarios ad Pentecosten
et quatuor denarios ad festum sancti Martini. Et quod predictus
Rob[ertus] poterit heredare quemcumque uoluerit de predictis
terris sicut de perpetua et propria possessione sua.   Sciendum
uero est quod ego Symon et heredes mei guarentyzabimus predictas
terras prememorato Roberto et heredibus suis contra omnes hom-
ines. Et ut hec donatio ra[ta et] firma permaneat in perpetuum .
idem Rob[ertus] dedit mihi in gersum quadraginta solidos.   His
testibus . magistro Willelmo de Gillinge . Henrico de Pinkeni .
Nicholao Murdach can[onicis] . Stephano . Willelmo . Absal[om] .
Hugone . Gileberto capell[anis] . Willelmo Ward . Waltero
Allem[an] . Roberto de Merkigton' . Radulfo de Nunewic . Roberto
de Mulwat . Waltero filio Bernardi . Symone et Henrico fil[iis]
Radulfi . Turoldo clerico . Philippo Baill' . Roberto de Lan[um] .
Waltero Besing . Willelmo de Biham . Matheo [?]Forest' . Roberto
fratre suo . Nicholao Parm[en]ter . Willelmo et Ada filiis suis .
Gaufrido Parm[en]ter . et Nicholao f[?ilio] eius . Willelmo Blundo .
Jordano fratre Tur [oldi] clerici . Ricardo clerico . et pluribus.

Tag for seal, missing.

Endorsed in an early hand : Northstaynlay (and the Arabic
numeral 1 or possibly 7).

This charter was entered in the fourth volume of the Fountains Chartulary which is now missing. This we know from the copy, without witnesses,
which has the number 1 in the North Stainley section in Add. MS. 18276,
f. 160d; see *Fountains Chartulary*, ed. Lancaster, ii, pp. 783-5, where other
charters of the grantor are entered.   The first three witnesses were canons of
Ripon, who witnessed a charter, also witnessed by several other witnesses to
the present charter, *c.* 1192. [1]

No. 345.

Omnibus sancte ecclesie filiis presentibus et futuris Simon
filius Gospatrici de Stanlei salutem. Sciatis me dedisse et presenti
carta mea confirmasse Deo et monachis ecclesie sancte Marie de
Fontibus in puram et perpetuam elemosinam septem acras terre
in terrura de Stanlei scilicet in his locis . in crofto quod fuit matris
mee deuersus le Nort . et ad caput crofti mei . et ad Cumbedene .

[1] *Memorials of Ripon*, i, 199; and for the date see the note on William
de Gilling in *ibid.*, ii, 254. That charter includes Robert and Matthew the
foresters among the witnesses; this supports the doubtful reading of *Forest'*
in the text above.

et ad Cumbedenerane . et in Westcroft . et super Scalleberg . et ad Henganderane . et ad Goditrane . et ad Hermitrane. Concessi etiam et confirmaui prefatis monachis sex acras terre que fuerunt Roberti de Seuerbi et quietumclamaui eis seruitium quod mihi inde facere consueuit. Confirmaui etiam eis tres acras terre que fuerunt Aldus de Scipton' . cum tofto quod ipsa habuit in uilla de Stanlei . et cum tofto Roberti de Seuerbi . in eadem uilla . et quietumclamaui seruitium quod predicta Aldus mihi facere consueuit . in perpetuum. Hec omnia dedi concessi et confirmaui ecclesie de Fontibus cum omnibus pertinentiis et aisiamentis et cum communa infra uillam de Stanlei et extra . scilicet quantum pertinet ad unam bouatam terre . in Stanlei . tenenda de me et heredibus meis in puram et perpetuam elemosinam solutam liberam et quietam ab omnibus seruiciis et terrenis exactionibus . ita quod facient de his omnibus quicquid uoluerint sicut de sua propria et perpetua possessione. Et ego et heredes mei hec omnia monachis de Font[ibus] garentabimus acquietabimus et defendemus ab omnibus contra omnes in perpetuum. Concessi etiam eisdem monachis et confirmaui quicquid habent uel habere poterunt de feudo meo in Stanlei . pro salute anime mee et omnium antecessorum et heredum meorum tenenda sicut carte uel scripta que inde habuerint testantur. His test[ibus] . Waltero Aleman . et Will[elmo] fratre eius . Will[elmo] de Castellun . Aufredo . de Stanle . Rob[erto] Brun.

Tag cut off and seal missing.

Several endorsements in medieval hands : (1) Stainleya. (2) huic immediate adiungenda est Regia . . . . que . . . . . per. F. (3) Sciendum quod hec carta confirmat omnes alias cartas hic signatas per . F . de Staynlay . et melior est omnibus. (4) Symonis de Stanlei fil[ii] Gospatrici. (5) Northstaynlay (and the Arabic numeral ? 2 or possibly 5).

This charter is entered in Add. MS. 18276, f 161, without witnesses; see *Fountains Chartulary*, p 785, no. 17.

INDEX

Place-names, when identified, are indexed under their modern spelling. Field-names, local names and unusual words, when indexed, are printed in italics.

An asterisk (*) indicates that the name occurs in more than one document on the same page, or in a single document and a footnote. The letter "*n*" indicates that the name occurs in a footnote and not elsewhere on the page concerned.

tone, 49; Roger, 21-2; Will. de, 139;
Will., 34
Anabull, Rob., 152
Andreuflat, 136
Andrew, Adam son of, 59, 61; John,
79
Anglehill, Thos. de, chapn, 30
Anlaby, Anlak-, 43*
———, Thos. de, 7
Anna, 75
Annesley (co. Nottingham), -leye,
34
———, Sir John de, 34
Anston, -stan, 138, 151; North, 3*
———, mag. Will. de, 141
Anwyk, Joan, 147
Apesceg', Alice wife of Hugh, 89;
Agnes her dau., 89
Appelby, Appil-, Apel-, Alan de, 36;
John, bailiff of Hackness, 72; Rob.
de, 174-5; Will. de, clk, 175-6;
and see Eppleby
Appellgang, le, 56
Appilby, *see* Eppleby
Appleton, Apel-, Appel-, Walt. de,
120-1
Appleton-le-Moors, Apelton, Wod-
appelton, 3*, 4*
———, John son of Walt. de, 4;
Mabel dau. of Ric. son of Benedict
de, 3; Ric. her father, 3; Simon her
bro., 3; Stephen son of Margery
her sister, 3; Will son of Savari
de, 3n
Appleton Roebuck, Apeltun, Appel-
ton, 74, 135
Araines, Bern de, 74; *and see*
Daraynes
arament, 21
Archbishop, Rob. the, 76
Arches, Arche, Alan de, 135; Juetta
de, 135
Arci, Arcy, *see* Darcy
Ardsley, Ardeslay, Erdeslay, 31, 33,
170
Armitage, Armyttage, -eg, Hermyt-
tage, Giles, 50; John, 23, 112*,
113n
Arms, *see* Bellew, Brus, Clotherham,
Coneysthorpe, Fairfax, Fauconberg, Fowbery, Gate, Gower,
Meinill, Revill, Ros, Salvain,
Sandford, Stainton, Upsall, Wyott;
unidentified, 31n, 52n, 84n, 101n,
119n, 140n, 144n, 147n, 163n,
164n, 171n, 178n
Arnald, Walt. son of, 75
Arnold (E.R.), Arnale in Holdre-
nesse, Arnall, Harnaal', 4*, 5*,
108
———, Hugh de, 5; mag. Ric. de, 135

Arnys, Adam, bailiff of Pontefract,
98
Arrowez, John, 41
Arthyngton, dame Eliz., 102
Arundellus, chaplain, 182
Ascill, *see* Assill
Asenergap, 139
Asilby, *see* Aislaby
Aske, Ask, Simon de, 91*-2*;
Ymania his wife, 92; his seal,
91n; Will. de, 92*; Amice his
wife, 92
Askham, Aske-, Walt. de, 178; Walt.
son of John de, 176
Askwith, -wyth, Aske-, Will., 104-5
Aslabeck, 93*
Asshelay, 74
Assill, -il, Ascill, Will., 51*-2
Assylcroft, 139
Assyngby, Anne dau. of Will., wife
of Rob. Westerdale, 47
Aston, -tun, 5, 6, 25; parish, 26;
rector, *see* Poppleton; *see also*
Canonthorpe, Cranem
———, Alex. son of Will. de, 6; Hugh
son of Joan de, 6; John son of
Nich. de, 5, 6, 26; Ralph son of
John de, 6
Asty, Hen., justice, 32
Astyn, Rob., 44
Atewik, Athewike, *see* Adwick
Atkynson, Alice, wife of John
Nykson, 87; Nich., 87; Ric., 80-1,
106; Thos., 87
Aton, Athon, *see* Ayton
Attehalle, *see* Hall
Attehesses, Attehesches, Rob., 3*, 51
Atwell, Aty-, Atye-, Attewelle, ad
fontem, John, 3*, 51*-2; Will., 90
Audesley, John, 115
Auggill, Thos., rector of Elston, 32
Aughton (Aston), Achton, Acton,
5, 6*
———, Eliz. dau. of Geoff. de, 6;
Matth. de, 6; Ralph de, 6
Augustin, 121
Aula, de, *see* Hall
Aunay, *see* Dawnay
Auneye, Ralph del, 117
Aunger, Thos., 18
Authen, Albert son of, 75; Geoff. son
of, 75; John son of, 75; Will. son
of, 75
Avenel, Avennel, John, 52; family,
181n
Axholme, Haxiholm, Peter de, 177;
and see Belton
Aycolt heued, 155
Ayer, John, 149; *and see* Aire
Ayleward, Rob. son of Will., 148-9
Ayl(e)wardegarth, 91, 93*

Buttre, Chris., 81; Edm., 81
Buttyll, Will., 48
Bygott, *see* Bigod
Byland, -lond, Bella Landa, abbey,
  19*, 24, 58; abbot, 24; charters of,
  in B.M., 58*n*
Bylardley, 18
Bylby, *see* Beelby
Bylclif, *see* Bilcliff
Bylton, *see* Bilton
Bymanroshathe, 117
Byndlowse, Rob., 125*
Bynglay, *see* Bingley
Byrke royd, 112
Byrkelands, 48
Byrlayston, Will. de, 26
Byrsay, *see* Bursea
Byrthinsty, 12
Byrthwayt, *see* Birthwaite
Byrton, *see* Bretton, Burton, Kirk-
  burton
Byry, *see* Bury
Byscopton, *see* Bishopton
Byset, Adam, 56; John, 56
Bythebrok(e), -bruk(e), Bethebrok,
  Bithebrok, -bruk, be la Brouk,
  juxta le Broke, per le Bruke,
  Roger, 27*-30*; Margery *or*
  Magota his wife, 27, 30*, 33; Rob.,
  27*; Stephen, 27; Maud his wife,
  27; Thos son of Stephen, 27*, 29,
  30; Joan his wife, *see* Crigglestone

Cadeby, 115
Cadicroft, 118
Cailly, Caili, -y, Cayli, -y, Caylly,
  John, 51*, 138; Thos., 3*
Caitwike, *see* Catwick
Calais (France), Calesia, 67
Calamyn, Rob., 177
Caldengleby, *see* Ingleby
Caldwell (wap. Gilling West), Calde-,
  16, 57
Calfrod, le, 48
Calington, Calyng-, Rob. de, 136, 138
Calthorn, *see* Cawthorne
Calueton, *see* Cawton
Caluwerod, le, 61
Calverley, -lay, Cauuerlay, 25;
  vicar, *see* Henry
——, Will. de, called Scoticus, 25;
  Alice his dau , wife of Simon de
  Otley, 25
Camblesforth, Camelsford, Cameles-,
  Camlesforthe, 135-6
——, Berard de, 135; Rob. de, 73*;
  Simon de, 73; Will. de, 73
Cambridge, Maud countess of, 20
Cambridgeshire, *see* Ely, Gamlingay
Campanar', Will., 96
Campynot, John, 21-2

Cance, John, 108
Candler, Thos., 110
Canonthorpe (Aston), Caunpthorp,
  25-6*
Cant, -e, Caunntte, Cauntte, Charles,
  81, 110*; John, 81
Caperoun, Adam, 99
Capetour, John, 20
Capon, -oun, -un, Cuthbert, 85;
  John, 85-6; Sir Rob., 85
Caprone, 58
Carcroft, 115-6
Carhouse (? Greasbrough), Carre
  hows, 20
Carias, Geoff., 93*
Carkelowe, 132
Carlell, Rob., 125*n*
Carlton (Snaith), 135-6
Carlton, Carle-, Karle-, Geoff. de,
  11; Geoff. son of Eudo de, 16;
  Sir John de, 121; Roger de, 173
Carlton Miniott, Carleton Mynyot,
  26
Carpenter, -punter, Geoff. the, 75;
  Gilb. le, 52; Hubert the, 96; Hugh
  the, 53; John the, 168; John the
  (son of Adam son of Maud), 156-8;
  and see More; John son of Robert
  the, 168; Rob. son of John the,
  157*-8; Agnes his wife, 157, 161*,
  163, 168; Eliz. her sister, 161
Carre, le, 45; *le West*, 45; *cf. leker*
Carter [?], Rob. le, clk, 151
Cartewrith, Hugh le, 52
Castellun, Will. de, 185
Castelwelleing, 90
Castleford, Castel-, Will. de, 65
Caton, *see* Cayton
Cattal, Little, Cathal, 135
Catteflatte, *over* and *nether*, 85
Catwick, Caitwike, 132
Cauerle, Sir Will. de, 74
Caunpthorp, *see* Canonthorpe
Cauntte, *see* Cant
Cauuerlay, *see* Calverley
Cave, North, 36-47; South, 41;
  vicar, *see* Wels
Cave, Cava, John de, 18; John de,
  chapn and clk, 177*; Will. de,
  canon of York, 182
Cawod, 8
Cawood, -wod, John de, 18; Walt.,
  110*n*
Cawthorne (W.R.), Calthorn, 21
——, Thos. de, 33
Cawton, Calueton, Thos. de, 176
Cayli, *see* Cailly
Cayliwod, Cayly-, 139*
Cayton (Pickering Lythe), Caton,
  47*n*, 111; chapel, 111
Celdehanwe, 90

-floketon, Ovir Flocton, 61, 63-4, 66-9
———, ———, Adam son of Chris. de, 63; Adam son of Martin de, 59, 60; Alice dau. of Adam son of Chris. de, 63; John son of Adam de, 61
Flynthill, Flyntill, John de, 82; John, 56, 82; Ric., 20*
Fodirgill, Ric., 127-8
Foghel, Will., 83
Foghou, 117
Folby, 26
Folby, Thos., clk, chapn of chantry of Thorpe Salvin, 145-6*
Folebert, Simon, 4
Folkton, Folke-, Hen. de, 76
Follifoot, Folyfayt, Alan de, 134, 136
Fontaignes, *see* Fountaygnes
Fontaynesgate, -eynesgate, 83-4
Fonte, Everard de, 75; Stephen de, 75
Fontem, ad, *see* Atwell
Fontibus, de, Funtayns, Sir Berard de, 91; John de, 85; John de, jun., 85; John de, steward of Skelton, 85; *and see* Fountains, Fountaygnes
Forcett, Forset, -sete, -seth, 16; church, 11, 12*; vicar, *see* Gilbert
———, mag. Gilb. de, vic. of Gilling, 11; John de, 12
Fordoles, le, 63, 65
Forest [Frost], Rob., vic. of Sandal Magna, 49
Forester, Hugh the, 69; Matth. the, 184*; Reg. son of Ralph the, 90; Rob. the, 184*; Will., 88
Forman, John, 51*
Formby, 84
Forster, Joan, 46; Thos., 94; *and see* Foster
Forteborem, 12
Forthe, John, 79
Forthgatez, lez, 132
Fosham, 44
Foss, Fosse, river, 177
Fostall Crofft, 21-2
Foster, Forstar, Rob., 8, 9
Fouke, Nich., bailiff of York, 174
Foulbridge (Pickering Lythe), Fow-brygg, 47*n*
Fountains, -ance, de Fontibus, abbey, viii, 121, 130, 184-5; abbot, 123; monk at gate of, 83-4
Fountaygnes, Fontaignes, Giles bro. of Berard de, 135; Peter de, 135; *and cf.* Fontibus
Fournyvall, *see* Furnival
Fowbery, Foulberye, -burye, John, 47-8; arms, 48*n*
Fowbrygg, *see* Foulbridge

Fowforth, Alice dau. of John, wife of Chris. Seggefeld, 72
Fox, James, 80; John, 59
Foxholes, John de, 61; Ric. son of Will. de, 117
Foyer, John, 51*
Franciscans, *see* Richmond
Franciscus, Rikeman, 77
Francois, Ric., 7; Alice his wife, *see* Alan; John his son, 6; Ric. his son, 7
Frankish, -ys, -ysch', -ysh, Anth., 106; Geo., 108; John, vic. of Warmfield, 49; Will., 101*-2; Will., bailiff of York, 177
Fraunceis, -ceys, Walt., 174; Will., 78
Fraunfer, -fre, Framfer, Ric. son of Thos., 152; his seal, 152*n*; Thos., 52*
Fraunk, -e, Perceval, clk, 2; Will., 2, 94
Fraunklayn, Roger, 39
Frauntenant, Rob., 173
Frebois, *see* Fribois
Frechewell, Peter, 146
Freissant, 75
Freman, John, 6; Rob., 5, 6; Roger, 6
Frerbroyer, Rob. le, 120; Margaret his wife, 120
Frere, Frer, Aunger *or* Anger (son of John), 98*-100*; Joan his wife; Isolda wife of Rob., 99; John, 17*, 18, 97*-8; Margery his wife, 18; John, clk, 100; John son of Aunger, 99, 100; Rob. son of John, 17
Freredik, le, -dyk, 60, 62*-3, 65
Fribois, Frebois, -boys, John de, 5; Will., 136*-8
Frisbi, *see* Firsby
Friston, Thos., 21
Frith, Fryth, 20
Frodingham, Frothyng-, Will. de, 108*
Frost, *see* Forest
Froste, Will., 49
Frubber, Will., 94
Fugel', Will., 84
Fulfen, 117
Fuller, Hugh, 109*n*; John the, 25, 98
Fulthorp, -e, John de, 85-6; Roger de, 107; Roger de, justice, 32; Will., 86
Funtayns, *see* Fontibus
Furacris, 12
Furnival, -yvall, Fournyvall, lord de, *see* Talbot; Ivo, 100; Joan dau. of Thos., 149; Thos., 149
fustum et baculum, per, 182
Fylay, Fyue-, *see* Filey

Fymmer, *see* Fimber
Fyncgale, John, 97
Fynche, Will., chapn, 66-7
Fyngale, *see* Finghall
Fyrthe, *see* Firth
Fyshburn, *see* Fishburn
Fysshe, Will., 110
Fytton, Feton, Rob., 55*
Fyxby, Will., 36

Gaile, Gaylle, Thos. ın le, 1*n*; Will.
in le, 1; Aubreye his wife, 1
Gainesforth, John, 130
Gaitford, *see* Gateforth
Galoufeld, Galofelde, le, 93-4; *-dick,
le,* 93
Galphay, -ghagh, -haghe, Eleanor
dau. of Thos. de, 83-4; Thos. de,
83-4; Thos. son of Simon de, 83
Galthefeld, le, 91
Galway, Roger de, 83
Gamlingay (co. Cambridge), 181*n*
Gant, Gilb. de, 75; Reg. de, 76;
Stephen de, 76*
Gardham, Garthom, Ger-, Hen. de,
40*n*; John, 44; Symonde, 47
Gare, Rob. del, sheriff of York, 178
Gargrave, Gayr-, John de, 114
Garriston, Gerthes-, John de, 177*
Garth [?], Thos., 47
Garthesdalle, John de, 94*n*
Garton, Adam de, chapn, 83
Gascoigne, John, 134; Sir Will., 134
Gascryk, Will., 18
Gaselandes, 84
Gate, Gates, Edw., 110-1; Sir Hen.,
111; Rob. 10*, 11; Eleanor his wife,
10; Rob. son of Rob., 10; arms, 10*n*;
family, 10*n*
Gatecotegap, 123
Gateford, Gayte-, John de, 149;
Will. de, 149
Gateforth, Gaitford, 74
Gaterigg, Gayt-, Will. de, 83
Gaunt, Peter, 118; Thos., clk, 178
Gaunton, 21
Gaushyll, Nich., 145
Gayhtfurht, Thos. de, 94
Gaylle, *see* Gaile
Gayrgrave, *see* Gargrave
Gayteford, *see* Gateford
Gaytsforde, 106
Gelle, John, 77
Gelow, *see* Gillowe
Gembling, Gemelyng, 108
Gene, Rob., 151
Genne, John, 179
Geoffrey, Rob. son of, 16; Thos. son
of, reeve of Richmond, 91-2*
Gerewel, Rob., 12

Gerford, Will. de, 15*
Gerland, Thos., 59
Gertheston, *see* Garriston
Gerthom, *see* Gardham
Gerwell, 15
Ghill, John, 52
Gibb, Thos., 145
Gilberd, John, 151
Gilbert, mag., vic. of Forcett, 12;
Hugh son of, 182
gilda, 76
Gildersome, -oshome, Gyldosom,
Will. de, 165, 167-9
Gildhousdale, 150
Gildingwells, -anwell, 69
———, Ranulf son of Roger de, 69
Giles, Gyles, John, 141-2*; John,
chapn, 136*-8*
Giliot, Gyliot, Gyllyott, John, 83-4;
Will., chapn, 115-6
Gill, Gille, Bern., 99; Ric., 36
Gillemyn, Hugh, 96
Gillepighel, 73
Gilling (wap. Gilling West), vicars,
see Adam, Forcett; (wap. Ryedale),
par., 183
Gilling, -e, mag. Will. de, canon of
Ripon, 184*
Gillinggat, 93
Gillowe, Gelow, Reg., 105; Rob., 105;
Roger, 104-5
Gilly, Gilli, Gylly, Alice dau. of John
143; John, 138, 145; Margery,
137; Ric., chapn, 140-2*; Ric. son
of John, 145
Girlingham, -tun, Laur. de, 13, 14;
Nich. son of Laur. de, 13
Girrick (Skelton in Cleveland),
Grenerig, 69*
———, John son of Hugh de, 69
Giseburn, *see* Guisborough
Givendale, Great, 71
Glaphowe, -hou, Matth. de, 117
Glasyn, Thos., 102
Gledhill, -hyll, -ill, -yll, Gleydehill,
-hyll, John son of Rob., 16; Rob.,
23, 69, 113*n*; Thos. son of Rob., 22
Glew, Roger, 104
Glover, Phil., 101-2
Gocelin, Goselin, Alex. son of, 6;
John son of, 5; *and cf.* Pecto
Gode, John, 56
Goderker, 165*
Godfray, Rob., 33
Godholis, 91
Goditrane, 185
Godsawe, Thos., 41
Godson, John, 83
Godwin, Hugh son of, 75
Godyer, *see* Goodyere
Goldale, *see* Gowdall

Lindric, Thos. de, 69
Linelandes, Lynlandis, 12, 13, 15; *-endis,* 12
Linthorpe (Middlesbrough), Leuigthorp', ix, 83
Lisia, mag., canon of York, 182
Litelholm, 77, *-more,* 133
Lithum, *see* Kirkleatham
Litonell, Simon, 151
Litster, Lites-, Littes-, Lytes-, Christiana, 86; John, 83; Simon, 86; Will., 98, 121-2
Littelenge, le, 88; *-ferthing,* 26
Littellayrlandes, 117
Litylwestwod, 53
Loereng, Lohar-, *see* Loreng
Lofthouse, -hous, Lofftus, Loufthouse, John, 128, 178; Thos., 8, 110
Loftscough, wood, 150
Lokoc,, John, 73; his seal, 73n
Lokwode, -wod, John, 180; Will., 110n; Will., town clerk of Scarborough, 109
Lomby, *see* Lumby
Loncaster, Arcules, 129
londez, 134
London, 68*, 79, 131
London, Adam de, 2; *and cf.* Lundon'
Longbalk, le, 134
Longden, Thos. de, 51
Longevilers, Sir Thos. de, 149
Loreng, Loer-, Lohar-, Loher-, Roger, 76; his seal, 77n; Will, 76n
Lorimer', Lorymer, Rob., 108; Will., 72; Joan his wife, *see* Hastings
Loskehowe, 137
Loste, Ric., 76
Louerd, Stephen, 88
Loufthouse, *see* Lofthouse
Lounde, John (de), 122-3; Joan his wife, 122-3; Roger son of John, 123
Louth (co. Lincoln), Luda, 137n
Lovell, Thos., 143
Lovet, Will., 143-4; Agnes his wife, 143-4
Lowthorpe, John, 48n
Luda, *see* Louth
Luddygton, Thos. de, 53
Lumby, Lomby, Rob. de, 52, 152
Lund, Hen., 41
Lundon', Will. de, 77, *and cf.* London
Lutonhoo (co. Bedford), Luton Hoe, 10n
Luuecoc, Geoff., 25
Lygeard, *see* Ligeard
Lyghtolores, Will., 34
Lyghtorese, Nich., 154
Lyle, Roger, 112

Lymkylne, Lyme-, 126*-7, 130
Lynberghflat, 24
Lynby, *see* Linby
Lynedale, 84
Lynlandis, *see* Linelandes
Lytester, *see* Litster
Lythom, *see* Kirkleatham
Lytlehowe, 137
Lytulbretton, *see* Bretton

Mabley, Rob., 131
Machell, -ill, mag. Hen., 20-1
Machon, John, 179; Thos., 17
Madson, Thos., 42
Maheuridding, 6
Makerell, Ralph, 20
Mala Palude, Palu, Will. de, canon of York, viii, 182-3; Beatrice his mother, 71, 182-3; Matth. his bro., 182-3; his seal, 183
Maland, Will., 10
Malger, Mauger, Roger son of, 76; Walt. [?] son of, 76
Malincroft, 157; *-rod,* 28
Malkynson, Rob., 28
Mallum, -om, Thos. (de), 94*; Agnes his wife, 94
Mallyng, John de, 28
Malory, -e, dame Eliz., 127, 130; Sir Will., 130
Malsard, 164
Malson, John, 100
Maltby (W.R.), Malte-, 90, 139
Maltby, Maltebi, -by, John de, 107; Rob. de, 76; Will. de, 24
Malton, Peter de, 98*; Rob. de, 78*
Maltster, John, 178
Man, Miles, 130
Maners, John, 126*; Joan his wife, *see* Dalle
Manfield, -feld, Mane-, mag. John de, 14; Odenellus de, 117
Mankyn, Thos., 128*
Manors (in Yorkshire), *see* Alwoodley, Bretton, Cliff, Dinnington, Eastburn, Eston, Grimthorpe, Harthill, Hemsworth, Hollinhurst, Marske, Notton, Nunwick, Ripon, Rise, Rykenild Thorpe, Shelley, Shitlington, Skelton, Thornton, Thorpe Salvin, Thrintoft, Treeton, Upsall, Whiston, Whorlton, Wilstrop, Withernwick
Mansell, James, 146n
Manston, Alfred, 134
Mappels, John son of John de, 86
Mappleton, Mapil, Thos. de, 108
Marais, -ays, John, 173; Peter le, 172; Beatrice his wife, 172
Marbury, Reg., 147
March, Rob 23

Muleton, *see* Moulton
Multon, Will., 147
Mulwith, -wat, Rob. de, 184
Munceaus, -cell', John de, 74; Lucy
  his wife, 74; Sir Rob. de, 91; Will.
  son of Gilb. de, 74
Munckeby, *see* Monkby
Munckton, Munke-, *see* Monkton
Munk, *see* Monk
Murdac, -ach, Hugh, canon of York,
  182; Nich., canon of Ripon, 184
Muredyke, le, 94
Murrok thyng, 57
Muskeld, *see* Mouskeld
Mychel, John, chapn, 66
Myckelthwayth, *see* Micklethwaite
Myddilton, Mydil-, *see* Middleton
Myddilwod, *see* Middlewood
Mydelham, *see* Middleham
Mykelker, 84
Myllgaytt, John, 83
Mylner, *see* Milner
Mylnes, *see* Milnes
Myre, *see* Mire
Myres, Leon., 80
Myrescogh, *see* Mirescogh

Nabbe acre, 112
Naburn, 177
Naper, John, 10n; Sir Rob, 10n
Nasse, Alan, 142
nayler, 65
Necoll, John, priest, 130
Nedderacastre, Nether Acaster,
  see Acaster Selby
Nederflokton, *see* Flockton
Neleson, Neyl-, John, 9; Will., 102
Nelson, John, 78; Thos., 52; Will.,
  55, 90; Will. son of John, 7
*Netaldewaht,*12
Netewath, 15
Nettelhoulandes, 14
Neuton, 152
Neville, -ell, -ile, -ill, -yll, Newyll,
  Novilla, lord of, le, 58, 94n; Alex.
  de, 58; dame Eliz., 36; Hen., 36;
  Dorothy his wife, 36; Sir John, 35;
  Ralph, earl of Westmorland, 125;
  Ralph de, 76; Sir Ric., lord
  Latimer, steward of Ripon chap-
  ter, 129; Rob. (le), 73; Sir Will.,
  lord (de) Fauconberg, 86, 119*;
  Joan his wife, *see* Fauconberg; Sir
  Will., 30
Newall, Laur., 108
Newark (co. Nottingham), -arch, 32;
  Milnegate in, 33
Newbald, -bauld, -bold, 39, 41, 44-5*,
  48*
Newbigging (Sandal Magna),
  -byggyng, 112

Newby (Stokesley), Neuby in Cly-
  veland, 86-7*
Newby, Neu-, John de, 78*; Agnes
  his wife, 78;* Ralph de, 97; Roger
  de, 87; Thos. de, 84; Will. de,
  chapn, 78; Will. son of Thos. de, 84
Newe close, le greate, 36; *litle,* 36
Neweclos, le, wood, 38
Newekroft, 29
Newland (Drax), Neuland on Ayer,
  55, 87*-8
Newland, Neu-, Rob. de, chapn, 119
Newport, Neu-, Will. de, rector of
  Spofforth, 78
Newryddyng, le, 55
Newton, Neu-, Humph., 23; John de,
  2, 141-2; Joylen de, 5; . . ., 131
Newton, Potter, Neu-, 58
Newyll, *see* Neville
Neylson, *see* Neleson
Nicholas, John son of, 5
Nikson, John, 1; *and cf.* Nykson
Nitherafne, Ralph de, 75
Nobilrode, 170
Noel, Ric., 75
Nonewyk, *see* Nunwick
Norfolk, the Duke of, vii, viii; John,
  duke of, 70; *and see* Norwich
Norh'kirlae, Norkirlae, *see* Skir-
  laugh
Norland, *see* Butterworth
Normanby, -bi, Rob. de, 76
Normand, -aunt, Margery le, 26*;
  Joan her dau., 26
Normanvill, Roger (de), 177*
Normavile, Ralph, 115
Norrays, le, -ais, -ensis, Norais, -ays,
  -eis, Alan son of Geoff., 13, 14;
  his seal, 14n; Geoff., 11*-14; his
  seal, 13n; Geoff. son of Geoff.,
  13*-15; his seal, 13n, 14n; Joan
  dau. of Geoff., 14; Roger, 56
Northamptonshire, *see* Marram,
  Peterborough, Sulgrave, Ufford
Northclif, *see* Cliff
Northeby, John de, sheriff of York,
  178
Northelmesall, *see* Elmsall
Northferyby, *see* Ferriby
Northinby, Northyby, Walt., 5, 121
Northmancroftys, 18
Northorpe, -ppe, 49
Northrode, le, 170; *-ryddyng, le,* 82;
  -wode, 34
Northskirlaw, *see* Skirlaugh
Northstead, le Northstede by
  Scharburgh, 79
Northumberland, earl of, 110; *and
  see* Biddlestone
Norton, Hen., 105; Sir John, 124;
  John, 21-2; Simon de, 34

Thekiston, John, 127
Theuest'uyc [?], 151
Thirkleby (Kirby Grindalythe), Thurkel-, 132
Thirlsay, 72
Thirntoft, *see* Thrintoft
Thirsk, Tresk, 150
Thixendale, de Sexdecim vallibus, Nich. de, 174
Thocotes, *see* Tocketts
Tholesun, Hugh son of Ric., 85
Thomas, the reeve of Wales, 151; Adam son of, 16; Hen. son of Will. son of, 136; John son of, 156, 159, 163; Peter son of, *see* Richmond
Thomasflat, 153
Thomfeld, le, Thome-, 54
Thomlynson, Will., chapn, 129-30; *and cf.* Tomlynson
Thompson, Thomson, Ralph, 110*; Rob., 127*; Thos , 110; Will., 87*; *and cf,* Tomsone
Thoresby, Ric. de, 178
Thornaby, Thormot-, -modebi, Rob. de, 83, 91
Thornburgh, Sir John, 110-1; Margaret his dau., 111
Thorncroft, 161
Thorne, John de, 4
Thorner, -our, Torner, ix, 132*-4*; church, 133; cross, 132; rector, 133; *and see* Swalowe; windmill, 133
———, Adam de, archdn of York, 71, 182-3
Thornhill, -yll, 59, 63-4*, 114
———, John de, 63; Sir Ric. de, 59; Ric., 115; family, 59*n*
Thornougate, 12
Thornton (in Craven), Thorne-, 119; (on the hill), on le hyll, 43; (? le Clay), 71; manor, 71
Thornton, Thorne-, Rob., 36, 125; Thos. de, 58
Thoroph Rekynyll, *see* Rykenild Thorpe
Thorp Arch, de Arches, 134-6; mill, 135
Thorp Malsert, *see* Grewelthorpe
Thorpdale, 117
Thorpe (Ripon), by Rypon, 101*, 129-30
Thorpe, Thorp, Torp, John de, 119; John son of Rob. de, 13; Mich. de, 14; Rob. de, 13, Rob. son of Walt. de, 11; Thos. de, 91-3*
Thorpe, Nether (Thorpe Salvin), 148
Thorpe Langton (co. Leicester), by Langeton, x, 148*-9
Thorpe Rykenild, *see* Rykenild Thorpe
Thorpe Salvin, Salvan, -vayn, -veyn,

Thorpesilvayne, Thorppsalven, Thorpsilvan, Thropen, ix, x, 136-48*; bakehouse, 141; chantry, 143*n*, 146; adv. of, 146; chapn of, *see* Folby; lord (of Thorpe Salvin), 143; manor, 141, 143, 147-8; park, 148; schools, 144; Lady Cross by, 145
———, Rob. son of Isabel de, 143
Thorpeneg . . , 77
Thoucotes, *see* Tocketts
Thours, *see* Tours
Thrimhowes, 12
Thrintoft, Thirn-, 71; manor, 71
Throapham, Thropon', 51
Thurkelby, *see* Thirkleby
Thurnscoe, -keughe, 23
Thurstonhagh, 172
Thwartergate, 87
Thwatesfeld, 133
Thwaytez, lez, 133
Thwayts, Edm., 71
Thweng, Thweyng, Tweng, John, 87; Lucy dau. of Rob. de, 24*; Rob. de, 176; Thos. de, rector of Kirkleatham, 177; Thos. son of Sir Marm. de, 119
Thwing, Thueng, Thwyng, 79, 80
Thwychel, le, 62
Thyes, *see* Tyas
Thykthorndale, 18
Thyrnoue, 117
Tibthorpe, -thorp, 135
Tichill, Ric. de, 176
Tickhill, Tikehil, Tyckill, Tykhill, -hil, 52; castle, 140*; castle-guard at, 140*n*; honour of, x, 51*n*; soke, 69
Tindale, *see* Tyndale
Tirel, *see* Tyrell
Tirsale, *see* Tyersall
Tochet, John, 78
Tocketts, Thocotes, Thoucotes, -cotys, Tocotes, Tou-, Tow-, Tokotes, James de, 85*-6, 119; James, 86, 120; Sir John de, bailiff of Ripon, 96*; John de, 85, 116*; Mich. de, 117
Todd, -e, John, 45, 71
Todwick, Tatewick, -wyk, Tote-, 50
———, Will. de, 151; Will. son of Greg. de, 3
Tofecoster, John de, 91
Toftes, le, 64; *-endis*, 12
Tolby, Rob. de, 136
Toller, Nich., 177
Tomlynson, Will., 68; *and cf.* Thomlynson
Tomsone, John, 33; *and cf.* Thompson
Tone, Toon, Ric , 101*; Will., 101*; Will. his son, 101*
Topcliffe, -clyf, Topeclyfe, -clyft, Toppcliff, 80, 124*n*

For EU product safety concerns, contact us at Calle de José Abascal, 56–1°,
28003 Madrid, Spain or eugpsr@cambridge.org.

www.ingramcontent.com/pod-product-compliance
Ingram Content Group UK Ltd.
Pitfield, Milton Keynes, MK11 3LW, UK
UKHW010731190625
459647UK00030B/681